METROPOLITAN UNIVERSITY

Planning for a sustainable environment

About the TCPA

The Town and Country Planning Association is an independent charity which campaigns for improvements to the environment through effective planning, public participation and sustainable development. Founded by Sir Ebenezer Howard in 1899 to spread the message of garden cities, it is Britain's oldest independent voluntary organisation concerned with planning and the built environment. Its membership is drawn from a wide range of firms, voluntary organisations and interested individuals as well as most of the local authorities in the UK. It has promoted many successful campaigns and initiatives and has had a worldwide influence on planning policy, law and practice. The Association has an extensive programme of conferences and seminars and weekend schools for councillors, publishes two periodicals, *Town and Country Planning* and *Planning Bulletin*, and provides a book service for its members.

Its current concerns include how to apply the principles of sustainable development to new and existing settlements and urban regeneration projects; campaigning for sustainable new settlements to ensure that regional strategies and development plans include new communities as a solution to problems of over-development; advocacy of an effective strategic planning framework throughout the UK and in relation to Europe; promoting policies to alleviate inner city deprivation and regional disadvantage; and proposals to secure social as well as economic benefits from such major projects as airports and the Channel tunnel, with minimum damage to the environment.

The TCPA is committed to the principle of social equality, enabling everyone to participate fully in the creation of a sustainable environment. The fundamental aim of the TCPA is to promote a better world for the enjoyment of present and future generations.

Planning for a sustainable environment

A report by the
Town and Country Planning Association

Edited by Andrew Blowers

TCPA

Town and Country Planning Association

DAVID LOCK ASSOCIATES
TOWN PLANNING URBAN DESIGN AND DEVELOPMENT

EARTHSCAN
Earthscan Publications Ltd, London

The authors gratefully acknowledge David Lock Associates and Eagle Star Properties Limited for their generous support for the publication of this work.

First published in 1993 by
Earthscan Publications Limited
120 Pentonville Road, London N1 9JN

A catalogue record for this book is available from the British Library

ISBN: 1 85383 145 X

Typeset by Saxon Graphics Ltd, Derby
Printed and bound in Great Britain by
Biddles Ltd, Guildford and King's Lynn

Earthscan Publications Limited is an editorially independent subsidiary of Kogan Page
Limited and publishes in association with the International Institute for Environment
and Development and the World Wide Fund for Nature.

Contents

Sustainable Development Study Group

ANDREW BLOWERS is Professor of Social Sciences (Planning) at the Open University, a member of the TCPA Council and Chair of the Study Group. He has been active in local politics as a Bedfordshire County Councillor for over 20 years. His three main books – on the limits of power, pollution and the international politics of nuclear waste respectively, are based on his experience as a participant observer of local conflicts. He has also published widely in books, articles and Open University courses on environmental themes. His present research is on the role of non-government organisations in setting international environmental agendas. He is a member of the Radioactive Waste Management Advisory Committee (RWMAC).

MICHAEL BREHENY is currently Professor of Applied Geography in the Department of Geography, University of Reading and a partner in the economic and development consultancy, Spatial and Economic Associates. He is a chartered town planner, having worked in local government before taking up an academic career. His interests are in planning theory and practice, in industrial and regional development, in local economic initiatives, in planning and sustainable development, and in locational aspects of retailing.

PAUL BURALL was for some years responsible for environmental issues at the Design Council where he organised the pioneering 'Green Design' exhibition at the London Design Centre in 1986. Now working as a freelance writer and journalist specialising in the interactions between business, design and the environment, he lectures regularly on these issues both in the UK and elsewhere in Europe. His book *Green Design* was published in 1991. He is a member of the TCPA Council.

MICHAEL CLARK is Lecturer in Human and Economic Geography, Environmental Management, Development Studies and Waste Management at the Department of Environmental Management, University of Central Lancashire. His research interests are in environmental assessment, planning evaluation and coastal planning issues. He co-edited (with J Herington) *Environmental Impact Assessment and the Planning Process* (Mansell, 1988). He is a member of the TCPA Council, former vice-chair of the TCPA North-West Forum and represents the TCPA on the Lancashire Environmental Forum and working group.

CHRIS GOSSOP was Deputy Director of the TCPA from 1984 to 1991 during which time he was responsible for much of the Association's policy work. His previous background was in local government, most recently with Leicester City Council where he was closely involved with that authority's inner city and environmental work. He was secretary of the sustainable development study group from its beginning in July 1990 until September 1991 when he left the Association to join the Planning Inspectorate Executive Agency as a planning inspector.

RAY GREEN retired as City Planning Officer of Exeter in 1986 having had previous experience mainly in shire counties and small cities, and he also worked for a period in local government in Nigeria. His principal interests have been in rural economic and social change and he is the author of *Country Planning* (Manchester University Press, 1971). He was Chair of the TCPA Countryside Planning Working Party, 1988–91.

MICHAEL GWILLIAM has been County Planning Officer for Bedfordshire since 1988 having previously worked for Surrey and Leicestershire. He has a particular interest in sustainability and its implications for development planning. Through his membership of national and regional advisory bodies he has pressed the case for sustainable policies in transportation, waste and minerals. In Bedfordshire he has lead the establishment of the Marston Vale Community Forest.

DAVID HALL has been Director of the TCPA since 1967, prior to which he worked for Hertfordshire and Durham County Councils mainly on planning policy and research, following two years in industry and extensive overseas travel. He served on the (former) Social Science Research Council Planning Committee (1975–78), was Chairman of the Council for Urban Studies Centres (1973–83),Visiting Professor in the Department of Geography and Environmental Engineering at Johns Hopkins University, Maryland (1975), and President of the Habitat International Coalition (1984–89). His consultancy work has included projects for the National Capital Planning Commission, Canberra and the Government of Quebec. He has lectured and written widely on planning and environmental matters.

TOM HANCOCK is the Principal of Hancock Associates. He has been responsible for many sheltered and social housing schemes and the master-planning of large schemes. These include the master plan for Peterborough, the first proposals for Canary Wharf, the Earthlife City scheme in Docklands and the Greentown proposals at Milton Keynes. Waterfenton, a proposed new town near Cambridge won first prize in the TCPA 1991 New Communities competition. His practice won the Garden City Heritage award in 1993 and was placed second in the Olympic Stadium Eastlands area competition in Manchester. His visiting academic posts include the University of Baroda, India; Columbia University, USA; and the Open University. He is a member of the TCPA Council and represents the Association on the Environment Council.

MICHAEL HEBBERT directs the postgraduate programme in Planning Studies at the London School of Economics. Trained as a historian, he is an expert in the history of town planning and in the comparison of different planning systems around the world, particularly Spain and Japan. Since the abolition of the Greater London Council he has written several studies on London's government and planning. Bicycling daily between east and west ends of London, and relaxing at weekends on a vegetable allotment on the Isle of Dogs, he is an enthusiast for sustainable urban living.

JOHN HOLLIDAY is a planner and landscape architect who has worked in English local government and overseas. He was Head of the Department of Urban and Regional Planning at Coventry Polytechnic (now Coventry University) and has since been engaged in consultancy and writing. He is a former member of the TCPA Council and of the TCPA Countryside Planning working party.

HELMUT LUSSER has been Assistant Chief Planner of the London Borough of Sutton since 1986 where he has made a major impact by introducing a wide range of environmental initiatives. He is a member of the local authority associations' Good Environmental Practice Group and represents the Association of Metropolitan Authorities on working groups with government on eco-audit and the Environmental Charter. He is a member of the TCPA Council.

PETER ROBERTS is Professor and Associate Dean at the Leeds School of the Environment, Leeds Metropolitan University, prior to which he was Professor and Head of the Department of Urban Planning at Leeds Polytechnic. He has researched and lectured on a wide range of issues including local and regional economic development policies, initiatives and strategies; environmental management and environmental policy in the UK and Europe; and the management of environmental, economic and social change in coalfield areas. He is past chairman of the Regional Studies Association, joint managing director of the Yorkshire and Humberside Regional Research Observatory, and a member of the TCPA Council.

RALPH ROOKWOOD is a Canadian who trained in economics in Canada before coming to Britain where, after post-graduate training in town planning, he researched into development trends for the London County Council. He then returned to Canada to take up the post of Director of Town and Rural Planning for the Government of Alberta. Back in England he was involved in preparing development plans for Cambridgeshire, Greater London, the City of Westminster and the London Borough of Lambeth, as well as the Advisory Plan for Central London and the Covent Garden Plan. He was successively Leader of the Covent Garden Planning Team, Deputy Chief Planner for Westminster, Director of Planning for Llewelyn Davies Weeks Forestier-Walker and Bor, and Assistant Chief Planning Officer for Lambeth. Since retiring he has been an active member of the TCPA Council and a member of various working groups. He is now Chairman of the TCPA Council and Chairman of the Trustees of the Neighbourhood Initiatives Foundation.

BRENDA and ROBERT VALE are chartered architects and lecturers in architecture at the University of Nottingham. They have been interested in buildings that have little or no environmental impact since their days as students, and wrote their first book, *The Autonomous House* in 1975. Their most recent book, *Green Architecture* was published simultaneously in Britain, the USA and Germany. In 1992 they were awarded the 'Green Building of the Year Award' by the *Independent on Sunday* for their Woodhouse Medical Centre in Sheffield. They are currently building their own house which will be self-sufficient in water, waste treatment, heating, cooking and electricity, in the centre of Southwell.

ADRIAN WEBB was Deputy Director of the TCPA and Secretary of its Sustainable Development Study group, 1991–92. Previous posts have been with University College, Cardiff, the Institute for European Environmental Policy and the Policy Studies Institute. He is the author of three special reports on European environmental politics for the Economist Intelligence Unit and contributes the 'Environment Report' to its quarterly publication, *European Trends* as well as other specialist articles. He is currently a consultant in the principles and implications of sustainable development.

Foreword

This report is one of the most significant pieces of work carried out by the Town and Country Planning Association (TCPA) for many years. We are greatly indebted to Professor Andrew Blowers, the chairman of the study group which produced the report, and to all its hard-working members.

The idea for a study of this kind grew from a feeling that some important considerations were missing from the debate that started in the late 1980s on environmental matters in general and the concept of sustainable development in particular. The Brundtland Report had stressed the need for the right balance to be struck between the protection of the environment on the one hand and development needs on the other.

However, the Town and Country Planning Association felt that, in the subsequent debate, rather too much emphasis was being placed on the need to protect the natural environment and not enough on that part of the Brundtland concept of sustainable development concerned with meeting the 'needs of the present without compromising the ability of future generations to meet their own needs'. Both the social dimension and the forward-looking, or planning, dimension were missing.

This study therefore seeks to rectify those omissions. In particular, it argues the need for social equity to be seen as an integral component of policies for achieving sustainability; and it recommends a new kind of environmental planning that would incorporate such issues as energy conservation, pollution control and waste management into the development and land-use planning processes at all levels.

The report should not be regarded as the Association's last word on the subject of planning for a sustainable environment. There is still much work to be done in making the concept fully operational and, above all, in achieving the political and public support for the very difficult and unselfish decisions that will have to be made. I am sure that the Association will wish to participate fully in the continuous process of education, lobbying and consciousness raising that will be required.

David Hall
Director, TCPA
March 1993

Preface

The notion of sustainable development was popularised, if not invented, by the Brundtland Report in 1987. By the time the TCPA's Sustainable Development Study Group was first convened in the summer of 1990 the notion of sustainability was widely used, though little understood. It was being adopted as a principle for environmental management and was a key theme in the British government's white paper, *This Common Inheritance: Britain's Environmental Strategy* published later that year. By the time of the Earth Summit at Rio de Janeiro in 1992 sustainable development had become the *leitmotif* linking environment to development on a global scale. The Rio Declaration on Environment and Development pronounced that 'In order to achieve sustainable development, environmental protection shall constitute an integral part of the development process and cannot be considered in isolation from it.' Sustainable development had become a fully established objective on the national and global environmental agenda.

The rhetoric was appealing, but the meaning of sustainable development was elusive, for the concept is at once vague and complex. Its vagueness encourages environmentalists, business people, politicians and consumers all to claim to be pursuing sustainable goals while failing to comprehend the conflicts and contradictions in their attitudes and actions. Its complexity stimulates a wide range of potential definitions which can be used to support divergent objectives.

Sustainable development is not something to be achieved on the margins, as an add-on to current policies, but requires a fundamental and revolutionary change in the way economies and societies are developed and managed. Sustainable development is an integrating concept, bringing together local and global, short and long term and environment and development. It argues the need for action *now* to defend the future. Continuation of current paths will eventually bring disaster in various forms including depletion of the ozone layer, global warming, nuclear proliferation, loss of biodiversity and desertification.

The chances of taking avoiding action may seem politically unrealistic, for economic rather than environmental issues are the primary concern of most governments. Mere day to day survival is the priority over most parts of the world and the collapse of the Soviet Union has revealed a state of economic distress coupled with environmental degradation on a vast scale. The affluent countries of the West, pressed by demands to finance sustainable development in the South and, at the same time to cut back on their own conspicuous consumption of resources, still pursue the path of sustainable growth, putting pressure on resources and the environment: a very different objective from sustainable development with its emphasis on conservation and control of pollution. In an unequal and divided world, national self-interest inevitably overwhelms the longer term need for cooperation in the effort to secure mutual survival.

Yet there are signs of change. Recognition that economic health depends on environmental conservation is the prelude to effective action. Sustainable development is becoming entrenched in policy making at various levels. Rio was an impressive demonstration of global concern about the environment. The Declaration of Principles and the two conventions on climate change and biodiversity signed at Rio, together with Agenda 21, which set out in detail the areas for follow-up action, set the agenda. What remains is for the principles to be put into practice and the agenda to be implemented.

While the framework for action must be developed at the international level, it will be within countries that the detailed interpretation and implementation of sustainable development will have to be worked out. Much of the impetus and motivation has come not from governments but from environmental groups, non-government organisations (NGOs) and local communities working on specific issues in particular places. The impact of the Chipko movement in conserving forests as an integral element in a sustainable community in India has shown what can be done. Greenpeace's campaign against the dumping of radioactive waste at sea is another different example. At the Rio Global Forum 6,500 NGOs from all over the world representing a myriad of different environmental concerns gathered together to demonstrate the common interest in environmental protection.

This report represents the contribution of one NGO with particular environmental concerns about the interpretation and implementation of sustainable development. The Town and Country Planning Association has for almost a century campaigned for the principles of environmental conservation and the balanced development of town and country. It is concerned about the relationship between environmental quality and social equality and the need to promote public participation to the fullest possible extent. The TCPA believes these objectives can be secured only through effective, long term and strategic planning of environmental management and development.

These enduring concerns of the TCPA are at the heart of contemporary concern with sustainable development. It was a logical step for the TCPA to take a lead in charting some of the ways in which sustainability principles can be built into planning practice at every level. In a sense the concept of environmental planning developed in this report is the natural evolution of a more comprehensive and strategic approach to environmental management. But in another sense it marks a major shift in ideologies, political institutions, life-styles and behaviour, a shift that may be difficult to contemplate in a world obsessed by markets. But as the needs of the future begin to press more urgently on the present so the desirability of planning over the longer term will become more evident. Environmental planning is an idea whose time must come if we are to avoid the abyss.

This report is very much a collective endeavour put together over a space of three years by a group from different backgrounds finding time in busy lives to debate and write and comment. We were encouraged by our publishers Earthscan and by generous grants from David Lock Associates and from Eagle Star Properties Limited. I am immensely grateful to my colleagues on the Sustainable Development Study Group who provided the stimulus, the motivation and the commitment essential for such a project to succeed. The report springs from a intense concern about the way we are shaping our world but also from a willingness to try to do something about it. The report combines broad perspectives with quite practical proposals. Many of the issues and ideas that are raised here will need further evaluation and development. The report is not an end but, we hope, a stimulus to further discussion and debate: a debate in which we intend to participate. After all, our common future depends upon our present actions.

Andrew Blowers
Bedford, April, 1993

1

The Time for Change
Andrew Blowers

A thousand years ago, as the first millennium approached, there was a widespread fear –
or hope – of the Second Coming by which divine intervention would bring to an end the
earthly existence of human beings. As we approach the second millennium, in a more
secular age, there is a growing concern that life on earth is imperilled by the destruction
of nature wrought by human intervention. While the menace of nuclear warfare has
(perhaps temporarily) receded it has been replaced by the threat of environmental
global catastrophe.

The prognostications of disaster if present global trends continue are now familiar,
although the precise causes and consequences are much debated. The hole in the ozone
layer threatens a substantial and widespread increase in cancers and cataracts and a
major impact on food production. There is the prospect of global warming bringing
drought, floods and climatic hazards that will vary over time and place but that may
fundamentally alter the natural resource base for human activities. There are the
unpredictable and unknown problems that may result from the loss of biodiversity. The
dangers of radioactive and hazardous wastes present problems for current and future
generations. With the world's population expected to grow from the present 5 billion to
8 billion by 2025 – with 90 per cent of that increase being in the developing countries –
there will also be immense pressure on energy, food, forests and other natural
resources.

Meanwhile, the richest countries of the Organisation for Economic Co-operation and
Development (OECD) – with only 16 per cent of the world's population – consume about
eleven times more energy per head and create half the carbon dioxide from fossil fuels,
three-quarters of the industrial waste and four-fifths of the hazardous wastes. Such
conspicuous consumption must be greatly curtailed if environmental catastrophe is to
be avoided. As one writer has observed, 'We are sawing through the branch that is
holding us, and if we carry on as before, it may break and bring us crashing down with
it'.[1]

There are wide contrasts in the use of resources and the quality of the environment
between rich and poor, between East and West, and between North and South. In the
developing countries the struggle for survival is paramount: 'Poverty reduces people's
capacity to use resources in a sustainable manner; it intensifies pressure on the
environment'.[2] But there is also the need to reduce the corruption and gross
maldistribution of wealth which is rife in many countries. In the East, the end of the Cold
War and the collapse of the Soviet system has revealed the massive environmental
pollution, degradation and dereliction that was the price paid for the rapid exploitation
of resources in the effort to industrialise.

Within the affluent West, air pollution has caused acidification affecting seas, rivers,
lakes, trees and buildings. Although there have been reductions in sulphur dioxide,
chlorofluorocarbons (CFCs), particulates and lead in the atmosphere, the burden of
carbon dioxide, nitrous oxide and carbon monoxide is rising. There has been an overall
improvement over time in water quality but in many areas soil quality is deteriorating.
There is ground water pollution and a loss of habitats. Locally, in cities, towns and the

countryside, pollution, noise, litter and congestion testify to the waste of resources and the impact of this on the environment.

Environmental problems are both widespread and localised. Social inequalities are often reflected in the environmental squalor of the decaying inner cities or in the risks borne by those living near hazardous or polluting industrial plants.

By the end of the 1980s the environment seemed to have become a major political issue at local, national and international levels. The United Nations Conference on Environment and Development (UNCED) held in Rio de Janeiro in June 1992 established a detailed agenda (Agenda 21) for future international action. The conflicts between the natural world and human development, between conservation and growth, and between rich and poor were firmly established as issues for political concern and action. The need to achieve social and economic development without detriment to the environment is clear. But this is a long way from securing political commitment among conflicting interests to defend the environment in the common interest. Appropriate action will involve fundamental changes in both attitudes and behaviour. Human activity must be organised in ways that are socially and environmentally sustainable.

Within this broader global context this report focuses on the UK and seeks to take into account the economic, political and social changes that will be required if sustainable development is to become a reality. There can be no doubt that major changes will be required; but the nature and extent of change will only be revealed by experience. Our report concentrates on the range of responses which we anticipate will be necessary. We have focused on the practical problems across the range of policies and on actions that need to be taken now to achieve a sustainable future.

The concept of a harmonious relationship between people and their surroundings has been an enduring concern of the Town and Country Planning Association (TCPA) since its foundation nearly a century ago. The ideal of the 'social city' was delineated by Ebenezer Howard and, in modified form, was put into practice in the early garden cities.[3] The social city requires an interdependence between settlements and surrounding countryside that neither depletes resources nor harms the environment. Its physical design is planned in order to create a healthy environment and encourage social equality and participation. The increase in land values through development is used to enhance the city region rather than for private profit. The self-sufficiency of the social city as envisaged by Howard is obviously incompatible with greater mobility and the global economy which has broken the close links between town and country that he envisaged. But the principles of conservation, balanced development, environmental quality, and social equality secured through public investment, participation and planning that were inherent in the social city are equally relevant today. Contemporary concern about sustainability makes this a propitious moment to demonstrate the part that planning can play in achieving sustainable development.

A PROPITIOUS MOMENT

There are many examples in the UK of political action by communities to prevent environmental hazards or protect environmental features. They may fail, as celebrated cases such as Twyford Down demonstrate. But there have been notably successful campaigns. Although sometimes dismissed as expressions of self-interest (the Not In My Back Yard – NIMBY – response to environmental threat), some campaigns have combined local protectionism with more altruistic concerns, as the example in Box 1.1 demonstrates. Increasingly, environmental campaigns are challenging the necessity, not simply the location, of locally unwanted land uses.

There are grounds for believing that political action on environmental issues can be successful at all levels. At the grass roots level there are many examples of successful campaigns to prevent environmental hazards or to protect valued environmental features. While many of these have been motivated by NIMBY and have simply protected certain areas at the expense of others, other campaigns have combined self-interest and more altruistic concerns, as the example in Box 1.1 demonstrates.

BOX 1.1 The Battle of the Dumps

During the 1980s proposals to build repositories for the disposal of radioactive waste were opposed by local communities. In 1983, Elstow in Bedfordshire was chosen by the Nuclear Industry Radioactive Waste Executive (NIREX) as a site for a shallow repository for low-level wastes and a disused anhydrite mine in Billingham on Teesside was selected for a deep repository for intermediate-level wastes. Billingham fought a campaign uniting all groups in the community against the proposal, which was dropped in early 1985.

Bedfordshire also opposed the plans and persuaded the government to undertake a comparative evaluation. As a result, three additional sites – South Killingholme on Humberside, Fulbeck in Lincolnshire and Bradwell in Essex – were nominated. In each community, action groups cutting across class and party lines led the opposition and the four communities combined with Billingham to form Britons Opposed to Nuclear Dumping (BOND) backed by the expertise of three of the county councils acting in coalition.

The campaign culminated in the summer of 1986 when blockades of local people (dubbed by *The Times* as 'middle class, middle-aged hooligans from middle England') prevented contractors entering the sites to undertake exploratory drilling. Although entry was eventually achieved, subsequent critical reports and continuing adverse publicity led the government to withdraw its plans on the eve of the General Election in 1987. It was decided instead to seek a site for the co-disposal of intermediate and low-level wastes in a deep repository.

NIREX undertook a consultation which revealed a general lack of enthusiasm to host such a facility. There was less hostility in the two 'nuclear oases' of Sellafield and Dounreay which were (predictably) selected for investigation. Sellafield was eventually chosen as the site most likely to be publicly acceptable. But it still has to be proved to be technically feasible to satisfy stringent safety requirements.

This example shows the ability of communities to mobilise across conventional social and political divides and to form a united front with other embattled communities. The opposition was not simply motivated by a desire to avoid the repository, it also argued against the principles of the policy and the way it had been imposed without adequate consultation. In the end, the successful resistance of the four communities reduced the options and made the choice of Sellafield the inevitable and expedient choice.

Source A full account of the case is given in Blowers, A, Lowry, D and Soloman, B (1991) *The International Politics of Nuclear Waste*, Macmillan, London

---

There are, too, hopeful signs that behaviour can shift in response to environmental concerns. In many countries the separation of waste streams at source is becoming an accepted practice. When environmental concerns combine with health issues, quite radical changes in behaviour can result. For instance, organic farming is becoming more popular in response to the demand for healthy eating and a sustainable environment. Sunbathing, especially in Australia, has been much reduced as a result of fears of skin cancer through depletion of the ozone layer. The increase in cycling and walking indicates a shift towards healthy and environmentally benign transport. These changes in behaviour are at present largely confined to a relatively well-off and environmentally conscious minority, but they may spread as people become more aware of the dangers to health and well-being inherent in existing life-styles.

Government and industry are also giving greater emphasis to environmental initiatives. At a local level, many councils have developed environmental charters, initiatives, audits, programmes and action plans. There is a new emphasis on recycling, conservation of habitats, improvement of landscapes and planting of woodland. The UK government has undertaken fundamental reforms in pollution control through the Environmental Protection Act (1991) and published a major white paper (1990)[4] that includes a commitment to the publication of annual monitoring statements. The EC has promulgated over a hundred environmental directives and drawn up its fifth environmental action programme focusing on sustainable development.[5] Although there have been long delays, action has been taken to reduce acid rain, to clean up beaches, to reduce pollution in the North Sea and to regulate international trade in toxic and hazardous wastes.

At the worldwide level, there have been agreements to phase out CFCs to protect the ozone layer and various agreements to restrict the trade in hazardous wastes. At UNCED, a Declaration on Environment and Development containing 27 principles was adopted and over 150 nations signed a Framework Convention on Climate Change and a Convention on Biological Diversity. Rio was a process in which more governments participated than ever before and which drew in 6500 non-governmental organisations attracting 15,000 participants to their own global forum. Despite its failures (the USA's refusal to sign the Convention on Biological Diversity and the inability to secure a convention on forests), Rio confirmed that environment and development were inseparably linked issues for global international action. Outside government, the business community has proclaimed its commitment to sustainability at the Second World Industry Conference on Environmental Management in Rotterdam in March 1991, while individual companies have changed production processes, initiated new products, reduced pollution and undertaken environmental audits in the effort to introduce cleaner practices.

It is tempting to exaggerate the changes in policies and practice. There is a natural tendency to postpone difficult choices which impose costs and hardship, especially if the changes appear to be unnecessary. After all, the threat to the environment from global warming or ozone depletion may be invisible, something that can be ignored for the present. Political horizons are relatively short, often five years or less. Governments are aware of the need to deliver economic goods and security, although the environmental consequences may be severe. Environmental problems tend to be relegated, especially in the face of economic pressures and problems. Restraint on the use of cars, on energy, or on agricultural production – whether through controls, prices or taxation – are inherently unappealing to politicians.

There are other obstacles to political action on the environment. One is the difficulty of apportioning blame and allocating costs. Another is the distribution of the costs and benefits of policies. A third is the problem of gaining agreement on policies and on effective machinery for implementing them. Part of the difficulty of dealing with the environment is the fact that environmental processes cut across physical (land, water and air), political and policy-making boundaries.

These political obstacles to action are considerable but, in our view, not insurmountable. As the consequences of inaction become more obvious, so the need for policies for sustainable development will become urgent. This report presents proposals that the TCPA believes would both encourage ways of living that are sustainable and would be politically realistic and feasible to implement.

THE MEANING OF SUSTAINABLE DEVELOPMENT

Since the publication of the Brundtland Report in 1987, sustainable development has achieved widespread popularity. It is easy to dismiss the concept, as some have done, as too vague to be useful. There has been a tendency to use sustainable development as a device for mobilising opinion rather than as an analytical concept for developing specific policies. But it is becoming clear that sustainable development is not simply a passing fashion but, rather, a fundamental goal. If we are going to propose policies for achieving sustainability, it is important that we have a clear understanding of what is meant by the term.

Much of the discussion has derived from one short statement in the Brundtland Report:

> *Sustainable development is development that meets the needs of the present without compromising the ability of future generations to meet their own needs.*[6]

Within this statement are three concepts that require more precise definition. They are *development*; *needs*; and *future generations*.

Development is often confused with *growth*. Growth conveys the idea of physical or quantitative expansion of the economic system. By contrast, development is a qualitative concept incorporating notions of improvement and progress and including cultural and social, as well as economic, dimensions. Sustainable development requires that we have regard to the earth's regenerative capacity, the ability of its systems to recuperate and maintain productivity. Thus the conservation of resources is a strong component of sustainable development.

The question of *needs* introduces into the definition of sustainable development the issue of the distribution of resources. In another passage, Brundtland defines sustainability as 'meeting the basic needs of all and extending to all the opportunity to satisfy their aspirations for a better life'. For many people, growing affluence has made luxuries into needs; yet the least well off are unable to attain basic necessities, let alone satisfy their modest aspirations. On a world scale, the environmental costs of supporting the standards of the rich while meeting the needs of the poor may prove impossible. Meeting needs is a moral issue: it means redistributing resources and is therefore a looming point of conflict. Even redistributing *increases* in wealth in order to reduce inequalities has seldom been achieved. Redistribution may take various forms, including technology transfer, financial aid, and compensation to prevent environmental degradation. Greater social equality for both moral and practical reasons is becoming a key issue in achieving sustainable development in both the developed and developing countries.

There is also a moral imperative in the idea of stewardship to protect future generations. As the 1990 White Paper *This Common Inheritance*,[7] says 'We have a moral duty to look after our planet and to hand it on in good order to future generations'. This should not be interpreted as maintaining the status quo. Clearly, if the criterion of needs is to be satisfied it will not be enough simply to hand on the environment as it is now to the next generation. It behoves the present generation to hand on a better environment in those areas where it is heavily degraded or socially deprived, such as the inner cities. It is also desirable to avoid irreversible damage, a criterion already breached with the destruction of certain species. In addition, the future will inevitably have to bear the environmental risks that have already been created by the production of nuclear and toxic wastes. A major component of sustainable development is the principle of inter-generational equity.

In order to ensure environmental conservation for present and future generations it may be necessary to restrict development of environmental assets such as important habitats, high quality landscape, forests, non-renewable resources and so on. The principle of equity suggests the superiority of communal or common rights over those of the individual or nation-state. At a national level, conservation of landscape was, in the past, based on private ownership and, therefore, restricted access. Access should either be open to all or denied to all. Furthermore, if access rights are restricted, those who are denied access should be compensated by a fair share of the resources that are available.

At a global level it can be argued, for example, that developing countries which agree to restrict the utilisation of their rainforests should, in return, enjoy access to the exploitable resources in the developed world. Just as rainforests can be regarded as a global asset, so it can be argued that 'the resources in developed nations are the property of the global community, and as such must be handled in a way that benefits everyone fairly'.[8] Sustainable development involves seeking to maintain areas of high environmental quality for the general benefit and, where possible, to enhance environmental quality in areas of deprivation.

For the purposes of this report, the aim of sustainable development is defined as follows.

To promote development that enhances the natural and built environment in ways that are compatible with:

1. *The requirement to conserve the stock of natural assets, wherever possible offsetting any unavoidable reduction by a compensating increase so that the total is left undiminished.*
2. *The need to avoid damaging the regenerative capacity of the world's natural ecosystems.*
3. *The need to achieve greater social equality.*
4. *The avoidance of the imposition of added costs or risks on succeeding generations.*

THE GOALS OF SUSTAINABLE DEVELOPMENT

For development to be sustainable, we have identified five fundamental goals that should guide all decisions concerning future development and in pursuit of which effective policies need to be developed. The purpose of this report is to explore what these policies should be and to indicate the means for their achievement. The five goals are outlined below.

1. RESOURCE CONSERVATION

Sustainable development involves the continuing supply of resources for future generations. It means the efficient use of non-renewable energy and mineral resources through higher productivity, recycling, the development of alternative technologies, and substitution where this is possible and not environmentally harmful. It also requires the protection of biological diversity, thereby maintaining the potential of species and habitats to assist the development of agriculture, medicine and industry. Only a minute proportion of species have been scientifically investigated in detail (1 in 100 plant species and less than that for animals). There is a need for detailed surveys of land and resources in rural and urban areas (a problem addressed in Chapter 3). The goal of resource conservation can be summarised as: *to ensure the supply of natural resources for present and future generations through the efficient use of land, less wasteful use of non-renewable resources, their substitution by renewable resources wherever possible, and the maintenance of biological diversity.*

2. BUILT DEVELOPMENT

This goal is concerned with the use of physical resources (natural and manufactured) and their impact on the land. Resource conservation requires patterns of development that minimise energy consumption, maintain the productivity of land, and encourage the re-use of buildings. The size, density and location of human settlements that is most appropriate for sustainability will vary in the light of technological developments in energy, building, manufacturing and transportation. (These are the subject of Chapters 4, 6, 7 and 8. The form and structure of sustainable settlements is examined in Chapter 9.) The goal of built development is: *to ensure that the development and use of the built environment respects and is in harmony with the natural environment, and that the relationship between the two is designed to be one of balance and mutual enhancement.*

3. ENVIRONMENTAL QUALITY

Development must also respect environmental quality. At the very least this means that processes must be avoided which degrade or pollute the environment and thereby reduce its regenerative capacity. Therefore, a third goal is: *to prevent or reduce processes that degrade or pollute the environment, to protect the regenerative capacity of ecosystems, and to prevent developments that are detrimental to human health or that diminish the quality of life.*

It must also be an aim to improve and enhance environmental quality, especially in those areas already degraded or grossly polluted. This brings us to the fourth goal, social equality.

4. SOCIAL EQUALITY

Under present economic arrangements, patterns of trade, aid and investment are largely shaped by the demands of the richer countries. Implicit in these patterns are inequalities that intensify the pressure on the environment through resource exploitation, the destruction of ecosystems, and the creation of pollution. Promoting greater equality will not, of itself, achieve sustainability, since both rich and poor degrade the environment. But the conflicts that arise through inequalities are a major obstacle to co-operation.

There is also the need to bequeath to the future environmental resources at least as good as those which exist today. This is the principle of equality between generations. Therefore, policies which seek to reduce social inequalities and moderate conflicts within and between countries are in the long-term environmental interest of rich and poor alike. Sustainability is a moral and social as well as a physical concept and a further goal is, therefore: *to prevent any development that increases the gap between rich and poor and to encourage development that reduces social inequality.*

5. POLITICAL PARTICIPATION

Greater equality means basic changes in patterns of consumption, the allocation of resources and, consequently, life-styles. Contemporary patterns of living in the developed countries based on individualism, competition and conspicuous consumption are simply not sustainable. A shift towards sustainable development will involve a revival of notions of community, collective provision and intervention. A sustainable environment cannot be achieved without the political commitment to make the necessary changes. The changes envisaged in the way we lead our lives are radical in their scope and implications. A move from economic and social organisations based on the exploitation of the environment and material consumption towards a post-industrial society focused on social equality, conservation and resource management cannot be achieved quickly, however imperative the need.

In the longer term, major institutional changes may be needed, involving the surrender of some sovereignty to international institutions. However, in the short term, the nation-state, with its administrative, economic and military resources, remains the most powerful form of political organisation. Without the co-operation of a substantial number of nation-states, agreement on global environmental issues is impossible. Agreements will certainly be required among the rich nation-states if there is to be any significant redistribution of resources from rich to poor countries to facilitate sustainable development strategies.

Change cannot be ordained from above alone; it must be stimulated from below as well. Devolution from the central state to the regional and local level will encourage greater dispersal of responsibility for sustainable practices and policies and will increase the opportunities for initiatives and innovation. Any move towards the greater regional satisfaction of regional needs, which could be a consequence of the new emphasis on reducing the demand for energy and transport, would have as its corollary a regional political dimension. Progress towards necessary institutional change is likely to be incremental but cumulative, and a pragmatic approach is needed. This report outlines actions that can be taken now that will contribute to the more fundamental changes that are, as yet, but dimly perceived. Values must engage with practice at the individual level if social change is to mature. Our fifth goal, therefore, is: *to change values, attitudes and behaviour by encouraging increased participation in political decision making and in initiating environmental improvements at all levels from the local community upwards.*

Policies for achieving sustainable development which incorporate these five goals will, in the view of the TCPA, require co-operation and co-ordination through planning, in a broad sense, if they are to be fulfilled. This does not exclude the use of market mechanisms nor does it presuppose particular political and governmental systems, although a participative approach can only prosper within accountable institutions. It does involve the role of law and regulation in appropriate cases, the introduction of inspection, monitoring and enforcement where necessary, and the use of controls over land use, rural and urban. The principles for a planned approach to sustainable development are set out in the last part of this chapter, where we present our proposal for the introduction of a new style and approach to planning – which we term *environmental planning* – and the changes that are necessary to bring it about.

ACHIEVING A SUSTAINABLE SOCIETY

Environmental planning is necessary to overcome the problems created by the market. Under contemporary economic arrangements, natural environmental resources are depleted rather than conserved. Consequently, some economists argue the case for strong sustainability, with natural and human capital stock being regarded not as substitutable but as separate. Natural capital stock possesses the characteristics both of irreversibility – once destroyed it is lost for ever - and of diversity – when available in abundance it is resilient to shocks and stress.[9] Sustainability involves replenishing renewable resources such as soils threatened by erosion, drought or over-cultivation, and conserving non-renewable resources through recycling, increased productivity or product redesign. But sustainability also requires us to avoid overburdening the regenerative capacity of natural systems. We may have reached a stage where pollution and environmental degradation have become so widespread that 'industry must now reproduce the conditions and resources which were previously considered part of nature and therefore free'.[10] To ensure survival it is necessary to avoid the creation of waste and pollution burdens that can result in the deterioration or destruction of the earth's ecosystems.

The criteria of sustainability are difficult to meet under contemporary market regimes of economic organisation. The description of these regimes as a 'free market' is a misnomer, since there are many forms of intervention designed to increase the efficiency of market operations, ranging from the imposition of safety standards and the regulation of restrictive practices to the setting of interest rates and the subsidising or guaranteeing of prices. The fundamental purpose of the market is to achieve economic growth in the short term by encouraging the increase of profit, and the creation of material wealth through competition. The goals of sustainability require new market mechanisms and controls designed to achieve environmental efficiency, the conservation of natural resources, the maintenance of health and the enhancement of social equality, where such are possible.

As the market is presently organised, income and expenditure are measured within individual organisations or within countries and are defined by the boundaries of ownership or sovereignty. Whatever occurs within the boundaries of a company determines its profits or loss. Similarly, sovereign states seek to develop their resources of people and materials in order to maximise national wealth. But some of the costs of a company's or a nation's activities fall outside the boundaries of company ownership or national jurisdiction and are termed 'externalities', strictly speaking 'negative externalities' since they impose unwanted or unforeseen costs on third parties. It is these to which the quest for sustainability has drawn particular attention. Among the most publicised externalities are the discharge of agricultural fertilisers into watercourses; the emission of sulphur dioxide from power stations creating acid rain; effluent flowing into sewerage systems; the congestion and noise imposed by traffic; the need for new school places consequent upon housing, and so on. These external costs most often have to be met by other organisations relying upon statutory charges, taxation, or appropriate legislation. Attaching external costs to individual owners underlies the popular principle of 'polluter pays' but there are many practical difficulties in its application. In some instances, 'planning gain' may be used as a means of recovering some of the costs imposed on the community by development.

Externalities reflect the inability of markets to allocate resources in sustainable ways. Pollution and wastes are discharged to the air, the sea, lakes, rivers and land at rates beyond the capacity of the environment to receive them. Resources are exploited at rates greater than they can be replaced. Pollution imposes a public cost for a private benefit.

This has led some economists to advocate extending market principles by applying values to hitherto uncosted environmental factors. With this approach, environmental values would be added to normal financial transactions and appraisals of gross national product would be revised to ensure that natural environmental losses and gains were entered into the assessments. Market-based incentives – such as pollution charges or taxes and incentives – would be needed to supplement traditional approaches: 'Essentially this means getting the true values of environmental services reflected in prices, rather than having them treated as "free goods"'.[11] Others argue that there are no techniques which give acceptable valuations to the natural environment and that the market cannot achieve the shifts in distribution that are necessary for current or future generations to follow sustainable paths. In practice, a combination of market-based principles and regulation is likely to be deployed. In this report we recognise the role of the market but place it within an overall planning framework to ensure that environmental priorities and protection can be achieved over the longer term.

PRESENT CONFLICTS AND FUTURE PRIORITIES

Environmental degradation is a feature of both wealth and poverty. The preoccupation with the daily need for food, water, shelter and energy robs the poor of concern for the protection of environmental quality or the longer term conservation of resources. Survival is the priority. As population pressure mounts in the developing countries the problems of deforestation, soil erosion and flooding become endemic in an increasing number of areas. As industrial development proceeds, the volume of carbon dioxide (CO_2) released into the atmosphere – and the consequent risk of global warming – will increase as fossil fuel power stations are commissioned, especially in the large countries of China and India.

In the rich countries, the per capita consumption of natural resources and production of CO_2 is a measure not only of wealth but of destructive power. The increasing needs of the poor and the demands of the rich for the earth's resources are a disastrous combination for the environment. The conflict between North and South was a central theme of the Rio Conference. The poor are unlikely to be impressed by exhortations for birth control and a reduction in CO_2 emissions unless these are backed by financial aid and technology transfer from the rich. They will also expect a massive reduction in the share of resources and atmospheric pollution taken by the advanced industrial countries. Conversely, the rich nations will resist the higher taxes, higher costs, restrictions on cars and other impacts on their living standards that will be required to ensure sustainable development.

The solution to the problem does not lie, as some would argue, solely in dealing with the problem of social inequality. That is a moral issue and is at the heart of social conflicts between and within countries. While removing conflict will obviously be politically important in creating the conditions for co-operation, changes in economic practice are also needed. Under contemporary economic regimes the pressure on the environment comes from rich and poor alike. The problem must be addressed by the adoption of sustainable practices in all countries. Such a shift must, over time, be fundamental and 'will call for new policies in urban development, industrial location, housing design, transportation systems and the choice of agricultural and industrial technologies'.[12]

This report is a contribution towards identifying those policies needed for sustainable development. But it is not enough simply to define the policies; it is important to understand the constraints and conflicts that obstruct their adoption. Consequently the proposals we make are intended to be feasible within a range of time-scales.

ASSUMPTIONS AND TRENDS

The strategies, policies and methods needed to ensure sustainable development will be determined by assumptions about the future. Assumptions have to be made about time-scales, about degrees of uncertainty, about social organisation and about values. They require a combination of forecasting, intuitive reasoning and imagination – what might be described as 'reasoned conjecture'. The future is unlikely to be an extrapolation of past trends; if it were, then, 'projections of the trends of the 1880s might have shown cities of the 1970s buried under horse manure'.[13] (See Box 1.2.)

BOX 1.2 Limits to Growth?

The Club of Rome's report, *The Limits to Growth*, published in 1972 took a pessimistic neo-Malthusian view of environmental prospects. It based its argument on the concepts of exponential growth and doubling time. These views have been revived in *Beyond the Limits* (1992): 'In the global system population, food production, industrial production, consumption of resources, and pollution are all growing. Their increase follows a pattern that mathematicians call exponential growth...Exponential growth is the driving force causing the human economy to approach the physical limits of the earth'. This suggests that trends which are, in the early stages, almost imperceptible, in the later stages become overwhelming and can only be checked by natural limits such as lack of land, exhaustion of resources and pollution resulting in famine, disease and death.

This argument has been challenged on two basic grounds. First, there is little evidence that all resources are becoming scarce; indeed, there is some evidence to suggest an increase in the resource base as a whole in response to economic growth. Even non-renewable resources have expanded through new discoveries, substitutes and better utilisation. Second, there is little reason to suppose that the future will behave in the same way as the past. *The Limits to Growth* suggests that all trends must inevitably be in an adverse direction whereas there is evidence that, in some parts of the world, population growth has slowed, the incidence of disease has reduced, agricultural land has increased and pollution has diminished. Action can be taken to avert disaster.

Of course, there is also evidence in the other direction. Certain resources are fixed in supply and there are signs of exhaustion. Global warming and the depletion of the ozone layer indicate that catastrophic consequences for human society may occur, possibly within the next one or two generations. The possibility of conflict over resources involving nuclear war cannot be ignored. Thus, while the gloomy prognostications of the neo-Malthusians are not inevitable, a sustainable future does depend on taking precautionary action now.

Again, the impact of the motor vehicle on urban form, social relationships, resource exploitation and pollution could not have been foreseen 100, or even, perhaps, 50 years ago. Sustainable development is a long-term and global problem, although it is affected by short-term, localised decisions. Policies need to be related to different time-scales, and it is necessary to be clear what we mean when referring to these. In this report, we use short, medium and long term as defined below.

Political horizons tend to be *short term* – five years or so – reacting to electoral or economic cycles, or, in the recent past in centrally planned economies, to the five-year plan. Prediction for the short term relies heavily on extrapolation in both capitalist and planned economies. Different rates of growth may be forecast but changing technology or innovation is not usually incorporated into short term forecasts. People need pay-offs whether in the form of re-election, material gratification or a sense of achievement. Pay-offs tend to be measured in terms of short term growth, income and consumption but may also result in environmental degradation. The short-term does not rule out all environmental pay-offs and can include reduced pollution levels, cleaner cities, lower noise levels, tree planting and so on.

BOX 1.3 An Example of Medium-term Planning

The Dutch National Environmental Policy Plan (NEPP) is based on a detailed survey covering forecasts over the period 1985-2010. It places the Netherlands in its wider context by analyzing environmental problems and their interrelationships at increasing spatial scales – local, regional, fluvial, continental and global. Sustainable development is to be achieved by closing the cycle of production to minimise or eliminate waste and pollution; by saving energy and using renewable energy resources; and by quality improvement at all stages to 'prolong the usage of substances in the economic cycle'. Policies, priorities and measures are assessed in terms of different scenarios including major shifts in economic and social behaviour. Significantly the plan is supported by a policy statement setting out the measures that need to be taken in the short-term to ensure sustainable development. 'The objective of not leaving problems to be solved by future generations can only be achieved if our present patterns of production and consumption are altered. This requires a departure from the existing trend in our behaviour, which must bear fruit within the term of office of the present government'.

Translating the plan into effective policies is difficult, even in Holland where there is widespread recognition of the environmental problems caused by agriculture, traffic and pollution of the Rhine. Achievement of objectives will depend on the development of appropriate technology, changes in consumer behaviour and, crucially, on the extent to which other countries strive for the same objectives.

Sources Public Health and Environmental Protection, Netherlands
Netherlands Second Chamber of the States General (1989) Environmental Policy Plan, *To Choose or to lose* The Hague
National Netherlands Ministry of Housing, Physical Planning and Environment (1990) *Environmental Policy Plan Plus* The Hague, p5

The *medium term* covers the period up to some twenty years hence: the foreseeable future for most people. Planning for the medium term requires taking into account the potential implications of different scenarios of growth, agricultural and industrial production, and technological innovation. Techniques such as surveys of attitudes and values, structural analysis of change, scenario building, risk analysis and managing uncertainty will all be needed. Hitherto, such forecasting in the field of government (as distinct from business) policy making has been highly speculative and has had little impact on short-term decision making. Within the next two decades, it is conceivable that such innovative technologies as renewable energy, nuclear fusion, new materials, genetic manipulation of plants and animals will revolutionise production, transportation, consumption, health and pollution patterns. It is also possible that such changes, if not carefully managed, will intensify the damage to the environment. In certain respects the medium term is the most critical for achieving significant changes of course. It is periods of ten to twenty years over which a convincing description can be given of what might happen if present trends continue and of the desirability of taking action to avoid environmentally damaging consequences.

Sustainable development is a *long term* objective ensuring 'continuous development in which the quality of the environment is not affected by the use mankind makes of it'.[14] The long term is dependent on decisions taken now. Any fundamental shift in policies must be related to – indeed, preceded by – a change in values. There have been changes in policies in the past in response to perceived and palpable threats to the environment. Certain pesticides were abandoned after Rachel Carson's *The Silent Spring*[15] spelled out the dangers. The oil crisis in 1973 encouraged smaller cars and lower speed limits, although over time these have been relaxed. Damage to the ozone layer is bringing the phasing out of CFCs. Thinking about the long-term future requires considering values and behaviour very different from those we have now. Global warming, in particular, forces us to think much further ahead, far beyond the next generation. It alerts us to the prospect of catastrophe but also to the hope of improvement. Action is required at all levels to reduce the harm and risks to the natural environment and to resources.

There are some areas where inaction may be preferable to avert decisions that could impose risks on future generations. A good example is that of radioactive wastes. Permanent disposal in an engineered repository – the currently favoured solution – would certainly reduce the costs of management imposed on future generations. On the other hand, should long-lived and dangerous radionuclides reach the accessible environment, the risks to distant generations from a long-forgotten repository could be extremely serious. Consequently, some environmentalists argue that the prudent course might be to maintain the retrievability of these wastes until a safe method for their management has been demonstrated. The problem with this is that it is improbable that there could ever be a guarantee against risk whatever method of management was used.

THE ROLE OF THE STATE

The problems of environmental risk and uncertainties over space and time can only be managed by a range of political institutions, some transcending national frontiers and others reinvigorating local participation and responsibility. As was argued earlier, the nation-state must surrender some of its powers upwards to international institutions and downwards to sub-national governments. The sovereign power of the nation-state appears to be a major obstacle to sustainable development.

National sovereignty can imperil the environment in two respects. First, sovereignty provides the nation-state with the power to exploit resources within its jurisdiction free from outside interference. Thus China can drown the Yangtse canyons; Malaysia can permit the cutting down of its rainforests; and, the wilderness of the peat moors of Scotland's Flow Country can be transformed into lugubrious coniferous forest with impunity. Other countries may protest, but they cannot prevail against a state unwilling to accede to international opinion. But sovereign states are not immune from the trans-boundary impacts of their neighbours' activities. Radioactivity may seep into the Irish Sea; acid rain may travel to afflict the Nordic nations; pollution may be distributed down the Rhine. At a global level, the use of CFCs creates a hole in the ozone layer and the combustion of fossil fuels creates climate change. Nation-states are quite literally capable of invading each others' sovereign territory without warning and without retaliation. It is difficult, if not impossible, to erect defences against the invasion of environmental externalities.

Solutions to environmental problems, whether at a global or local scale, cannot be achieved without the agreement of nation-states. The nation-state, organised on capitalist lines and with a sophisticated administrative apparatus and military force, is by far the most powerful and universal political organisation.[16] Nation-states can provide the means for organising, regulating and enforcing international agreements to protect the environment. But nation-states have conceded some power to suprana-tional bodies in the interests of international co-operation on the environment. The EC has been especially active in promoting community-wide environmental policies. As a result of various agreements forged at Rio, states will have to agree targets, accede to monitoring and, in the case of the richer nations, provide resources for implementation.

The nation-state must create the framework within its territory to ensure the implementation of sustainable development policies and to enable local initiatives to flourish. In the final section of this chapter we focus on the role of the nation-state in promoting sustainability through environmental planning within its own territory but consistent with global needs.

Sustainable development can only be achieved by policies that take into account society's needs in the long term and are capable of being implemented by an efficient and effective system of government. The TCPA believes that a system of environmental planning is needed to fulfil three functions:

1. The co-ordination and creation of policies over different time periods and spatial scales.
2. The identification of appropriate targets and methods for implementing them.
3. The monitoring and evaluation of results.

The principles of such a system of environmental planning are set out in the final section of this chapter.

THE PRINCIPLES OF ENVIRONMENTAL PLANNING

Environmental planning as defined in this report envisages achieving the goals of sustainable development through a system of co-ordination and control organised through participative democratic processes of government at all levels. Environmental planning is a comprehensive approach to environmental management which has three basic features:

1. It takes account of future uncertainty by a precautionary approach.
2. It reflects the integrated nature of environmental processes and policies.
3. It takes a strategic view of decision making.

We shall look at each of these in turn.

The *precautionary principle* urges that action should be taken 'where there are good grounds for judging either that action taken promptly at comparatively low cost may avoid more costly damage later, or that irreversible effects may follow if action is delayed.[17] The danger of delay is, as the story of the 'tragedy of the commons' (see Box 1.4) clearly demonstrates, that it may then become too late to prevent environmental degradation afflicting the health and productivity of regions and continents and even of the whole planet.

Therefore, precautionary action may be needed 'even where scientific knowledge is not conclusive'.[18] Responsibility for the future should make us cautious in the present. We also need to develop now those policies for sustainable development which will bear fruit in the medium and longer term.

AN INTEGRATED PROCESS

Integrated environmental planning has three dimensions. The first, is the *trans-media* nature of environmental processes. Pollution can adopt different forms and pass through different environmental pathways of air, land and water. This has led to the adoption of Integrated Pollution Control (IPC), bringing together the different pollution control inspectorates under Her Majesty's Inspectorate of Pollution (HMIP). This generic approach will eventually be taken a step further with the introduction of the Environment Agency[19] that will incorporate the National Rivers Authority (NRA), and the waste regulatory functions of the local authorities.

BOX 1.4 The Tragedy of the Global Commons

The well known analogy of overgrazing the commons has been extended by Garret Hardin to show how it is in the individual self-interest of nations to pollute the global commons beyond the point where it is necessary in the common interest to prevent deterioration of the environment.

The global commons are the atmosphere, oceans and land into which wastes and pollution (negative externalities) can be discharged at no cost to the individual nation. At a certain point the carrying capacity of the commons will be exceeded and deterioration will set in. But individual nations, able to avoid the cost of the externalities they create, may still continue to benefit from the increased wealth from production despite an overall decline in environmental quality. 'Since this is true for everyone, we are locked into a system of "fouling our own nest"'.

Of course, the argument assumes that there are no restraints on access and that all nations pursue their own interests single-mindedly. This is not the case, as the negotiation of international agreements which require nations (and companies) to accept limits and regulations indicates. But the tragedy of the commons does indicate a tendency for conflict between the national economic and the common environmental interest. The problem is how to secure restraint in the short term in order to achieve long term sustainability.

Source Hardin, G (1968) 'The tragedy of the commons', *Science*, vol 162, pp 1243–8

The TCPA proposes that this integration should go further still by integrating pollution control, waste management and land-use planning, thus recognising that these are interdependent processes. Land-use policies affect the location of polluting activities. Plans for recycling, waste minimisation and pollution control all have a land-use component. This interaction between land use and environmental policies is already recognised in the environmental programmes of many local authorities and it is now time to bring the separate traditions together to create a proper environmental planning process.[20] The implications of this proposal are set out in later chapters.

The second dimension of integration is the *trans-sectoral* nature of environmental policy making. Environmental issues cross traditional policy boundaries and, as a result, tend to be neglected in sectoral policy making. Among the most obvious areas of policy affecting or affected by the physical environment are transportation, energy and agriculture, each of which relates directly to resource conservation, environmental quality and land use. The need to take the environment into account in all aspects of policy making is being recognised by the EC, and the British government has issued a guide on environmental policy appraisal to all government departments.[21] In some cases, horizontal policy integration can be achieved directly. For example, land-use transportation studies and energy plans can have a much stronger environmental component.

The *trans-boundary* nature of environmental processes – their ability to cross political frontiers – is the third dimension of integration. Consequently, policies must be integrated vertically between different levels of government. Some progress has already been made at the international level. As a result of UNCED, there is now a need for agreement on targets and on monitoring and verification procedures to prevent global warming and species destruction. The prospects for similar agreement on deforestation appear to be slender, at least in the short term. Within the UK, a strategic planning framework is required to achieve the vertical integration of policy making between national, regional and local levels.

A STRATEGIC APPROACH

The third feature of environmental planning is its *strategic approach*. This should apply at all levels of government, for there is a danger that policies for sustainable development will founder on the rock of increasing centralised power and the emphasis on short-term political priorities. Some environmental policies must be enacted at central state level but there are others that require competent and effective supra-national authorities. And, below the level of the nation state, the powers of local and regional governments need to be reinforced if they are to promote initiatives and facilitate the implementation of policies for sustainability. The principle of *subsidiarity* – taking decisions at the lowest level compatible with attaining required objectives – will maximise participation and effectiveness. Therefore, a major theme in this report is the need for institutions to be created at appropriate levels with sufficient authority to introduce policies in the short term that will ensure the long-term sustainability of the earth's environmental resources.

At each level there should be an *environmental plan*, a policy statement of objectives that sets targets, identifies methods for achieving them, and establishes criteria for the regular monitoring of progress. At the nation-state level, the National Environmental Plan would translate EC and other international agreements into specific policies and targets and identify the methods for implementing these. For example, the plan would demonstrate how central government action would ensure that the agreement to stabilise CO_2 emission levels by the end of the century is to be met.

The National Environmental Plan would also provide the framework for subsidiary regional and local plans, setting targets to be achieved through local action. For instance, the government's target of recycling half the recyclable household waste (ie a quarter of all household waste) by the end of the century would be set in the National Plan but implemented through subsidiary plans. The National Plan would also ensure that environmental assessments are carried out for all projects, programmes and policies undertaken by central government ministries, departments and agencies. Monitoring would be an integral element of the plan, including an annual 'state of the environment' report. The government has begun issuing annual monitoring statements indicating progress on environmental objectives and has issued a statistical report on the environment.[22] These reports provide an important base on which to judge progress. We envisage a much more far-reaching process with reports linked to plans and showing the costs of policies in terms of resource depletion and pollution.

In the view of the TCPA, a regional level of government is necessary to identify the land-use and environmental implications of sectoral policies in agriculture, energy, industry, housing, transportation, the provision of infrastructure, and waste management. It is at the regional level too that the relationships and balance between the economy and the environment can be articulated in terms of sustainable development. Yet strategic planning at the regional level is the missing dimension in the UK. The TCPA believes that this essential level of environmental planning can be achieved fully only through a system of regional government with sufficient powers to interpret and integrate the policies of the various sectors. But there seems little prospect of such regional government in the near future so, in the meantime, the TCPA believes that it is vital to strengthen existing regional policy guidance, to develop regional planning conferences such as that covering the South-East, and to enhance the regional dimension in bodies responsible for the environment such as the National Rivers Authority (NRA), HMIP and, when it is formed, the Environment Agency. The potential relationship between regional economic and land use planning is explored in Chapter 8.

Within this system of environmental planning, the detailed implementation of policies for sustainable development would be set out in local environmental plans produced by local authorities. Within the two-tier structure of existing local government, these plans would succeed the structure and local plan system. As unitary authorities come into being there would be a need only for a single environmental plan. But the local level is not merely the point where national and regional policies are administered. The local level has a far more dynamic role, for it is here that there is enormous scope for innovation, initiative and participation. It is at the local level that the involvement of the community can be developed and that co-operation between environmental groups and local authorities is commonplace: the next chapter includes examples of environmental projects from a wide range of communities. But the erosion of local authority finances and powers by nearly two decades of centralisation has reduced their effectiveness. In times of restraint it is often environmental initiatives that are cut.

PRIORITY FOR THE PUBLIC INTEREST

Policies for sustainable development can only be achieved if there are resources to back the commitments contained in environmental plans. In part, these resources will have to come from levying taxes and charges on industry (eg the 'polluter pays' principle) which will be reflected in prices. Other resources will no doubt come from public and private borrowing. Options such as local income tax could be explored. A carbon tax seems likely to tackle global warming, although it could be fiscally neutral in so far as the tax burden is shifted from income or other taxes. Such a shift might produce a change in life-style (less car use, more energy saving etc) but not a reduction in the standard of living. However, the addition of VAT to domestic fuel introduced in the 1993 UK budget cannot be hailed as a 'green' tax as no parallel resources have been provided to help improve energy efficiency in homes. Overall policies to protect the environment – such as waste recycling or the promotion of public transport – will require an increase in public investment and expenditure.

One way of providing resources for public investment in sustainable development policies would be to resuscitate the idea of a tax on the increased value of land identified for built development. As the next chapter shows, 'betterment tax' has been tried three times since the war and has been repealed for political and technical reasons on each occasion. Among the practical problems are the need to ensure equalisation between areas with vastly different development potential and the requirement to provide sufficient incentives for necessary development. The TCPA considers that betterment tax in some form would provide some of the resources to help meet the goals of sustainable development, especially in conjunction with local development plans. This is discussed further in Chapters 2 and 9.

At a broader scale, the issue of private and public property rights is at the heart of the problem of sustainable development. This issue was discussed earlier in the context of stewardship for future generations. Sustainability may require restrictions on the use of private property, denial of development and the limitation of access to resources. Compensation may be justified for the loss of property rights which create hardship. But it is difficult to organise payments to discriminate between hardship and windfall gains. In the case of agriculture, compensation to farmers for not destroying protected marshes, heaths, woodlands or habitats may be unnecessary, inequitable and costly. A more effective approach, as argued in Chapter 3, would be through extending some form of control to development in agriculture and forestry and providing more resources for the protection of the countryside. Compensation should also be introduced for those communities that have to bear a disproportionate share of the environmental risk or degradation created by society. We shall return to this issue in Chapter 5.

The principle of placing the property rights of the community above those of private interest can be extended to the international level. As was suggested earlier, restraint on the exercise of national sovereignty may be necessary to ensure the protection of such environmental resources as rainforests or to prevent the trans-boundary effects of polluting and hazardous processes. The principle of equity suggests that compensation should be provided where restraint imposes hardship on developing countries. Such compensation may take the form of appropriate technology transfer, aid, positive trade discrimination, or access to alternative resources.

CONCLUSION

Sustainable development will require substantial changes in behaviour at every level, giving priority to such unfashionable ideas as planning, community and greater equality. Existing patterns of consumerism, private ownership, individualism and the free market are deeply rooted in Western society and have spread far across the globe. Attempts to uproot them may seem hopelessly idealistic. But we are reaching the point where self-interest and a common interest in survival converge. Already changes are occurring in local communities, in the world of business, in national policies, and in international relations. There is a need to realise the goals of sustainable development outlined in this chapter by developing practical and politically realistic policies that can be achieved now at local and national level. This is the task we have set ourselves in this report.

Deeper currents, but dimly perceived, are flowing, as yet only creating small perturbations on the surface. It is from these that the grander, more far-reaching, changes will grow. As the poet Arthur Hugh Clough put it:

> *For while the tired waves, vainly breaking,*
> *Seem here no painful inch to gain,*
> *Far back, through creeks and inlets, making,*
> *Comes silent, flooding in, the main.*[23]

The author wishes to acknowledge the help of Ray Green, Adrian Webb, John Holliday and Ralph Rookwood in the preparation of this chapter

2

The Planning Background

David Hall, Michael Hebbert and Helmut Lusser

As we have explained in Chapter 1, this report sets out the case for environmental planning. In the UK, planning has been limited to the statutory land-use planning system usually known as town and country planning. Our purpose in this chapter is to provide a historical background, to show how the town and country planning system has evolved, to explain its purpose and its limitations, and to indicate its role and relevance to the much wider system of environmental planning that we propose.

'Sustainable urban development is a new goal', write Tim Elkin and Duncan McLaren in *Reviving the City*.[1] So it is, but the issue of sustainability, under different names, is deeply rooted in the past. The TCPA itself was founded a century ago to challenge the greed and waste of big cities and to campaign for an alternative pattern of living and working in decentralised, small-scale communities that were in balance with the natural environment.[2] The conservation movement has its roots in late-nineteenth-century USA, when the closing of the last pioneer frontier brought home to a small group of scientists and reformers the realisation that public policy would be required to protect the land and its finite resources from excessive private exploitation 'if our descendants are to have transmitted to them their heritage not too greatly diminished'.[3]

From the outset, conservation implied planning, so that natural resource protection and city planning were soon intertwined. Sustainable urban development – in sense if not in name – was a central theme in the writings of the Scottish biologist turned town planner, Sir Patrick Geddes (1854–1932) and his disciple the American urbanist Lewis Mumford (1895–1990). Both were formative influences in wartime Britain, when conservationists such as John Dower and Julian Huxley joined forces with urban reformers in the great debate about the role of planning in postwar reconstruction.

So although the words 'sustainable development' are new, the underlying concept is already a familiar one in British land use planning. The planning system as we know it – based on the 1947 Town and Country Planning Act – was designed in and immediately after the war years in a context of intense public concern about the balance between urban development and agricultural, forest and open land resources. It has unique features found nowhere else in Europe:

- an absence of legally binding plans;
- local discretion;
- a national appeals system;
- a national policy.

As originally envisaged, the system was to be run from Whitehall by a cross-sectoral ministry, and its plans at regional or county level were to be broad-brush documents, defining an integrated strategy for the use of land and water resources over the medium term.[4]

In Britain as elsewhere, town planning had grown up as a local system of zoning control designed to avoid bad-neighbour problems and to hold down municipal costs.

The 1947 Act was a radical departure. In its all-embracing character, flexibility, and scale (national direction and co-ordination with local implementation), it bore a marked resemblance to the systems of intervention that are being devised in response to today's environmental crisis. These features were introduced with all-party support in 1947 precisely in order that the implementation of a national environmental policy dealing with the preservation of fertile agricultural land for essential food production, the protection of upland and wildlife habitats, and the greening of towns and cities, would not be compromised by parochialism and the claims of private property rights.

THE LIMITATIONS OF TOWN PLANNING

How has the postwar planning system performed from an environmental point of view? In practice, it has been an effective instrument for achieving the policy objectives of the 1940s, particularly the demarcation of built-up areas from the countryside and the designation and protection of national parks, landscape areas, and nature reserves.

But it has been far less successful in responding to new kinds of environmental concern. Once established as a regular branch of government at central and local levels, land-use planning became set in its ways. Its place in the scheme of government was assured but circumscribed. It was not allowed to trespass on the preserve of agricultural policy, which has an exceptionally tight political nexus with the farm supply, farming and food industries. So the town and country planning system has protected the rural land resource from building development but not from some of the uglier side-effects of agribusiness.

The same applies to the control of noise, noxious emissions and wastes from manufacturing and extractive industry. The planning system set up by the 1947 Act had the potential to place local authorities in a key role in the control of industrial pollution. It gave them powers to determine the nature, as well as the location, of new development; a statutory responsibility to consult and co-ordinate (with pollution control agencies) in plan making and development control; and an ability, through positive planning, to co-ordinate environmental improvement on a broad scale.

But this 'comprehensive range of techniques...for pollution control', as Christopher Wood describes it,[5] was left largely unused. Wood analyses the reasons why: inadequate training, poor information, lack of central guidance, professional jealousies, and the fear – explored particularly in Blowers' study of pollution and planning in the brickfields[6] – that a tightening of local planning controls would lead to local job losses. There was also an important institutional factor. Industrial pollution control was the domain of the Alkali Inspectorate, now Her Majesty's Inspectorate of Pollution. In a later comparative study[7] of pollution control and planning in the UK and the USA, Wood documented the comparatively cosy relationship of Britain's national inspectorate with client industries and its tendency to discourage planning authorities from consideration of the environmental impacts on air and water of new industrial development. As the Royal Commission on Environmental Pollution said in 1976, 'Our concern is not that pollution is not always given top priority; it is that it is often dealt with inadequately and sometimes forgotten altogether in the planning process'.

Transport figures large in current environmentalism. Part of the original purpose of the postwar planning system was to reduce the wasteful transport of people and goods. The ideal was to reverse the trend towards big cities and enlarge the opportunity for small-town living. 'Decentralization means real homes for families within walking distance of pleasant work places and of playing fields and countryside', suggested an exhibition screen designed for the TCPA by Rose Gascoigne in the 1940s. The vision of balance and self-containment was partially realised in the postwar new towns. These great publicly financed projects were direct descendants of the garden city tradition. The original combination of the words 'garden' and 'city' implied something close to the heart of sustainability: modern manufacturing industry purged of its grime, in balance with its natural setting. The new towns carried to an extreme the nineteenth-century hygienic desire for space, order (particularly the orderly segregation of land uses) and openness. However, they also sought to provide a good social and economic environment with a full range of the necessary social, community and welfare services and high levels of employment. As such, they were exemplary solutions to the nineteenth-century problems of pollution and overcrowding, although in the context of the late twentieth century they can be criticised. New towns, like all other towns, have no specific relationship with their surrounding countryside and draw much of the population, industry and financial resources from further afield. In their efforts to accommodate the car – and Milton Keynes, with its low density grid system designed to create areas free from through traffic is a good example – they are no more sustainable than other towns. Inevitably, the new towns can be criticised when judged against criteria of sustainability that take a harsher view of car use; but in terms of open space and the design of residential areas they provide good examples of environmental quality that is accessible to a broad population.

Looking at much postwar development with the benefit of hindsight, we can see how town planning was forced astray in its response to rapidly rising car ownership and road transport. Effort was put into well-engineered new roads encompassing traffic-free precincts with concrete underpasses while neglecting the inequitable distribution of the car by class and age, as well as its heavy material demands and destructive environmental effects.

An attempt to show how car growth could be accommodated while protecting the urban environment was made by Sir Colin Buchanan in his famous report *Traffic in Towns* in 1963.[8] Unfortunately, his central thesis has often been misunderstood or misinterpreted. He was arguing that it was essential, first, to determine the standard required in the urban environment and then to face up to the consequential, and inevitable, high cost of accommodating the car within that objective.

No doubt the potential was there in the postwar planning system to shape new developments in the interests of equity, personal safety and environmental quality. In too many areas, life has become less convenient, with services, schools and shops less accessible and with fewer facilities within walking distance of home. An increasing proportion of activities are structured for the benefit of the car-owning majority of households for whom, for example, the weekly trip to the supermarket has brought real benefits in terms of price, and the range of goods, as well as convenience. But there has been a price.[9] Mayer Hillman's research over several decades documents the erosion of local living environments by the motor car. Not all the blame lies at the door of retailers and service providers. It also reflects a failure of regulation and public policy. By comparison with neighbouring northern European countries, British planning has been remarkably slow to promote pedestrian and bicycle circulation.

As with pollution control, the potential for planning to direct transport policy into more environmentally sustainable directions remained dormant for a combination of political and administrative reasons, among them the low position of environmental generalists in the professional pecking order. As a result the most prominent shaping of public policy in new developments has been the wasteful and excessive standards imposed by engineers in the interests of vehicle flow and service maintenance. We have the worst of all worlds: undersized houses amidst oversized suburban roundabouts, car parks, mown verges and turning circles.

PLANNING AND THE LAND-USE QUESTION

In assessing the performance of the postwar planning system in Britain in terms of sustainability, one final factor that cannot be ignored is the failure to capture for the community any significant proportion of the profits from the increase in land values that arise from the granting of planning permission for development. This failure enfeebles moves towards sustainability in two ways. First, it tends to make the development of greenfield sites more attractive than the redevelopment of existing sites, as the gain in land values for the former can be enormous: agricultural land given planning permission for housing can increase a hundred times or more in value (as well as often being easier and cheaper to develop than, for example, a contaminated inner city site). Second, the failure to tax satisfactorily increased land values has removed the one direct source of finance available to the community to pay for much of the investment needed to mitigate the environmental effects of the development, ranging from the provision of public transport and waste recycling facilities to the planting of sufficient trees to absorb the carbon dioxide produced by the energy used by the development.

Much of the increase in land values derives from action by the community in, for example, extending services towards the site and it has long been argued that this 'betterment' should be reclaimed by the community once planning permission has been granted for development. There have been three attempts to collect betterment since the present planning system was introduced in 1947 but each has been abandoned for political or practical reasons. Opponents have criticised the collection of betterment as inflationary, as double taxation when associated with capital gains tax, and as a disincentive to the free operation of the market in land.

The first attempt to collect betterment was made by the postwar Labour government in the 1947 Town and Country Planning Act. This imposed a development charge of 100 per cent of the increase over 'existing use' value. This was followed in 1967 by the Land Commission Act, which provided for a 40 per cent levy on the added development value, with discretion for the government to increase this levy progressively. This failed because it proved to be a bureaucratic nightmare. 1975 saw the introduction of the Community Land Scheme, which provided both for development land to be brought forward at the appropriate time and in the appropriate place and for a development land tax to be charged at 60 per cent of the added land value. This was abandoned in two stages in the early 1980s, again mainly for political reasons.

Since then, planning authorities have turned towards 'planning gain', an officially recognised means of seeking voluntary contributions from developers to the cost of off-site infrastructure and other external costs. But, being voluntary, this has proved to be an unreliable tool that has too often resulted in minimal advantage for the local community. Since planning gain is negotiated with developers, it is usually dealt with as part of a planning permission. The process thus tends to be developer led and, in some circumstances, effectively amounts to the sale of planning permission. The present situation is inequitable both in not restoring to the community the increased land values that community action has created nor in compensating individuals harmed by decisions taken on behalf of the community. Sustainable development demands that these deficiencies be rectified, in the first case to provide for the investment necessary to offset the environmental impacts of development and in the second to make the planning system more just in its allocation of benefits. To these ends, a new sustainable land fund to be sourced from a betterment tax is proposed in Chapter 9.

Of course, any kind of betterment tax was anathema to the free market radicals of the Thatcher government. Indeed, a decade of radical neo-Conservative government in the 1980s further weakened the environmental basis of the planning system in several important respects. Public transport was hit by bus deregulation and by an aggressive road building programme. Local government in big cities was reorganised, with the removal of all traces of the intermediate or regional level of government which elsewhere in Europe has been a prime protagonist in environmental protection. Enterprise zones and urban development corporations gave ostentatious proof of the government's hostility to planning. During this period, the government came very close to a significant deregulation of land-use planning, and particularly of green belts; all that held it back was the mobilisation of the conservationist forces within the Conservative party. Paradoxically, the decline of British manufacturing industry in the 1980s had a beneficial side-effect for the environment, evident in the improving indicators of water and air pollution in the statistics published in the regular *Digest of Environmental Protection and Water Statistics*. But the indicators of urban sustainability showed the 1980s as a decade of decline.

SUSTAINABILITY – A NEW FOCUS FOR PLANNING

The end of the last decade was also the turning point towards a rediscovery of sustainable urban development. The shift occurred at all levels of government. Within Whitehall, the White Paper *This Common Inheritance*[10] and the Environmental Protection Act of 1991 were important milestones, marking the retreat from any further environmental deregulation. Also in 1991, the European Commission published its *Green Paper on the Urban Environment*.[11] The EC's initial incursion into urban policy – prepared by a newly formed urban division within the Environmental Policy Directorate, DG XI – was bold and controversial. It established a strong policy link between urban planning and environmental policy. The arguments for and against the compact townscape which the EC paper identified as most environmentally virtuous will be considered in Chapter 9. But whatever the argument for the sustainability of different urban forms, the importance of the Community's intervention is that it has re-established the old nexus between town planning and sustainable development issues.

The EC seems likely to maintain an active role in this field. The door is being opened for extensive intervention by the Environment Directorate in the interests of pollution reduction and energy saving. The Commission has proposed enlarging the scope of its 1985 directive on Environmental Impact Assessment from individual projects to entire public programmes; and there are proposals to bring development plans into the net. However, progress has been slow. There have also been rumours of initiatives to standardise the present diversity of property and land-use regulation within the Community, proposals that would certainly be controversial.

Meanwhile the British government's latest policy guidance[12] has established sustainability as a consideration for town and country planners at all levels of government – district, county and national. Energy generation and renewable energy are listed as key topics for consideration in strategic planning policy. 'The sum total of decisions in the planning field as elsewhere should not deny future generations the best of today's environment', says the guidance note.

SUSTAINABLE PLANNING AT LOCAL LEVEL

Already many local councils have been laying foundations for a more environmentally sensitive approach to their own activities and a strengthening and more critical approach to the use of the regulatory and control powers available to them. These powers were significantly reinforced by the Environmental Assessment Circular of 1988 (implementing the EC Directive of 1985) and the Environmental Protection Act of 1991.

The purposes to which these may be put are set out in a growing array of Environmental Statements, Environmental Strategies, Environmental Action Plans and Green Charters. The new wave of environmental concern affects urban areas as much as rural, and local councils of all political persuasions. Researchers at Heriot Watt University[13] in July 1991 found more than two-thirds of Britain's 514 planning authorities to be engaged in some kind of 'green planning' initiative, with Liberal Democrat and Labour-controlled councils in the lead.

Early in 1991 the TCPA carried out a postal survey of its own local authority members to see how environmental concern was being reflected in current practice. Fifty-four authorities responded, and the results – in combination with other surveys by the local authority associations (the Metropolitan Planning Office Society, 1990, the Association of County Councils/Association of District Councils/Association of Municipal Author-ities, 1990 and the London Boroughs Association, 1991) – give a good overview of the scope for green planning and of its limitations.

We first asked councils to name and rank their five most important green innovations in order of environmental significance. The response, summarised in Table 2.1, shows the most frequently occurring innovations. No less than three quarters of respondents list 'recycling schemes' and the establishment of a recycling officer among their top five green innovations. The second most popular innovation listed was the introduction of a green plan or policy. More than half of the 54 responses listed specific plans among their important green innovations.

Table 2.1 *Survey of 54 local authorities to establish what environmental initiatives had been taken*

Green innovations	Cited by (%)
Recycling schemes/recycling officer	74
Environmental strategy/statement	54
Promotion of unleaded petrol	17
Tree planting and landscape improvements	17
Environment sub-committee/officer	15
Traffic-reducing measures (park and ride, cycleways etc)	15
Environmental audit	13
Energy-efficiency measures	11
Pollution monitoring	11
Environmental clean-up (litter and graffiti removal)	9

Source: Survey of 54 TCPA member authorities (1992)

There was less consistency on other matters. Clearly, local authorities vary greatly in their priorities for environmental action. Ten of the 54 respondents attached greatest significance to the planning framework, whether through the introduction of green policies through local plans or through the issuing of non-statutory environmental guidance (the response was evenly divided on this score). Twelve authorities put their emphasis on administrative changes, some setting up new officer posts or new committees, others instituting managerial devices such as green audits. It is clear from this and other surveys that there has been some competitive jockeying between local authority departments for the lead on green issues. The Metropolitan Planning Officers Society (MPOS) found in 1990 that half of its environmentally active member authorities had designated an 'environmental co-ordinator'. However, in the majority of cases this individual was not located within the planning department.[14]

As for policy content, the largest group of authorities in the TCPA survey, nineteen in all, have pursued the new emphasis on sustainable practice through specific programmes: their actions range from urban fringe improvement (two) and tree planting (three), through traffic reduction and energy conservation (three apiece), to recycling initiatives (rated top priority by eight authorities).

The greening of policy reflects public attitudes. Respondents were asked to pinpoint the main implications for planning of public interest in sustainability. Transport was the key issue for more than half, followed by energy efficiency in the use of land and design and buildings (twelve respondents).

Several authorities showed awareness of the political implications of the new policies. Bournemouth planning department suggested that a greater public interest in environmental issues was bound to result in fewer applications being approved, more appeals, and consequently more decisions being made centrally by the Department of the Environment. The point was echoed by Thamesdown, who argued for clear government guidance on environmental considerations in planning which local authorities could then implement secure in the knowledge that their case would be upheld on appeal. More than one respondent voiced the need for environmental policies at a national, as well as county and local scales.

The most conspicuous example to date of environmental benefits secured from the bottom up, without central guidance or participation, is the negotiation by local authorities of Section 106 (formerly 52) agreements to provide landscaping and, in some cases, endowments for its maintenance. The rapid increase in the use of agreements during the 1980s was an unpremeditated response to a rising property market at a time of public retrenchment. The negotiation of agreements has, since the repeal of the Community Land Act, also undoubtedly served as an informal, if irregular, device for the local capture of betterment.

The majority of planning gains go into infrastructure, such as road or car parking contributions. But two-thirds of respondents had made use of agreements with a specific green aspect. Several examples were given. In the City of London, a large number of open spaces have been created and secured through planning gain; in Blyth Valley (Northumberland), when a large area was earmarked for housing at South Beach, individual developers entered into a Section 106 agreement to provide open space and, within the same authority, at New Hartley a Section 106 agreement was used to ensure the proper maintenance of an adjacent Site of Special Scientific Interest (SSSI); and in Melton Borough, Leicestershire, a proposal for a new village was adapted using a similar agreement to include a common, 120 acres of passive recreational land, structural landscaping, and a village green and other facilities.

Many authorities who use Section 106 agreements highlighted the problem of enforcement. Several noted the need to distinguish planning gains from bribes. Of the third of the sample who claimed to make no use of them, some instead opted for more stringent conditions attached to the approval of a planning application. A few identified other devices similar in principle, such as agreements under Section 9 of the Bournemouth Corporation Act to secure the improvement and management of landscapes in the area. South Somerset planning authority identified Section 39 of the Wildlife and Countryside Act, which it uses to achieve similar goals.

LOCAL INITIATIVES

The picture presented by our survey is a familiar one in the history of modern Britain. New challenges are stimulating a variety of policy responses among local governments, which are more flexible and sensitive than the central state.[15] Some of these initiatives are staking out new roles for the market and regulator and imply significant redefinitions of private property rights and public interest. The green development guides published by authorities such as Stockport and Sutton are well in advance of legislation and are issued in full awareness that a holistic sustainable planning policy cannot be achieved within current parameters set by law and national guidance.

It is therefore not surprising that the TCPA survey identified recycling – traditionally not an area associated with town planning in its narrow sense – as the environmental initiative most frequently cited. It is an area where a national target has been established, where government resources are specifically being directed and where there now exists considerable scope for invention, imagination and progress. Reduction and recycling of waste were high on the agenda of several authorities. Oxford County Council has adopted waste reduction targets of 50 per cent by 1999, while the London Borough of Sutton intends to reach the same target four years earlier.

Other action programmes with good chances of acceptance by the planning inspectorate seem to be those dealing with landscape, its protection, enhancement and stewardship. Urban forestry, community forests, landscape strategies, and tree planting appear to be at the forefront of action which can make an important contribution to more sustainable development patterns. More greenery means more biomass, thus helping contain soil erosion, act as absorber of CO_2 (the major greenhouse gas), filter fumes and dust particles from the air, and positively influence local microclimates.

The importance of energy conservation and efficiency is widely acknowledged. Activity in this field, as is shown in Chapters 4 and 6, needs to tackle two quite different problems: the upgrading of standards for new buildings and the retro-fitting of existing structures. While Milton Keynes catches the limelight with its promotion of new energy efficient buildings, several authorities – Newcastle-upon-Tyne and the London Borough of Enfield are two – are pursuing less glamorous but arguably more significant initiatives to improve the performance of their existing stock. Progress is constrained more by lack of money than of legal powers. Local councils cannot raise the capital resources needed to achieve future fuel economy, although it is estimated that they could save £2 billion from greater energy efficiency.[16]

Greening transport and reducing pollution in the process is an objective shared by many authorities. There has been more emphasis on shifting trips from private to public transport than on policies to reduce the length and amount of travel itself. While there are now widespread statements in support of better public and other alternative modes of transport, action by local authorities is restricted by cash limitations. Car-related investment in new highways and their improvement still takes the lion's share of all resources available for transport. Some planning authorities are using the development control process to negotiate improvements to public transport infrastructure and a view is emerging that in areas where congestion is already an issue, new development should help deal with traffic pollution by making a contribution to, for example, a commuted public transport fund. Much work will be needed in this area before a position has been reached which in any way can be described as contributing to a more sustainable future.

In the absence of powers for integrated environmental regulation, many councils have placed their main current emphasis on auditing and monitoring. Half the respondents to the TCPA survey had some experience of environmental quality monitoring, though the focus varied between air and noise pollution, the assessment of the impact of traffic management schemes, landscape quality review, and more general systems of environmental audit. Two authorities, Wansbeck and Salford, outlined environmental quality monitoring schemes of particular interest. Wansbeck planning department runs a scheme known as LEAF, or 'Landscape Enhancement and Forestry'. Through this scheme, the whole environment of the district is being assessed and a comprehensive landscaping and afforestation package to improve areas in need of upgrading is being developed. Salford planning department has developed numerous monitoring initiatives. To provide a baseline for monitoring future change these include: monitoring air and water pollution; energy use in council buildings; derelict and vacant land; output measures from environmental improvement schemes; landfill gas; and habitat surveys.

Information, public education and community involvement are essential ingredients in an environmental strategy. Nothing can come of policies for waste reduction, energy saving or the use of alternative means of transport without public support. Young people are already being involved widely in nature conservation, energy conservation, materials recycling and other issues. Their participation provides a growing ground for the budding environmentalists of the next generation.

FUTURE CHALLENGES FOR PLANNING

So much for current practice. What of the future? Our planning system was designed at the end of the war for cities, towns and country which appeared to be relatively self-contained entities. But the imposition of Green Belts, the location of new and expanded towns and the building of motorways was gradually changing the concept of the city into a much wider one of interdependent local economies that required some regional planning. This process of city diffusion has since continued until most of lowland Britain is part of one city region or another.

At the same time, a major international concern was impinging on the scene: the serious threat to the environment as a whole, in particular to the ozone layer, the climate, and biological diversity.

This last concern has altered for the better our view of planning and the environment. Instead of seeing town and country as needing separate policies, we now see the whole as one environmental issue, to be tackled anew. Planning for sustainable development implies a further widening of scope. Although land-use planning has undoubtedly sought to protect the natural environment from the impact of development, the main emphasis has been protection of wildlife habitats and enhancement of the landscape. Only limited attention has been given to the protection of the environment from polluting land uses and, in the case of pollution from agricultural activity, no planning considerations are made at all. Nor do planning considerations yet extend to resource management in the sense of conserving the natural resources that go into building materials, the energy required to make them and the buildings, and the scope for recycling wastes from development.

As the previous chapter argued, it is now necessary to envisage environmental planning as an integrated process which ensures that sustainability is built in as a primary objective at all levels across the range of policies – energy, transportation, pollution, industrial, agricultural and so on – that affect the environment.

Planning for the wider pattern of land use and transport remains weakened by the institutional vacuum, despite the best efforts of the county councils,[17] and of wider voluntary groupings such as the South-East Environmental Strategies (SEEDS), an environmental alliance of local councils in the South-East of England. As we envisage it, environmental planning must be extended to take in land use and transportation, the control and management of pollution, and the conservation of resources, including energy. Such goals imply real shifts both in the setting of priorities and in the evaluation of programmes across the whole range of government. The challenge of *Environmental Policies for Cities in the 1990s*,[18] as emphasised in the recent OECD report of that title, is to weave environmental considerations through the decision making of all sectoral ministries. This aspiration in part underlay the establishment of the British Ministry of Town and Country Planning 50 years ago and, a quarter-century later, reappeared in the brief merging of transport with environment, local government, planning and housing in an environmental super-Ministry. What is different this time around is the shift away from administrative restructuring towards the wider view and towards fiscal and financial mechanisms. Since the collapse of the command economies, governments are more likely to put planning into a proper perspective. Previous rounds of environmental concern placed too much expectation on town and country planning, and the result was tokenism. As the District Planning Officers Society (DPOS) observed of a call by the Council for the Protection of Rural England for energy conservation to be written into all development plans (as it since has been in Planning Policy Guidance (PPG) note 12): 'Telling planning authorities that this is something they can and must tackle will not of itself produce substantial results. Indeed it could be a soft option for Government which faces difficult and unpopular decisions on fiscal and regulatory measures'.

The challenge today is not to incorporate green objectives in the maps and texts of five-year plans, since experience shows how easily plans can be marginalised, but to establish them as factors to be taken seriously by all decision makers, private and public. This is the environmental planning system already outlined in the previous chapter. This system must be complemented by:

- *The modification of private property rights and liabilities.* Law that bears on ownership is perhaps the most powerful tool in the hands of legislatures and the most efficient means of effecting structural change under the capitalist system. The few short paragraphs in the 1990 Environmental Protection Act which lay a 'duty of care' for ground pollution upon owners, and the new duties with respect to litter, will have a direct and penetrative effect, just as did the 1947 Town and Country Planning Act's nationalisation of development rights in private property.
- *Taxes and charges*. Fiscal intervention adjusts price signals in the market to reflect externalities. It remains to be seen to what extent environmental policy can follow the *Blueprint for a Green Economy*[19] in relying on market responses to fiscal signals, as many of the instruments – polluter pays mechanisms, road pricing, tradeable emissions permits, energy/carbon taxes – are logical in principle but still relatively untested in practice.
- *Subsidies and grants*. As we argue below, sustainability cannot be had cheaply. It involves replacing much of our 'dirty' capital stock with environmentally friendlier buildings and equipment. The benefits will accrue to the public in the long run but may not be reflected in private return. Incentives can make viable what would otherwise be unattractive.
- *Monitoring and making the results publicly available*. This is a powerful instrument under democracy. Although the government's new series of environmental monitoring statements began in 1991, there is immense scope for the improvement of data availability and expertise at the local level, particularly if local councils are to be expected to assess development in terms of energy and pollution implications.
- *Regulation*. Technical regulation is the traditional basis of environmental control and will continue to provide the cutting edge in the transition to a cleaner, environmentally friendly economy. The trend (eg under the 1991 Environmental Protection Act) has been towards standards for environmental performance, leaving open how they are to be attained; these standards are nowadays likely to originate in European Community directives.

Town and country planning control has an assured place in the toolkit of instruments for sustainable development. From a strictly theoretical point of view it might be possible to pursue sustainability only through the application of environmental standards and the enforcement of polluter pays principles. But the effect would be highly regressive. Energy, shelter and travel account for more of the poor household's income than that of the rich, and it is these basic outgoings that will become more costly as environmental effects are taken into account. That is why we advocate a much broader environmental planning process that takes social equality as one of its primary goals. An equitable route to sustainability involves measures to protect and maintain the quality of community life. Potentially, town planning does this. Its basic unit of account is not the individual household but the neighbourhood, the community, the town.

America has shown the world how disintegration of the social and the physical fabric of cities goes hand in hand, at immense environmental costs to the world at large. Because of the scale of the problem, environmental legislation in parts of the United States is some of the most advanced in the world today, with tight regulation, sophisticated monitoring and subtle charging and incentive systems. What is missing is the capacity to reverse patterns of social polarization and automobile dependency that are deeply entrenched in land use and planning.

Such social problems certainly exist here, as Britain's inner cities for example, testify. But in some important respects Britain, like other European countries, faces the new agenda of environmental sustainability from a better position. Despite all that has been said in preceding paragraphs, British towns and cities have not been replaced by what a Californian geographer famously called 'the non-place urban realm'.[20] The settlement system remains relatively compact and viable for public transport. We still take for granted a system of policy making and intervention that introduces a wide range of public interest considerations into property development. The best attempts of Friends of the Earth to expound the 'new' concept of sustainable urban development represent a world that is familiar rather than futuristic.[21, 22] Later in this report we come back to the question of the pattern of town and country at which we should aim. But first, to understand how and why it matters, we take a sectoral approach in the following six chapters, looking at natural resources, energy, waste, building, transport, and industry. Chapter 9 reassembles the parts and re-opens the question, what pattern should we aim at?

Sustainability in action
Michael Gwilliam

INTRODUCTION

Some commentators have suggested that the town and country planning system in the UK is already well related to the concept of sustainable development. Conversely, others have dismissed its potential contribution to the sustainable approach as marginal. However, as suggested earlier in this chapter, the system does have potential to make a valuable contribution although, at present, it does so in an unacceptably limited and often haphazard manner.

This section focuses on the present system not because it is ideally constructed but simply because it exists and therefore offers immediate capacity for action. The need to make practical progress towards sustainable goals is pressing, and we cannot afford further inaction simply because 'the model is not right'.

Nevertheless, in focusing on opportunities to use the present system we do need to recognise that there are four basic mechanisms for changing behaviour: direct taxation; intervention in the market to affect product prices; regulation of action by government and its agencies; and positive action to bring about change by directly creating new facilities or opportunities.

Our greatest scope for change may actually lie in the first two. By contrast, our present planning system relies very largely on the third of these mechanisms, and even in this sphere other regulatory agencies play a significant, and not always closely co-ordinated, role. Positive action through the planning process should be a potentially powerful agent for change but in practice its scope has been much restricted over recent years. New towns are no more. Most local authority capital programmes are a shadow of twenty years ago. Urban Development Corporations continue on their uncertain path, as do inner city programmes such as City Challenge and some continuing transport investment. Some have sought to replace this direct investment by the use of 'planning gain', using part of the profit from private schemes for wider social goals. This mechanism can make a contribution during periods of economic growth. At times of recession, with falling real property values, its contribution is very uncertain.

It is precisely because of these limitations that we need to look at the contribution of our present planning system with a view to its closer integration with the work of other environmental agencies. If this begins to occur and is seen to bring forward achievements on a voluntary basis, it may in turn demonstrate how much more might be achieved by radical adaptations of the present system.

THE NEED FOR NEW TOOLS

If we are to bend the existing planning system towards a more sustainable approach we will, however, need some new tools to help us. We need to find practical and available mechanisms that can improve the basis of planning judgements at both the technical and political level. Some examples of potential 'tools' are set out in the following paragraphs, but they are no more than illustrative and will hopefully stimulate others to supplement them.

New Ways of Thinking

We must start to look at development issues with a greater sense of inquiry and awareness about resource concerns. At times we should examine a development need or an inquiry problem from 'the other end of the telescope' to see how it measures against sustainable principles and whether it might make better use of resources or reduce pollution by applying technology more imaginatively. Such ways of thinking already exist or are being developed and include:

1. *Best Available Technique Not Entailing Excessive Cost (BATNEEC)*. See Chapter 5.
2. *Minimum Necessary Specification (MNS)*. Recent government-sponsored research has demonstrated that construction projects, especially in the public sector, frequently over-specify materials and energy inputs for a given design solution. Alternative materials, such as those available from recycling, are not consistently considered. The challenge in future should be for construction engineers to adopt a 'lean engineering' approach (as has already begun to happen in areas such as car design) to create design solutions to construction problems that are elegant and economic in their use of natural resources.
3. *Net Added Value (NAV) assessment*. We need to ask what a project adds to our net resources/productivity/capacity for the longer term, taking into account its consumption of non-renewable resources and its effects through emissions. In some cases such an assessment should be used to determine whether or not a project should proceed. We are not capable of making such assessments at present and will need new information and skills to do so.
4. *Constant Time Accounting (CTA)*. Conventional Discounted Cash Flow techniques place a disproportionate value on benefits derived from projects over the short term, usually no more than ten years. Some projects, however, may continue to consume substantial amounts of non-renewable resources or create significant pollution for many years, whilst conferring apparently attractive short-term returns. Our project assessments therefore need to become more subtle.
5. *Environmental Management Standards*, such as BS7750. A growing body of expertise is developing from the application of this standard and, although not totally transferable, the approach could offer a useful perspective on some aspects of planning judgements.

Better Knowledge

We have not significantly improved our knowledge base for development planning in over twenty years. Our present knowledge base is stereotyped and inadequate for allowing us to assess the new questions. We can tackle this challenge in two ways: by using broader information bases and by interlinking the information that they provide.

We should raise our knowledge of the local environment, particularly its physical characteristics and focus on vulnerable dimensions and potential resource opportunities. We should seek to draw much of this information from the considerable amounts of data already being collected by other agencies operating at the local or regional level, such as the NRA, the Pollution Inspectorate, and the Ministry of Agriculture, Fisheries and Food (MAFF). These improved information bases should be used to understand better the interplay of key environmental and resource issues. Developments in information technology give us the opportunity to hold, manipulate and display data so as to allow the build up of three-dimensional models of key characteristics and their interplay. This is not an attempt simply to return to the 'heavy modelling' techniques of the 1960s and '70s, but it is to recognise that we need to use technology to introduce more rigour and perspective into our work.

Increased Skills

A concomitant of our use of new ideas and data will be the need to train and equip planning staff to obtain and make full use of the available information. Planning training will need to be reviewed and those in work will require some retraining. We may well have to go further and broaden the skill base of those involved in planning, looking to a more mobile and flexible workforce, with more secondments, transfers and use of contract and task groups for particular projects and much more interplay across traditional professional 'territories'.

Better Inter-Agency Working

If the planning system is to play an effective synthesising role at the local level and change attitudes about sustainability, it must operate more effectively with the other agencies – public, quasi-public or private – that operate at the local and regional level. This will require further efforts to improve local networks and co-operation, with more use of joint projects and combined operations, so that our networks become 'action networks'. A particularly important area will be the link between planning and pollution control.

Increasing Public Awareness

The planning system operates in a democratic environment and changed attitudes towards development and land use will not be achieved by planners operating in a technical vacuum, however good their knowledge base. We therefore need to see the involvement of local people as an integral part of the process of change. This requires sustained efforts to provide more information to the public about environmental matters, encouraging dialogue and gradually building an understanding of the need for behaviour change. This is not the same as fostering the narrowest form of NIMBY reaction to development, which planners too often face at present. Such attitudes can be characterised by little concern for any wider issues and needs and an unwillingness to change personal behaviour. Nor is it simply to join with the 'anti-development' lobby. We will have to sustain a very considerable degree of new development in the years ahead, and some of it will be locally unpopular. The key is to change the focus and terms of public discussion about the pace and scale of development. To do this will require clear thinking about the issues, distinguishing and focusing on those which are of real significance in sustainability terms. We should talk more about the nature and form of development, the quality as much as the quantity.

Political Perception

The nature of the democratic process – with regular election cycles – means that political time horizons are often very short. Sustainable development requires, and indeed demands, longer time horizons. It will also require some injection of new resources to allow the planning system and related agencies to make the quantum move forward proposed in other chapters of this book. In the present political and economic climate, this represents a very considerable challenge, although something may be achieved by a redirection of resources. A fraction of the 'peace dividend' – the resources released from defence needs following the end of the Cold War – for example, would work wonders, and the issues are surely significant enough.

There are, however, also some heartening indicators of changes in political attitudes. Sustainability is now on the political agenda at both the international and national level. It needs to be pursued at the local level, and the necessary analysis applied in a more consistent manner by all departments of national and local government. Planners must better articulate why they need support to take a longer-term perspective, and demonstrate the political attraction and indeed necessity of this approach. This will require more resolution and sense of purpose than the planning profession has generally shown in recent years.

TARGETING OUR APPROACH

In order to build confidence about a sustainable approach, we need to deliver some tangible successes. We can do this by searching out practical opportunities. These opportunities already exist across the whole spectrum of town and country planning activities. In order to illustrate the point it is helpful to look at the scope for action in terms, firstly, of the built environment and, secondly, undeveloped 'green' land.

The Built Environment – New Development

When preparing a development plan there should be an explicit effort to identify sustainability criteria and build them into decisions on the scale and location of development. For example: does the plan sustain or improve biodiversity; is the interaction between different land uses made easy by the way, say, homes and employment centres are juxtaposed; are public transport options good; will the plan assist in reducing pollution and meeting water and waste management targets? We should, however, beware of easy assumptions, such as the idea that high density development is inherently a sustainable concept and therefore desirable.

We should also seek to identify the most sensitive types of development in terms of sustainability priorities and then focus on these priorities in the Development Plan. In order to do this we will need more nationally sponsored research. We will then be able to evaluate the relative costs in sustainability terms (use of resources, pollution etc) of such developments as edge-of-town shopping developments or the relative importance of locating all new settlements on rail corridors and apply this national guidance at the local level.

In our Development Control and Building Regulations practice we should apply this thinking in greater detail by developing and applying 'sustainability indicators' which reflect the criteria set out in the Development Plans. In order to be practical, we need to use quite a coarse 'sieve', with a focus on a limited number of factors, using the principles described more fully in Chapter 9. Where an application was identified as sensitive by this process it would then be subject to a more detailed 'sustainability assessment'. Such an assessment would be an adaptation of the Environmental Assessment system. It is important that we do not seek to be over complex or 'comprehensive' in the initial stages of this approach or the process will become unviable. We also need to recognise that this knowledge base will have to be gradually built up over time.

Even in these difficult times, local authority development will still occur and it is essential that such projects give a clear lead in addressing sustainability principles. This has not been the case in the past. National government's record has been even more uncertain and the Marsham Street Headquarters of the Department of the Environment are themselves a notorious example of poor design and use of materials and energy. By contrast, planned developments such as Redditch New Town or the Odense City programme in Denmark show what can be achieved in integrating land use and transport systems. In the case of Odense, considerable energy conservation has also been achieved by the use of combined heat and power schemes.

The Built Environment – Existing Development

New development, though significant, is only a relatively small proportion of the total stock of buildings and infrastructure. It follows that the scope for changes of behaviour is in theory greater amongst this large existing stock. Unfortunately, the practical ability of the planning system to influence this stock is more limited than in the case of new development (although Chapter 6 puts forward some proposals).

Opportunities do exist through redevelopment schemes and the effects that new development can have on existing buildings and their use. A new housing development which includes good local facilities and public transport links could, for example, also provide them indirectly for older housing areas, allowing their residents to change behaviour patterns. A larger scale example would be to add an integrated local/national public transport link to an existing road-served airport, such as the proposed London/Luton Interchange with a new mainline rail station and a direct rapid airport link or the London Heathrow surface rail link. It is therefore important to apply the principles suggested for new development to redevelopment proposals and existing uses, when the opportunity arises. The new power to control some demolition of property gives planning authorities further scope. The reuse of existing buildings may sometimes better reflect sustainability criteria than their destruction and replacement.

Green Land and Non-renewable Resources

We should look at our underdeveloped land and our natural resources from a sustainability perspective. In the first instance, this means identifying the most vulnerable areas and types of physical resource and their associated pollution and depletion. We need to ask whether the present position of change is likely to give rise to problems if it were to continue in 50 or even 100 years' time.

This should lead to an understanding of the key interactions between the critical elements and between the built development and development needs. Environmental audits can assist this process of information and understanding. Lancashire and Bedfordshire provide early examples of such audits operating at the county level. They can, however, require considerable resources to prepare and will not always be appropriate. Nevertheless, they can reveal that topics such as water conservation or soil contamination are key problems, with consequences for development proposals. This information should be used to build up the sustainability indices referred to earlier and so be reflected in the appropriate Development Plan.

Specific targets should be proposed for the reduction of an important resource depletion or pollution problem, as it is essential to have some awareness of progress at the local level if we are to avoid simply making well-meaning statements of policy. In some cases the sensitivity of the issue may suggest that an absolute ban on development in an area would be necessary, going beyond present planning practice. This, however, is likely to remain the exception and could only relate to a resource of clearly acknowledged national importance.

The analysis of natural resources may also raise some questions about depletion of local resources when related to rates of depletion at a regional or national level. They may indicate that, cumulatively, the present rate of loss is unsustainable. In such circumstances, a policy of demand management will need to be considered. It would not usually be practical to advocate a demand management policy for a given resource covering only a single local authority area. But it may well be appropriate for an authority to advocate that a demand management policy is more widely adopted for, say, water resources, waste, transport or minerals extraction. Indeed, this advocacy role is an important element of local government planning's potential contribution to a sustainable approach. Authorities should articulate local concerns and draw government's attention to the practical consequences of present national and regional policies.

Such a demand management focus must, however, not be confused with opposition to development *per se* or a requirement to stop using non-renewable resources in the short term. This would not be politically realistic at the present time. We need to recognise existing needs but start to target provision more sharply and at the same time more fundamentally explore the options for meeting demand in the longer term. This will, however, mean choosing the initial cases for demand challenge carefully.

We also need to look at opportunities to increase the overall resource stock by restoring development land or non-agricultural land to an ecologically diverse and more stable mix of uses. For example, surplus agricultural land in a Community Forest area could become much more diverse ecologically with benefits for recreation activities, for the habitat resource stock, for water resources, and for our timber resource, giving a net gain in resource terms.

EQUITY

In moving towards sustainable planning policies and practice we need to be aware of the impact of such policies on society and its constituent groupings. Some policies, although well justified in simple sustainability terms, could well bear heavily on particular social, sometimes disadvantaged, groups. This is particularly the case where a policy or decision controls an economic activity and leads to a loss of jobs or reduces access to facilities. There is no easy answer to this issue. In some cases the sustainability requirement may be so important that such impacts are unavoidable. In other cases we may be able to ameliorate these impacts; in others, a more fundamental review of social policy may be required. The essential requirement is that these aspects are given explicit consideration when sustainability assessments are made.

A SELECTIVE FOCUS

As pointed out earlier, it is essential to focus and avoid the encyclopedic approach which in the past has been a weakness of planners. If we seek to catalogue and analyse all aspects of development and sustainability the system will overload, we will fail to act and the process will become discredited.

We therefore have to scan sufficiently broadly yet closely to identify the key sustainability questions and then focus measures on these elements. In doing this we should remember that, for an issue to be significant in sustainability terms, it probably needs to demonstrate that it threatens to generate one or more of the following problems in a manner that is of more than local significance:

- A loss of scarce natural resources.
- A substantial contribution to pollution.
- The destruction of biodiversity.

Of course, the cumulative effects of development are not always easy to detect and impacts may therefore only gradually emerge. Nevertheless, we need, initially at least, to follow Henry Ford's maxim, 'If it ain't broken don't fix it', if we are to start to manage complexity. We can always refine the process later.

CHOOSING THE LEVEL

Although the whole planning system needs to become imbued with sustainability principles, some topics may be more effectively addressed at different levels of the system. For example, energy and water issues may be particularly appropriate for action at the regional level while housing development decisions and air pollution may be better focused locally. Given the need to target limited planning resources most effectively, we should seek to identify the most appropriate level of the planning system to take action on a topic and then encourage the development of expertise therein as a part of a coherent planning response to sustainability.

FIRST STEPS

The most vital requirements are, firstly, a better collective awareness and understanding of the main questions that sustainability poses for planners, and, secondly, to make a start in applying these principles. We will find that a number of our existing policies and practices are inherently sustainable. Let us build from that base, using our local knowledge of vulnerabilities and seizing on simple practical opportunities as they arise. A few early successes will build credibility and provide useful experience. Planners can begin by:

- Focusing on the key issues and considering local targets.
- Publicising successes.
- Sharing best practice and information.
- Improving local links with other environmental agencies.
- Advocating changes in government policy based on their local knowledge.
- Identifying issues for national research.
- Devoting resources to environmental education, treating it as a key element of the planning system, not a makeweight.
- Initiating new training and secondment programmes.

How do we find the resources to do this? Perhaps by recycling a few 'sacred cows': but that's another story.

3

Ecosystems and Natural Resources
John Holliday

Throughout the world there is a revolution in thinking about the use of natural resources. No longer can the land, water, air, minerals and other resources be taken as 'free goods'. As population, waste and pollution put pressure on the biosphere, so society seeks ways to meet the challenge of climate change and to conserve resources. Chapter 4 looks at energy and Chapter 5 examines the problems of waste and pollution. This chapter concentrates on four areas:

1. The importance of recognising the ecosystem as a balance of man-made and natural resources.
2. The planning and management of resources.
3. The major land uses of agriculture and forestry.
4. The uses of water, minerals, recreation and localities of scientific, scenic and historic interest.

In doing this it is important to realise that the biological and resource base of the planet is not a fixed entity. It is dependent in part on human activity and in part on the changing nature of the biosphere. Their interaction results in a wide range of ecosystems, from those of developing countries where natural resources are fundamental to their economies, to rich countries where industrial and service economies play a major part in how the ecosystem is viewed. In the former, rich countries are often more concerned about global warming or wildlife than about the indigenous societies of the poorer countries. In the latter, what was once a 'natural' ecosystem has given way to one of inter-acting natural and social systems to produce a 'humanised' ecosystem. In this, the quality of life is dependent not only on conserving wildlife, landscapes and farming but also on the development of the whole socio-economic structure. This, in turn, means examining such aspects as property rights and the traditions of urban and rural land use. Within this world system we shall concentrate on the ways in which the UK should evolve and in particular on the role of planning in guiding that process.

ECOSYSTEMS

The concept of an ecosystem is taken to cover the interaction between people and other forms of life and the environment in which they live. It therefore includes urban and rural areas of varying scales and is concerned with the integration of activities and land use.

We should start by looking at the biological basis for humanity and the age-old attempt to 'conquer' the environment. We need to do this to be clear about the goals of natural resource conservation and the way in which human development takes placed so that robust directions for the future can emerge.

The history of modern science in the West shows the growing dominance of biology which has combined with human development to result in what has been called 'ecological determinism',[1] the destruction of many indigenous human ecosystems in the interests of the Western world. The continuance of this destruction gave rise to one of the major issues at Rio, a treaty on the conservation of biological diversity. The vital issue was the conflict between, on the one hand, the broad interests of conserving species and, on the other hand, more specific, Western, interests largely driven by multinational companies intent on using species for industrial development and claiming the right to retain intellectual property rights in transforming species into products such as pharmaceuticals. At the same time, developing countries challenged the West's right to exclusive use of the wealth from developing such products and also demanded compensation in return for any agreement to prevent their exploitation.

This conflict of interest underlies much of what this chapter is about. There are two major stances. One is that nature and the natural processes of the physical world – including people – must be kept 'in balance' or human activities will end up destroying the biosphere in which we live. The alternative view is that people have always altered the environment and that the ingenuity and power behind technology – and especially the emerging potency of biotechnology – will enable us to survive even though the balance is greatly altered to meet new demands. In the latter view the goal of balanced development is not dependent on what has gone before but on what new developments emerge in our efforts to provide a sustainable environment.

All would agree that there is an ultimate limit and that the chemical constituents of the air, land and water must be kept at levels which will support healthy life. But the way in which people see the issues are many, ranging from those who think the time left to us is very short to those who believe that the problems can be dealt with over long time-scales. A leading proponent of the technological fixers was President Bush's administration in the United States. The USA did not sign the Rio agreement on biological diversity; is by far the world's biggest consumer of resources and in many respects also the biggest polluter of the environment; and it has no national target for reducing carbon dioxide emissions. The new administration of President Clinton seems likely to change this picture significantly: one of its first actions was to announce its intention to impose an energy tax.

Characteristic of the doomsters is *5000 Days to Save the Planet*,[2] which claims to demonstrate the threat of continuing current human behaviour patterns. The Club of Rome publication *Limits to Growth*[3] and the subsequent *Beyond the Limits*[4] report also forecast inexorable catastrophe (as has already been summarised in Box 1.2).

On the other hand *The End of Nature*[5] makes clear that man has gone 'beyond nature' in the fields of mechanisation and genetic engineering. In other words, technological fixers are already fixing things.

The concepts of nature or natural resources are not easily defined. A common mistake is to view nature and the environment as something 'separate' from urban people, as no more than an attractive countryside outside the mainstream of social and economic life. This concept is dangerously inadequate: nature is an interacting system that is changing all the time; the environment is not something that is static and separate from the activities of urban people. Resources such as land, water, vegetation, wildlife and minerals are the basic constituents of economic life and they are spread across the country. Their location, when combined with the use of energy and with waste and pollution, determines the pattern of work and home. New communications are changing some basic characteristics of these relationships.

In this process we are increasingly aware of what can be called horizontal links in the ecosystem – environmental impact assessments are one example of measuring how development will alter relationships. But we are constantly being caught between today's decision and the needs of future generations. It is this challenge – how humanity gets from today to the future – that is central to the concepts of planning and management. It is one thing to see the damage now being caused by pollution, another to anticipate where the next threat will arise.

Our consciousness of this problem affects our future actions and raises questions about the directions of Western industrial development. But whatever the perspective, there is no doubt about the scale and recent speed of events: pollution and waste are now at the forefront of priorities in many countries. 'Green' activities of all kinds are being seen at all levels. The trend is clear. The developed world is moving towards more biologically sound processes in such things as waste minimisation and organic food, but the dominance of market values in a free trade era is slowing the trend, often working against these processes and allowing existing production systems to expand in old ways.

The conundrum reappears elsewhere. For example, the 'green revolution' which followed the UN World Food Organisation's effort to raise production in such countries as India was in many ways highly successful and there is now little doubt that growing populations can be sustained on less agricultural land. But, at the same time, the excessive use of fertilisers and pesticides has led to the pollution of ground water and other damage. This, in turn, has generated proposals to curb the use of such chemicals: for example, the Netherlands is turning to the biological control of pests. It is a question of how fast we can move and what are our priorities. But there is no doubt that we need to look a long way ahead, whether towards the effects of the loss of rainforest, or towards the scientific potential for keeping the planet in balance.

BOX 3.1 The task for the next few centuries

'An age of expansion is giving place to an age of equilibrium. The achievement of this equilibrium is the task of the next few centuries...The theme of the new period will be the resurgence of life, the displacement of the mechanical by the organic, and the re-establishment of the person as the ultimate term of all human effort. Cultivation, humanization, co-operation, symbiosis: these are the watchwords of the new world-enveloping culture.'

Source Mumford, Lewis (1944) *The Condition of Man*, Secker & Warburg

---

In this context any one country will be working towards a more sustainable future for the sake of its own survival. In a world in which resources must be more fairly shared, the idea and reality of scarcity will grow in importance. The conservation of resources does not merely add up to the protection of our environment: it implies a fundamental look at the way in which our land is used. The capacity of an environment to accept change can be much increased by the careful activities of people. Over the centuries, the capacity of much of Europe's agricultural land has been greatly increased by drainage and mechanisation, for example. We should see capacity as a movable target within the overall constraints of sustainability.

The capacity of any ecosystem to meet demands depends a great deal on technological advances. Improving the effective use of resources can be used to improve the quality of life.

Thus we can view the past and future of much of the land of Europe as having increasing capacity, and there is the possibility of increasing it further. There is also great biotic potential in much surplus agricultural land, provided that we consider its future use flexibly and allow changes. The lessons from ecology are that the diversity of life, the recycling of productive materials, and the efficient use of natural resources can improve the quality of the environment. But we will need to change our beliefs, values and approaches to development and nature.

BOX 3.2 Lessons from the ozone story

'One can draw many possible lessons from the ozone story, depending upon one's temperament and political predictions. Here are the ones we draw:

- Political will can be summoned on an international scale to keep human activities within the limits of the earth.
- People and nations do not have to become perfect saints in order to forge effective international co-operation on difficult issues, nor is perfect knowledge or scientific proof necessary for action.
- A world government is not necessary to deal with global problems, but it is necessary to have global scientific co-operation, a global information system, and an international forum within which specific agreements can be worked out.
- Scientists, technologists, politicians, corporations, and consumers can react quickly when they see the need to do so – but not instantly.
- When knowledge is incomplete, environmental agreements need to be written flexibly and reviewed regularly. Constant monitoring is needed to report the actual state of the environment.
- All the major actors in the ozone agreement were necessary and will be necessary again: an international negotiator like United Nations Environment Programme; some national governments willing to take the political lead; flexible and responsible corporations; scientists who can and will communicate with policy makers; environmental activists to put on pressure; alert consumers willing to shift product choices on the basis of environmental information; and technical experts to come up with adaptations that can make life possible, convenient, and profitable even when it is lived within limits.'

Source Meadows, Donella and Dennis, and Randers, Jørgen (1992) *Beyond the Limits*, Earthscan, London

THE PLANNING AND MANAGEMENT OF NATURAL RESOURCES

Human demands on natural resources are increasing to the extent that new approaches to their planning and management are needed. It is as well to list at the start some natural resources with which the United Kingdom is well endowed and which provide the particular environment in which to plan. The land is on the whole well cultivated and has high potential for food production. Water is plentiful and still relatively pure. The tides provide a vast potential energy source. There is also wide untapped free energy available from wind. The sun is also free, and not enough used. Britain has been fortunate in its supplies of coal, oil and gas but these are non-renewable and will to some extent give way to renewable sources. Building materials – clay, stone, sand and gravel – are in good supply but increasingly difficult to work in the face of other uses and environmental considerations. Vegetation is prolific: but, although climatic change is unlikely to alter the potential fundamentally, there is some evidence that small alterations are taking place already and there may be a modification of the species and of habitats for crops and wildlife.

These resources are not mean attributes: they provide the basis for sustainability. But only some are used and there are debits on the human side of the ecosystem. As the first modern industrial country, the UK still lives with an inheritance of big and often ugly cities. Land-use planning, as shown in Chapter 2, is still perceived in terms of 'town' planning. One of the legacies of nineteenth-century free trade and the Empire and the resulting ready availability of resources is that resource planning never developed in the UK. The countryside, in the words of Wiener,[6] was in the late nineteenth century 'empty' and available for use as an integrating cultural symbol. This developed into the view that the countryside, rather than being seen as a part of an urban land resource, should be 'protected' against development, a view that still holds despite the continued accommodation of resource demands on a one-off rather than any strategically planned basis.

Britain has a set of valuable resources which have been developed and used in ways more appropriate for an urban past than for a sustainable future – the lavish use and waste of pure water as a reaction against the degraded nineteenth century city, for example. Put simply, we need to look at our resources and build a long-term strategy around them. In particular, we need strategies for land, water, energy and the urban system. Assumptions about agriculture, about the use of water and energy sources, and about big cities, all need reconsidering in the light of future need. Energy is the subject of the next chapter. The question of urban form was opened up earlier in this report and will be discussed in detail in Chapter 9.

Changed assumptions need changed systems: we need to look at the way our resource stock is valued, how it is accounted for, how investment and returns are calculated, and for whom. The goals we set, if they are to be accountable, must have clear values put against them, whether monetary or otherwise.

At present we have three particular problems to tackle:

1. How do we adapt an infrastructure and attitudes that are unsuited to the future?
2. How do we integrate the variety of agencies that have been generated over the years to deal with a diverse, complex and specialised set of resources?
3. how do we tackle the new market and accounting system that has been developed to serve private and public interests, but often fails the public?

An archetype of the challenge facing us is the water industry. This developed in the nineteenth century as a public service to clean up the dirty industrial city. The two branches of water supply and sewage disposal had specific and clear objectives but the professionals concerned did not work effectively together in one organisation until the 1973 Water Act established the Regional Water Authorities alongside the existing water companies, all of which are now private bodies. Under the Act the authorities, based on catchment areas and river basins, were encouraged to think of relationships between the various stages of water use and disposal, with the aim of managing water as a public service to be provided to whoever demanded it. Water was not seen as a resource that played any positive role in influencing development type or location, except where obvious damage would be done to a catchment area.

Privatisation, introduced to shift the costs of this service from government funding directly on to the consumer, may improve efficiency but has not otherwise changed the direction of the industry. It is still a service based on inherited practices and concepts which do not treat water in new ways, except that there is a trend towards better river management, less new reservoir capacity, and some separation of clean and dirty waste, so that lakes and other features can be built into the environment. But the concept of a service is still resulting, among other things, in the over-abstraction of water, the drying up of rivers, and shortages of supply as demands increase unchecked.

The water industry is but one example. The same story can be told of every countryside industry, from agriculture and forestry to the newer recreation and tourist industries. Add in wave and wind generation, expanding activities to protect wildlife and so on, and a very confused picture emerges of a multiplicity of specialised demands and practices with no integrating agency of the kind familiar in built-up areas through urban planning. Planning as it applies to the countryside is ill equipped both in law and in expertise to do the job.

The failure of the various systems to meet up with the needs of the next century has at least been recognised, and some work carried out. In line with a market philosophy the *Blueprint for a Green Economy*[7] report offers a method. It advocates the valuing of the environment in monetary terms, not as an exact science but as a way of forcing us to a rational decision-making process. Even though many things cannot be given monetary values, they can nevertheless be considered within an economic framework. We can consider the future, and decide to what extent to discount it. We can develop a method for environmental accounting. Europe is moving to do so.

The current belief in the market must be seen for what it is: a means of assessing choices according to a monetary value but not necessarily for the benefit of life in general. In life, whether human or otherwise, non-market values play a role which ranges from a small part to the total sum of existence. In a recent report of an Environmental Ethics Working Party on *Values, Conflict and the Environment*[8] human beings are judged to count most, and a comprehensive weighting of environments (a modification of cost–benefit analysis) is accepted by a majority of the working party on this basis. But a minority rejected this conclusion on the grounds that some environments were intrinsically outside the possibility of being valued in the marketplace. There is in many quarters a strong resistance to the dominance of the market, cultural values always being cited as being incapable of monetary valuation. Of course, any measure of 'progress' is open to argument: for example, many would now argue that the traditional economic marker of Gross Domestic Product (GDP) is more a measure of how close to environmental disaster society has stepped than any gauge of progress in terms of quality of life.

The government white paper *This Common Inheritance*[9] reviews much of the ground which needs to be covered but falls short on translating aims into actions partly because cultural and political values obscure the economic realities. From Schumacher writing in 1974[10] to the more recent work of The Other Economic Summit (TOES), the changes in emphasis, values and approaches have been made, but little has carried through into practice. The Department of the Environment publication *Policy Appraisal and the Environment*[11] makes a start. A more striking example of thorough-going environmental policy change was seen in the objectives set by the Netherlands government in its 1988 National Environmental Policy Plan, quoted in Box 3.3, which required a general election before the government could act (see also Box 1.3).

BOX 3.3 The objective of environmental management

'The main objective of environmental management is to maintain the environment's carrying capacity on behalf of sustainable development.

The carrying capacity of the environment is damaged if the environmental quality can lead to irreversible effects within a generation, such as mortality or morbidity among people, severe nuisance and damage to well-being, the extinction of plant or animal species, the deterioration of ecosystems, damage to water supplies, soil fertility or the cultural heritage, and impediments to physical and economic development.'

Source Netherlands National Environmental Policy Plan (1989)

All these documents illustrate intention and, to some extent, method. They, like the Rio Earth Summit, mark a beginning to serious changes of direction. However, whenever we are faced with economic difficulties, priorities shift to the perceived needs of the market, privatisation and profit. Longer-term environmental imperatives – however crucial to life in the future – are cast aside in the search for short-term economic recovery. So we are still left with the three problems of a reliance on the market, an outmoded inheritance of ways of dealing with problems, and diverse agencies incapable of an integrated approach. How do we take a clear look at resource planning without continually being embroiled by day-to-day problems?

The difficulties cannot be underestimated and there are some serious blanks in the present picture. In spite of a new concern with the quality of our environment and some long term thinking about, for example, renewable energy resources, we have still to accept a conceptual shift in our view of the way in which the economy works and our aims relative to homes, work, production and consumption. The government Cabinet Committee on the Environment, set up following the publication of *This Common Inheritance*, could begin to pull together some of these strands and rethink policy, with the spur of those who have started the process, such as TOES.

One approach is to ask how the inevitable conflict between environmental aims and other policy objectives be resolved. Such a question is misconceived and is likely to lead to the wrong policy formulations, for it yet again separates the environment from other issues. The application of systematic thinking to our environment should start by considering man-made and natural systems as one interacting ecosystem. This immediately leads to an understanding that all resources, natural and otherwise, require managing and planning in ways which integrate the natural environment and that created by humans. Audits and surveys, analysis, policy development and implementation, use of the legal system, public participation in decision making, all would apply equally to buildings, communications, food, timber and energy, with the objective of meeting agreed demands on our resources. This should be the aim of environmental planning.

Complex as the task may be, this long-term integration is vital. The aims of this process were well described by a Royal Town Planning Institute report[12] as being to:

- manage uncertainty and complexity through systematic and continuous learning;
- respond quickly to the unforeseen through rapid contingency planning;
- open up rather than close options, exposing priorities for debate and widening choice;
- manage conflict creatively and thus foster acceptable social and economic change.

We welcome the initiatives seen in *This Common Inheritance* and hope that the full implications of what is said will be acted upon. For example, the section on countryside and wildlife has a heading 'Integrating the environment and the economy': but what is written in the section does not provide any sense of proper integration, which should go far beyond simply looking after landscape and wildlife. It ought also, for example, include looking after rural society in the way carried out by the Rural Development Commission.

Recommendation

Fully integrated urban and rural strategic guidelines that relate to the environmental policies recommended elsewhere in this report should be developed for regional and local bodies.

THE AGRICULTURAL AND FORESTRY LAND RESOURCE

Agricultural land is the most extensive and problematical resource and its future is likely to become more questionable in the light of European Community policy and world trade. Within the EC the UK has an exceptionally high use of agricultural land and a low percentage of forestry land, as Table 3.1 shows.

Table 3.1 *Percentage of total land in agricultural and forestry land use in European Community countries*

	Agriculture	Forestry		Agriculture	Forestry
Ireland	80.9	6	Netherlands	49.7	8
UK	76.8	9	Germany (West)	48.4	29
Denmark	66.7	11	Portugal	47.6	32
Italy	58.5	21	Belgium	46.6	20
France	57.4	27	Greece	–	–
Spain	54.0	25	Community (12)	58.9	24
Luxembourg	49.4	32			

Source European Community Maps and Office of the European Communities

The figures in the table cover a wide range of different conditions. The UK has a high percentage of hill land and rough grazing which, for example, Belgium has not, although it too is a small and densely populated country. There are also strong variations across Europe relating to cultural history and values. Germany, for example, has a high proportion of forestry land which holds particular significance for its culture. This heavily value-laden cultural – and therefore political – influence makes it difficult to alter the balance of land use. In the past, agriculture certainly had to do with the sustainability of a nation and its people, but it is now equally certain that for every country within the Community this is under question.

There are two broad sets of values to be tackled: market and cultural. The market situation has been questioned for many years now, not least because the Common Agricultural Policy (CAP) has taken up the majority of Community funds. In a world of 'free' markets, the protection and subsidies given to food production are likely to continue to be reduced, as they have been in the recent CAP review and as intended within the negotiations under the General Agreement on Tariffs and Trade (GATT) negotiations. This trend will be reinforced by the growing need to consider resources at home and to help poor countries abroad. As a result, the area of 'surplus' agricultural land in much of Western Europe will almost certainly increase. The current provision for set-aside can be seen as temporary, and is on the whole non-productive. So there is potential for switching land from food production to environmental improvement.

Left to a free market, agricultural land is already going to other uses. However, change is often strongly resisted, whether the new use is for housing, workplaces, power production, water resources or recreation. But if enough food can be grown on much less land and if there are other needs that are at present unmet or still to be ascertained, there is a clear requirement to look very hard at the method for assessing land use in the light of future needs. Obviously the best soil should be conserved, but there should be a harder look at practices that still use an excess of fertilisers and pesticides.

The Ministry of Agriculture's codes of good practice for the protection of water, air and soil go some way to controlling the problem, but much relies on voluntary effort. In the medium term, integrated pest control using biological methods will help to minimise pesticide use: once proven techniques have been developed, they should be encouraged by formal advice from the Ministry.

On less good agricultural land there will be increasing competition from other uses and it would be more helpful if we assessed relative values in a strategic way rather than dealt with farmland simply in terms of individual efforts to diversify. This requires resource planning rather than the familiar country planning. Although we have long experience in, for example, minerals planning, we have little in looking at the costs and benefits of wind power, the use of biomass, and other potentially valuable land-use alternatives to set-aside. Neither are our planning policies for rural areas always helpful to the sustainability of vital social and economic communities. Environmental protection and the encouragement of wildlife are welcome, up to a point, but we cannot afford to manage ecosystems which rate human needs too low. Biological diversity and economic activity are not mutually exclusive, and the capacity of much land could be increased. Too much land is held speculatively or as an investment hedge, and it has long been argued that over-investment in land-holding is damaging to the economy.[13]

In parallel with mainstream agriculture there are other trends. One is a movement towards smallholdings, both for commercial purposes and as a way of life. From Scottish crofts to lowland English farms, changes in the ownership of farmland are bringing new activities to agriculture. There is also a reaction to factory farming and a growth of new attitudes and practices in the use of farm animals. In the Cotswolds, for example, the husbanding of rare breeds of sheep is a developing industry. And there is also a trend towards the development of community-supported agriculture, in which people buy shares in a local farm's production. These and other moves – such as the 'eco' villages in Sweden and Denmark – suggest a reaction against mainstream high-tech farming, favouring instead small-scale community activity and the development of a much more diversified agricultural scene.

Recommendations

Agricultural land of high productivity should continue to be protected through the application of codes of good practice and with more attention to minimise the use of fertilisers and pesticides.

Less valuable land should be assessed for its most beneficial use, leading to guidelines for woodland and wildlife reserves, as well as for housing and economic development.

Proposals for future use should be included in strategic plans together with their justification.

Consideration should be given to the establishment by local authorities of 'countryside centres'[14] to guide, control and support activities in the countryside.

Forestry has a natural association with agriculture. Since the setting up of the Forestry Commission in 1919, the war time strategic justification of ensuring timber supply has changed to include meeting the needs of recreation, landscape design, and ecological balance. Much has still to be learned, for in this country – unlike some others – owners have long pillaged forests for cash and neglected long-term needs. But learning continues, although it is very slow as regards integration with agriculture and the newer problems of acid rain, fish life, water supply and ecosystems generally.

Forestry is an attractive investment for the future: it has a beneficial influence on climate, water supply and wildlife; it reduces pollution by absorbing CO_2 and filtering dust; it has an over-riding value in the design of the landscape and, in particular, in absorbing large-scale urban development and providing recreation; and, of course, it has an economic value that is made all the more important because, at present, Britain imports 80 per cent of the timber it uses. There is further potential in growing timber as a biomass crop for energy production. Not only does forestry offer these long-term advantages, but there is public acceptance of mixed forestry in lowland Britain.

However, since the last war there have been problems resulting from favourable tax policies for owners that have encouraged market-led planting, often with damaging effects on the landscape and ecosystems. Until the 1980s, grants and tax concessions were generous and encouraged massive clear-felling of hardwoods and the planting of large, monotonous, mono culture forests. This latter practice has not yet ceased.

There is growing concern about the use of grants for landowners and about rights of access. From the public attention now being given to the large sums of public money paid to landowners, it appears that some action may well be taken independently of any planning legislation.

Recommendation

Planning guidelines and strategies should be prepared in detail for all hill lands as part of the proposed new environmental planning system. The present weak control of the use of hill lands should be replaced by statutory requirements for the assessment and planning of land uses.

On hill land much has been done since the war, and gradually our forestry expertise (greatly neglected in the UK previously) has approached best practice in Europe. But there is still great scope for improvement, as there has been an absence of strategic planning in association with other major resources. There are one or two exceptions, for example in the Flow Country of Caithness and Sutherland (see Box 3.4). Here, the government asked the regional council to propose an indicative forestry strategy in the light of demand and the unique value of the area for wildlife, science and its world importance as extensive moorland. A strategy has now been largely accepted by the government (incidentally demonstrating the value of regional planning bodies).

BOX 3.4 Controlling forestry

'The Highland Regional Council (HRC) had for some years been facing one of the thorniest problems on land use in the counties of Caithness and Sutherland where the combined forces of the ecology, conservation and environmental lobbies were ranged against what they saw as the incipient spread of forestry. The HRC's Summary Report and Land Use Strategy published in January 1989 set a standard of impartiality and sound judgement which has placed a marker for others to follow...The Flow Country covered some 300,000 hectares and is as near to wilderness as could be found in any part of western Europe...

Accepting the majority of the report, the Secretary of State for Scotland accepted the majority of the HRC recommendations and indicated that permission would be given to allow afforestation up to 100,000 hectares, the level deemed necessary to establish viable upstream and downstream forestry related activities. He also agreed that 180,000 hectares of the two counties could be designated as SSSIs.'

Source Sinclair, John (1990) *Taking the Land in Hand*, Hebden Royd

---

In the past few years major plans have been made for community forests, together with a new forest in the East Midlands. Twelve new forests are jointly proposed by the Countryside and Forestry Commissions to cover about 200,000 hectares, mostly to be sited near urban centres. Their objectives are wide, ranging from timber production, recreation, encouraging scientific interest in wildlife and ecology, and integration with agriculture and settlements. When combined with proposals for green spaces within urban areas, these new forests represent a major change in the use of land in and around urban areas.

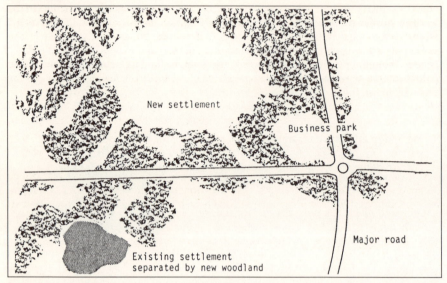

Source *Town and Country Planning*, June 1991, p189

Figure 3.1 *Planting woodland to enclose a potential site for a new settlement can create a high-quality periphery that will help to allay public fears about possible future sprawl*

While changes in forestry have been positive and show major gains, agriculture is in some disarray and has little to show by way of strategic planning apart from a slow movement towards social and environmental objectives. Some work has been done on the transfer of agricultural land to conservation[15], but very little guidance has yet been established.

BOX 3.5 Woodland and New Settlements

'The debate about new settlements has been dominated by developers seeking to impose them and planners seeking a public mandate to plan them properly. Entrepreneurial landowners could sidestep this debate and use new woodland to attempt to redistribute development hope value at the regional rather than the local level. Their objective would be to persuade consumers in the social marketplace (ie elected councillors on planning committees) that future development should be concentrated on their land rather than elsewhere.'

Source Pitt, Julian (1991) 'Community Forest Cities of Tomorrow', *Town and Country Planning*, June, TCPA

There is also an inheritance of rights over land which were curtailed in urban areas in the 1940s. There is little planning control over either agricultural or forestry operations.

Further, there is much use of devices not only to give special tax treatment (roll-over and access provisions) but also to pay heavy compensation for the curtailment of agricultural development in, for example, SSSIs.

This has happened partly because of different attitudes to the country and the town; in the UK, high value is attached to the look of the landscape and all it represents from the past. But much of the special treatment afforded to the countryside is tied up with vested interests. It is time for the rights and responsibilities of land and property owners in the countryside to be brought into line with those in the town.

There is much confusion in the use of the words sustainability, conservation and protection and they are often used interchangeably. But their meanings are not the same. *Sustainability* implies change and development for people as well as for the environment. *Conservation* also involves change but within the broad intention of keeping the environment more or less the same. *Protection* is against change and development. Protection is too often a smokescreen for perpetuating vested or blinkered interests instead of seeing the full material and spiritual use which is implied in sustainability.

It follows that, if we are to develop sustainable policies, traditions and public money cannot continue to be used to support existing landowners too extensively: their rights and eligibility for compensation should in equity be on the same basis as those who own property in towns. Further, over-protective attitudes in the countryside will have to give way to policies that see the land as a major resource. Rather than being subsidised for unproductive use such as set-aside, the land should be producing new employment in association with the development of other resources. In suggesting this, we are not advocating sprawl or poor quality design. These were major reasons for the 1947 Planning Act and, after 45 years of experience, we can now assuredly exercise good control over new development. There are many good examples which can be followed everywhere and forestry can play a much greater role in urban fringe areas (See for example Figure 3.1).[16]

Recommendation

As forestry development is especially valuable on urban fringe land and land which may in future be used for urban purposes, such sites should be part of strategic land-use plans. (Particular reference is made to the ideas set out by Julian Pitt.[17])

Legislation should be introduced as a part of an environmental planning system in order to:

- Define and allow for the control of certain agricultural development, including such operations as the destruction of hedgerows or historic sites. This would not control the choice of crops or similar operations.
- Extinguish rights to drain wetlands, plough up moorlands and damage other valued environments.
- Alter compensation provisions so that none would be paid where rights were extinguished.

OTHER NATURAL RESOURCES

WATER

Overall, there is plenty of water in the UK. But there are shortages in the South East because of lower rainfall and where higher abstraction to meet growing demands has depleted groundwater supplies. There is also a tradition in the water industry of providing a 'service' rather than thinking positively about strategic planning for sustainable development. There is a clear need for more attention to be paid to water supply and sewage disposal within strategic plans for regions as a determining factor in planning.

Shortages have been severe in some regions in recent years and it is possible that the movement of water from west and north to east and south will probably be necessary. Its cost at a few billion pounds is relatively cheap compared with expenditure on many other sectors and as a vital natural resource its priority should be high. At present, however, the government is putting more emphasis on metering, the prevention of leaks, and the use of showers in place of baths. Although such measures are useful, they in no way indicate any attempt at a fundamental review of the way in which water is used in society today. The principles of the current water infrastructure were conceived and designed for the Victorian era.

Elsewhere, some of the fundamentals of the current system are being challenged. There is some separation of clean and dirty water and the imaginative use of clean water run-off for the provision of new lakes; there are moves to increase the supply of treated sewage (from which toxic minerals have been recovered) for use as a fertiliser; there is the development of reedbed natural purification systems; and much is being done to manage and recycle river water rather than follow the pipeline process of reservoir, purification, use and disposal. Changes in the design and technology of supply and disposal are now necessary, together with changing policies.

Recommendations

The provision of water should no longer be thought of as a service that should be automatically available for development but as a resource to be managed in association with all development. Plans should be more positive about the consequences on the demand for water of the future of land use.

Strategies for water conservation on the basis of more separation of supply and disposal systems according to appropriate recycling techniques should be prepared as part of our system of environmental planning.

Domestic pricing policies which encourage waste of water should be phased out soon and replaced by charges based on metered usage, with allowances for the less well off.

MINERALS

Planning for mineral use has been a special concern since the war and is one of the most contentious development issues. The question of mineral extraction for power generation is discussed in the next chapter and for the building industry in Chapter 6. Rare minerals can be expected to continue to be in demand, although these are not extensive land users. County councils are required to prepare local minerals plans under the Planning and Compensation Act 1991.

The working of minerals highlights a particular planning problem, that of damage to the landscape. Their working is noisy and dirty and generates often-damaging traffic. Restoration is covered by planning conditions but a continuing problem of dereliction exists, in spite of government efforts and grants. Where the ownership of such derelict land is known, there would seem to be a strong case for taxing it in order to bring it into some use, for tree planting, for example; taxation would then cease. Where ownership is not claimed, such land should be taken into public ownership by local government or a trust, when it could be made productive.

Recommendation

All derelict land should be taxed, or where owners are not known, brought into public ownership (see also Chapter 5).

There is then the more general problem of design in the landscape so as to avoid unpleasant development. A major problem is that screening is rarely a satisfactory solution to a landscape design problem as this requires sensitive and large-scale planting, often across ownership boundaries. In fact, property interests in many cases mitigate against good practice and the question of rights and the use of public money is now becoming a major issue. Julian Pitt[18] has pointed the way to a solution with his ideas for advanced planting for future uses. The same technique is being used at Ardington and Lockinge in Oxfordshire, where planting is being carried out 30 years in advance of building on estates under one ownership.[19] The achievement of this solution is dependent on long-term planning and land purchase or on binding agreements.

Single ownership has in the past allowed for major long term design but is unlikely to be possible for many areas in the future. So this design role can only be achieved through long-term strategic planning. This could encompass not only minerals but all aspects of development. It would require agreements with many landowners but could be a next stage in the control of land use and the acceptance of change.

Recommendation

Long-term planting proposals should be part of strategic planning. Such planting over 20 or 30 years could absorb most ugly mineral, urban fringe, and similar development. It would be the responsibility of those wanting to develop land to undertake the work. Although planting could be done after consultation with the planning authority, it would not imply any planning permission and would in any case be an asset of value to the owner.

SPECIAL AREAS – SCIENTIFIC, WILDLIFE, HISTORIC AND SCENIC

The growth of legislation and policy relating to areas of special interest for their scientific, wildlife, historic or scenic value has been sporadic, of varying effectiveness, and uneven emphasis. Generally, law and practice has been inadequate to protect valuable sites, for compensation provisions have been too heavy for protectors. For the long-term interest, society will soon have to decide a number of priorities, given conflicting interests and new developments. The influences that will determine choices include:

- The value of scientific, wildlife, historic and scenic areas. As with buildings a grading system is desirable, for not all can be kept but some should be considered sacrosanct.
- The effect of climatic change on vegetation and on wildlife, which may require 'movable' site and grading priorities.
- The recognition that the management of ecosystems requires an integration of human and wildlife considerations and that culling, for example, will occur if human activities are to be considered.
- The recognition and designation of major historic land sites in the countryside, many of which are now unrecognised. Again some system of grading needs introducing more widely.

- The growing attraction of scenic areas. In some cases excessive use is leading to considerable damage and consideration needs to be given to restricting access to certain 'heritage' areas.
- The move towards the integration of many proposals by careful management, planning and the targeting of resources.
- The provisions for control and compensation.

It is inadequate just to 'protect' certain areas for reasons of landscape value. These are working and living areas of great variety and often in need of economic development. With agriculture, forestry, mineral and other development, they need to be seen for what they are, as part of the natural resource of the country and, like cities, requiring integrated planning and a recognition of the dynamic of change. At the same time, when protected status is given, the provisions for implementation need to be fair. Following the recommendations made earlier, the planning principles now applying to urban development need to be extended to include land resources in general.

Recommendation

Integrated land-use and design strategies should be a key part of our system of environmental planning. They should recognise the variation in value of different sites and the dynamic for change by climate and other natural, as well as socio-economic, factors and be part of the planning strategies already recommended for all land. They should be based on an environmental audit of all resources, as proposed in *A Time for Action*.[20]

RECREATION

Recreation has become a major industry which exploits our natural heritage and often spoils what it values most. For example, the sporadic siting of golf courses as a form of farm diversification can lead to demands for extensions and related growth that are not always in the right place. This is serious and needs to be put into the context of conserving resources for the future. Of course, an enormous amount of good work has been done in National Parks, Areas of Outstanding Natural Beauty (AONBs), coasts, country houses and other places, but broad policy treatment is very limited, being restricted largely to designation, access and design. This often prohibits more productive uses: for example, employment unrelated to tourism.

Existing designated areas provide a start, but in this highly specialised world they need to be refined to create niches in the landscape, localities that fit into larger areas. Thus, as SSSIs and other specialised areas are designated, so (in the context of transport, energy, agriculture and scenic factors), recreation needs to be thought about and put into a strategic context: appropriate in certain areas but not in all. Again, National Parks and some countryside practices show the way, as does work on the transfer of agricultural land to conservation areas[21]. Some pricing policies may also be appropriate, especially for commercial tourism. But at present the diffusion of tourism and recreation is too wide and the location of sites too arbitrary.

If we are moving towards a new view of our natural resources, we shall need to reconsider the general freedom of access to the countryside which exists – with resulting demands on road space and energy use – and fit these needs more sustainably into the landscape.

Recommendation

When proposals for recreation are being considered, an analysis of the potential for growth should be made, taking into account both landscape suitability and the likelihood of attracting unsatisfactory urban-style development.

URBANISATION AND THE COUNTRYSIDE

The inevitable spread of urbanisation across the land poses the question as to what kind of ecosystem will be formed to meet the needs of sustainable development. We would not go as far as H G Wells who, as a result of new communications, saw a countryside covered with houses and urban uses.[22] The human colonisation of 'natural' ecosystems will, however, continue. But we would stress that urban-related uses are likely to take unsuspected forms. The demand is for urban (or post-urban) people to use land in ways which seem right to them in an age in which agriculture is, after millennia of dominance, of declining importance as a land use in advanced countries. The shift of perspective which this implies is not the present shift to bland extensive landscapes, or the further 'protection' of the environment. It is a shift to a realisation that here is a major resource which can be used economically, socially, and environmentally for the fullest needs of the population.

The problem lies with resistance to change. The potential is great, but the resources of people and land are not used to the full. Some of the resistance comes from the myth of a landscape which has passed,[23] an attempt to protect from change something that is inevitably evolving. It has always changed with people's development. Land, water, wind, sun, vegetation and minerals: these are resources that urban populations must learn to use well, in new ways, and without the mind-sets which centuries of a certain kind of urban progress have instilled. We will need to plan and greatly raise the quality of design for the environment if we are to survive.

Nowadays, there is resistance to almost all development. This resistance will grow and the implication is that we will not make clear progress without very careful advanced thought and design. The design of sustainable ecosystems is a major challenge. It depends on vision, on sound planning and on investment. In the future of the advanced industrial economies, ecosystems will be more specialised and intensive; less concerned with food growing, more with other aspects of energy production. They will be more complex, more open to the public gaze and use, and more in need of careful planning and management. Land ownership will carry greater responsibilities. As the Countryside Commission suggests,[24] there will be a new map no longer relying on old processes to create attractiveness, diversity and ecological vitality. The Commission promises to press for a 'strategic approach at regional and local level'. Such an approach must accept change for sustainability as the basis for all planning.

This new map must also include human habitation, which cannot forever remain in the form created by past considerations. When swallows arrive in the New Year, many views will have to change.

The author wishes to acknowledge a host of people who, over the years, have provided stimulus and information for this chapter.

Towards a Sustainable Energy Policy

Adrian Webb and Chris Gossop

THE CHALLENGE OF GLOBAL WARMING

From the dawn of civilisation energy use has been the most important single material factor influencing man's activities, ranging from physical comfort and food supplies to every type of economic achievement. Without the use of energy, quality of life can hardly rise above subsistence level, or the necessities of bare survival. This fact is today readily apparent in many communities in the Third World.[1]

Unchecked, the profligate use of energy – particularly in the developed world – and the consequent and growing environmental effects threaten the survival of all of us in the long term. It is essential that we move towards a society which manages all its resources – especially energy – in a way that meets genuine human need but that also ensures a secure future for generations that follow.

In *Our Common Future*[2] the World Commission on Environment and Development highlighted the scale of this task. Reviewing prevailing energy trends, the Commission forecast an increase in global energy consumption from the equivalent of 10 billion tons of coal per year in 1980 to 14 billion by 2025, allowing for a population increase from some 4.5 billion to 8.2 billion and assuming the same per capita use and differences in use between the developed and less developed countries. But if people in the developing world began to use energy at the same rate as those in the developed world today, total consumption would rise to a staggering 55 billion tons. The implications of such an increase, or even a much lower one, are alarming. Supplies of fossil fuels on which the world currently relies are finite, and the options of renewable sources and nuclear power pose substantial problems of their own. For all their promise, wind, solar and tidal power remain largely untried as bulk sources of energy. Nuclear power raises questions of safety and waste disposal which have not yet been satisfactorily resolved.

However, the burning of fossil fuels leads, with present technologies, to the production of carbon dioxide, the prime source of global warming (the 'greenhouse effect'). The best estimate is that temperatures will rise by an average of 0.3°C a decade, giving a 1°C rise by 2030. Although the precise consequences of global warming are unclear, there is a scientific consensus that the effects will be momentous. Low-lying countries such as Bangladesh and the Maldives are likely to be affected by severe flooding, which could also threaten cities such as Hamburg and Shanghai; climate change will radically alter food-growing capacities in many parts of the world; and the resultant mass migrations of people will pose huge problems for world order.

The apparent unsustainability of such future scenarios led the World Commission to advocate a new low-energy path, the principal features of which would be a massive new emphasis on energy efficiency and conservation and an accelerated development of renewable sources 'which should form the foundation of the global energy structure during the 21st century'.

The measures required to move the world towards a sustainable energy path will profoundly affect both the developed and the industrialising countries. However, in the short term at least, the development needs of the latter imply additional energy consumption, even assuming significant improvements in efficiency both in the supply of energy and in its final use. We must look primarily to the developed countries, which presently consume the bulk of the energy used across the world (7.0 terawatts [TW] in 1980 compared with 3.3TW for the developing countries) to cut their energy demand and to assist others to develop benign energy strategies through technology transfer and financial assistance. There is no question that in the rich, developed world, the means exist now to achieve huge savings and, ultimately, to move away from harmful supply technologies. The problem is that, for a variety of economic, structural and political reasons, in most such countries this switch is yet to happen.

Our Common Future was published in 1987. It was favourably received by the governments of some 100 nations and a resolution of approval was passed by the United Nations General Assembly. However, the practical response was very slow and it took the findings of the Intergovernmental Panel on Climate Change (IPCC), published in mid-1990, before any real signs of action emerged. Based on the IPCC's scientific confirmation of the reality of global warming, a number of governments have set targets to stabilise or reduce their CO_2 emissions. Front runners include Germany – which plans to cut its emissions of carbon dioxide 25 per cent by 2005 – and Denmark, which plans to cut similar emissions by 20 per cent by 2000, both using 1987 as the base.

These plans must be seen against the estimate by the Commission that an immediate reduction of 60 per cent is necessary to stabilise atmospheric concentrations of the longer-lived greenhouse gases, carbon dioxide, CFCs and nitrous oxide.

While ahead of the United States – whose inhabitants are the world's greatest per capita consumers of energy and which has yet to commit itself to any timetable for action – the United Kingdom's response to the threat of global warming has been hesitant. It was the last of the EC member states to accept the Community's target of stabilising CO_2 emissions at 1990 levels by the year 2000, a most undemanding target given the scale of the threat and the enormous potential to achieve savings. The TCPA does not think that this gives remotely the right signal to the power generation industry and to consumers. On the other hand, a reduction of 25 per cent by the year 2005 would be a sign that, nationally, we were acting with more appropriate urgency.

Recommendation

The United Kingdom should commit itself now to equalling the highest level of reduction in carbon dioxide emissions set elsewhere in Europe and to not less than 25 per cent of 1990 levels by 2005.

The remainder of this chapter will look primarily at UK energy policy and at the sorts of changes which will be needed if we are to tackle CO_2 and other impacts effectively. Clearly, the UK will need to play a full part in securing the international agreements on emissions so vital to our long-term future. In parallel, however, there is much that the UK could do on its own or, preferably, in concert with its European neighbours to take a lead and show by example what can be achieved. Table 4.1 shows the main sources of CO_2. (Transport, acknowledged as a growing source of CO_2 and other emissions, is dealt with separately in Chapter 7.)

Table 4.1 *Main sources of CO_2 emission in the UK (by Final Energy Consumer)*

Households	26%
Industry and agriculture	56%
Commercial and public sector	15%
Road transport	21%
Other transport	3%

Source Department of the Environment (1993) *Climate Change*

A LONG TERM STRATEGY FOR ENERGY

Until recently, the UK government has had little patience with the notion that the meeting of our energy needs requires any form of long term planning. Instead, there has been a strong belief in market forces as being, in general, the most efficient way of distributing resources while the question of an appropriate energy mix is not thought to be one for the government but one which should emerge from the total decisions taken by individual consumers and producers in the marketplace.

However, the TCPA believes that the new environmental imperatives demand that future energy policy should be much more interventionist. The present market-dominated approach has given both producers and consumers too little incentive to invest in saving energy and, although there have been some encouraging initiatives, the total impact of these is as yet small. Evidence from most countries, including the USA, is that a mixture of public and private initiatives produces better results. Government sets the targets and standards, creating impetus and the right conditions – such as a level playing field – for the private sector to undertake progressive initiatives without suffering undue competitive disadvantage.

The TCPA considers that some key principles and areas for action will need to be adopted if Britain is to move towards a sustainable energy path. Above all, a long-term approach is vital. We propose that this should have the following components:

- The establishment, in concert with the EC, of national energy saving/CO_2 reduction targets.
- The development of a national framework reinforced by taxes and incentives to achieve these goals and within which local energy strategies would play a significant role.
- Over the short to medium term, fostering the most efficient use of fossil fuel reserves – predominantly gas, oil and coal – and the accelerated development of combined heat and power (CHP) networks.
- The phasing out of nuclear power.
- The preparation of a long term strategy for renewable energy with a view to meeting at least 20 per cent of the UK's energy demand by 2025 and the major part by the middle of the next century.

ENERGY TAXATION

Although both France and Germany have accepted the principle of energy taxation, agreement on implementation within the European Community remains elusive. In our view, energy taxation, coupled with energy efficiency and conservation standards for buildings and products, is the only realistic way to achieve major reductions in national energy use which considerations of global equity and environmental protection demand. Their introduction could be fiscally neutral and, to counter the regressive impact, would need to be coupled with a corresponding adjustment of the overall tax and benefits system and be supported by loans and grants to promote conservation and efficiency.

Recommendation

The EC, together with the UK government, should introduce energy and carbon taxes on a progressive basis as a means of encouraging greater energy efficiency, curbing CO_2, and reducing other impacts; such taxes should apply both to fossil fuels and to nuclear power in recognition of the considerable costs that both forms of energy impose on the environment.

POWER GENERATION – OPTIONS FOR THE FUTURE

A greatly stepped-up programme of energy saving reinforced by energy taxes could reduce significantly the need for new generating capacity. However, much existing plant will need to be replaced at the end of its economic life and decisions will be required on what form this should take. This section reviews the main options and the types of technology that could help put Britain on the path towards a sustainable energy policy.

FOSSIL FUELS

In the short to medium term – and certainly up to the middle of the next century – the UK will continue to rely heavily on fossil fuels, particularly natural gas and coal. This will make it particularly difficult for the UK to meet the IPCC Scientific Assessment that carbon dioxide emissions must be reduced by 60 per cent immediately if their concentration in the atmosphere is to be stabilised. Currently, coal is coming under increasing pressure from natural gas both as a direct source of energy and as a fuel which can be burnt to generate electricity – producing less carbon dioxide/sulphur dioxide in the process. Gas has emerged as the preferred fuel of the new generating companies for both economic and environmental reasons. These factors seem destined to reinforce the run-down of the coal industry and the continuing job losses in the coalfields, even if the massive closure programme proposed by the government in 1992 is reduced significantly. Given the freedom that the companies now have to import coal, the future for the domestic industry and for those areas that are still directly dependent on mining looks bleak.

The TCPA is disappointed that no real attempt has been made to exploit the lead that Britain once had in developing new coal-burning technologies such as fluidised bed combustion (FBC). FBC can reduce sulphur dioxide emissions by more than 90 per cent by trapping sulphur during the combustion process, with no need for flue gas cleaning.[3] Although not a greenhouse gas, sulphur dioxide is a major contributor to the acid rain that is causing major damage to forests and buildings throughout Europe. Within the past decade other countries have moved fast to introduce the new FBC technology, with several hundred FBC units now commissioned around the world. Environmentally, such plants represent a major advance on conventional coal-fired stations and could help change the public's perception of coal as an inherently dirty fuel. Abroad, many such plants have been built within central city locations, satisfying extremely stringent emission requirements; for example, a coal-fired fluidised bed CHP plant has come into operation in the centre of Stockholm.

FBC has two advantages over conventional combustion. It generates far less nitrogen oxide (NOx) – a greenhouse gas and cause of more local pollution damage – and it is highly flexible regarding fuels. With relatively little modification, virtually any fuel can be used, ranging from low grade coal to refuse and even sewage sludge. FBC is most appropriate in relation to smaller power stations and unit sizes ranging up to, say, 250MW. It has particular promise for combined heat and power applications, a technology dealt with below.

The use of FBC, the fitting of desulphurisation equipment and low NOx burners to existing coal-fired plant, and the burning of natural gas can drastically reduce sulphur dioxide and nitrogen oxide emissions, the major sources of acid rain. However, technological solutions which can eliminate or substantially reduce carbon dioxide emissions are thought to be a long way off. Given that we shall need to rely on fossil fuels for at least the next half century, the priority after reducing demand must be to ensure that energy is produced as efficiently as possible. While good progress has been made in stepping up conversion efficiencies with the latest combined cycle gas-fired plant – giving an efficiency of roughly 50 per cent – the fact remains that even with this new technology half the energy potentially available is still being wasted. These levels of efficiency also cast doubt on the wisdom of using gas for power generation at all, as far higher efficiencies (85 per cent and more) can be achieved when gas is used in condensing boilers for domestic and commercial heating systems.

The only real way to secure further improvements in the use of gas for electricity generation is through the exploitation of the heat that would otherwise go to waste through combined heat and power/district heating systems, widespread on the Continent but only now coming into their own in Britain.

COMBINED HEAT AND POWER (CHP)

In contrast to conventional electricity-only generating plant – where the excess heat is dumped, usually in the form of steam emitted from cooling towers – the heat produced by a CHP system after the generation of electricity is not wasted but is instead piped through district heating mains to housing and other users. By combining the production of electricity together with hot water for space heating as well as, possibly, steam for industrial processes, energy efficiencies of more than 80 per cent can be achieved.

CHP/district heating is particularly prevalent in Scandinavia, with one of the most extensive schemes being in the Danish city of Odense, where some 95 per cent of homes are heated directly through the city's CHP plant. A feature of such whole city schemes is their immense variety and flexibility. In Sweden, for example, the heat produced from CHP stations, generally coal or refuse fired, is often supplemented by waste heat from industry while, through the use of sophisticated technology, it can even be extracted from municipal sewage and from lakes.

Such local schemes tailored to meet the specific needs of the city or town in question contribute significantly to meeting Sweden's national energy objectives. District heating networks provide for about 30 per cent of Sweden's total heat demand while the municipalities which typically control the networks have a production interest in about 20 per cent of the electricity produced nationally. The applicability of local energy strategies in Britain is discussed in a subsequent section of this chapter.

In Britain there has been considerable development of industrial CHP in the wake of the 1989 Electricity Act and the stimulus that this has given to independent generators to sell electricity to the national grid. Total capacity at present stands at some 2000mw, a figure which will increase to some 5000MW assuming two current proposals come on stream. Of these, the larger – an 1800MW gas-fired station – is being built by ICI to provide power and process steam for its Teesside operation. Surplus electricity will be made available to the national grid.[4]

The TCPA welcomes such initiatives and hopes that further projects will come forward in the near future. However, we are disappointed that there has been so little progress in establishing city schemes, which have been the subject of government investigations and reports since the late 1970s. Despite all the considerable effort expended – which has demonstrated the clear potential for CHP in a range of urban areas – it is only in Nottingham and Sheffield that anything substantial has actually been built, although there is a proposed scheme in Newcastle-upon-Tyne.

Installing a CHP/district heating scheme from scratch in the heart of an existing city or town is a complex (and costly) process which will demand very close co-ordination between the developer, the local authorities, and the energy utilities with whom long-term contracts will need to be negotiated. If such obstacles could be overcome – it was the last of these which led to the failure of an otherwise extremely promising scheme for Leicester – CHP at the urban level could make a significant contribution to our overall energy needs and to the reduction of CO_2 and other emissions. At the same time it could make a useful contribution to the redevelopment of our larger cities where, because of the density of development, such schemes are likely to be most appropriate. We recognise that they may be more difficult to establish in the smaller towns and in the suburbs that are an enduring feature of the British scene.

A new emphasis on urban CHP would accord well with the objectives of the recent EC *Green Paper on the Urban Environment*.[5] This places much emphasis on the practical contribution that CHP could make as part of an integrated approach to tackling urban problems. The potential of CHP is one of the stronger arguments in favour of the 'compact city' concept espoused by the Green Paper, and CHP is at the forefront of measures now being advanced by the European Commission to cut CO_2 emissions, one objective being mandatory solutions to 'prevent all the residual heat from conventional power stations being simply released to the environment'.[6]

On these grounds it would make great sense to consider very carefully the case for locating new generating plant within urban areas or wherever it can be demonstrated that there is a definite market for the waste heat. In general this would entail a move away from the remote 'mega' stations of up to 2000MW to small and medium-sized CHP plant, generating perhaps 100–200MW and burning either natural gas or coal (or refuse) employing FBC technology. We share with the EC very strong doubts about whether permission should be given for any further electricity-only fossil fuel stations. Instead, promoters of power stations should be required to demonstrate that suitable provision is being made to exploit the heat which would otherwise go to waste.

We would like to see the government do much more actively to promote the development of CHP as an essential part of future energy policy and, where such plant can be located in deprived inner areas, as an integral part of the Inner City Programme (within which implementation would be relatively straightforward). That promotion would need to address the problem of the lack of legislative power to require potential consumers to connect to the system.

Recommendations

Promoters of power stations should be required to demonstrate that suitable provision is being made to make the fullest possible use of heat that would otherwise go to waste in the generation of electricity.

Local energy schemes that include CHP, should be eligible for City Grant where it can be demonstrated that they will contribute to inner city revival.

CHP schemes generally should come within the scope of the Non-Fossil Fuel Obligation (see below). (At present, only CHP schemes based on refuse incineration qualify.)

NUCLEAR POWER

The nuclear industry sees itself as a potential beneficiary of the identification of fossil fuel burning as a principal cause of global warming, arguing that nuclear power should be seen as the 'clean energy for the future'. Efforts are also being made to bring down costs by possibly extending the lives of the first-generation Magnox reactors and perhaps burying spent reactors under earth mounds following only partial dismantlement in order to reduce decommissioning costs.

However, this argument ignores the true costs of nuclear power, costs which must allow for the full implications of nuclear waste and for decommissioning, obligations that will endure for centuries. (The issue of radioactive waste is dealt with in Chapter 5.) We must remain alive to the problems that nuclear technology is creating for future generations, the risks of nuclear proliferation and the small though ever-present chance of a catastrophe of the magnitude of Chernobyl. (These issues are dealt with fully in Chapter 5.)

In the light of these considerations, the TCPA has concluded that nuclear power should be phased out when the existing nuclear power stations reach the end of their life. We appreciate that the practical realisation of nuclear fusion might revolutionise the situation. We question whether the profound risks associated with nuclear fission can be reduced significantly. Neither nuclear nor fossil fuels are compatible with the sustainable energy path that we need for the longer term. For that, we look to the renewables, which are covered in the next section.

Recommendation

Nuclear power should be phased out when the existing nuclear power stations reach the end of their life.

The opportunity of the government's forthcoming review of nuclear power should be used to carry out a full evaluation of all the energy options and the development of a coherent energy strategy.

RENEWABLE ENERGY

Of the European countries, Britain is one of the best endowed with potential sources of renewable energy, especially wind, wave and tidal power. Yet these have remained largely unexploited, with research and development spending on renewables accounting for only a small fraction of that spent on nuclear power. Certainly our past record is poor compared with such countries as Denmark, the Netherlands and the US (California), with their substantial wind programmes, and Sweden, with its support for innovative solar systems and energy forests.[7]

However, the last few years have seen an appreciable change in attitudes to sustainable energy. Some encouragement has come from the establishment – as part of the electricity privatisation legislation – of the Non-Fossil Fuel Obligation (NFFO), under which the supply companies are obliged until 1998 to contract for the output of the nuclear stations as well as a tranche of renewable energy. This has opened the way for a significant expansion of 'alternative' technologies.

Unfortunately, the nuclear industry has been the prime beneficiary of the NFFO, while privatisation itself has stimulated gas rather than renewables. A more important stimulus to the development of renewable sources has been the growing appreciation of the threat posed by global warming. In consequence, the target set by the government in *This Common Inheritance*[8] for the installation of a further 1000MW capacity from renewables by the turn of the century may well be exceeded. The Department of Energy estimated that by 2025 renewables could be meeting up to 20 per cent of the UK's energy demand and saving 11 per cent of total (not just electricity generation) UK CO_2 emissions in the process.[9] Undoubtedly there is the potential to go very much further.

The realisation of all this potential, however, faces a range of obstacles. In global environmental terms, renewables represent 'the ultimate clean energy supplies'.[10] However, they are not without their own local environmental impacts, as the controversies over the Severn Barrage and various wind farm proposals have demonstrated. They may also prove to present currently unsuspected practical problems.

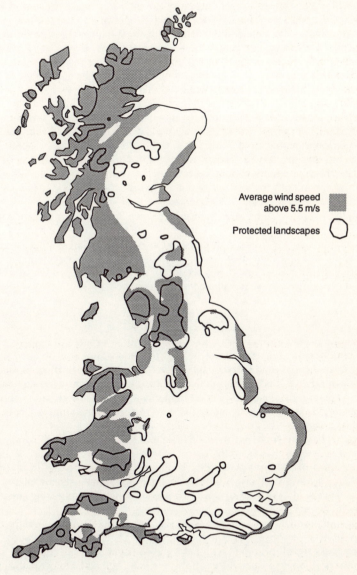

Average wind speed above 5.5 m/s

Protected landscapes

Figure 4.1 *Wind and tidal power in Britain: conflicts with protected landscapes*

WIND POWER

In the case of wind power, currently the front runner for widespread electricity generation from renewable sources, these conflicts have been heightened by the terms of the NFFO, which mean in practice that schemes are viable only where average wind speeds exceed 7.5 metres/second. In general, such sites are restricted to upland areas and the exposed coasts of Wales and the South-West (the NFFO does not yet apply in Scotland or Northern Ireland), areas which often coincide with regional parks, AONBs, or other sites of special protection (Figure 4.1). Under current EC rules, the NFFO runs only until 1998. However, the European Commission has indicated that it would consider a proposal to extend this deadline – for renewable energy sources only, not for nuclear power – 'with a generally favourable view'.[11] If a suitable extension were to be allowed, this would open the way for wind farms to be built in less environmentally sensitive areas. Friends of the Earth estimate that if areas with wind speeds between 6.5 and 7.5 metres/second were included in the area of search 'the percentage of exploitable wind energy in England and Wales would double from the present 36 per cent to 74 per cent'.[12]

While we are encouraged by the government's new commitment to renewable energy technologies, we would like to see a marked stepping up of both research and development with the stimulus provided by the NFFO and supplemented by income from an energy tax. As experience is built up of the operation of the first wave of schemes, the government should formulate a long term strategy for renewable energy looking ahead initially to 2025: one target might be to meet at least 20 per cent of energy needs in 2025 from wind and solar sources.

Coupled with this we believe that there is a need not only for guidance to planning authorities as to how they should handle planning applications for renewable energy sources but also for some national land use guidance indicating broadly where particular types of scheme may be appropriate. This would aid planning authorities in preparing their development plans, secure a consistency of approach, and help ensure that national targets for renewable energy can be met.

BIOMASS

One source of renewable energy that promises to be capable of making a significant contribution to meeting overall energy requirements without the obvious environmental disadvantages of wind farms or tidal barrages is biomass. Burning bio-fuels such as straw or wood does, of course, produce carbon dioxide; but growing such biomass as a crop – where a replacement is planted immediately after harvesting – ensures that this carbon dioxide is taken up again by the new crop, so eliminating any contribution to global warming.

Experiments elsewhere in the world have proved the potential of biomass. Probably the most successful has been the use of ethanol produced from sugar cane in Brazil, where a third of all of that country's 12 million cars use the fuel in place of petrol. Elsewhere, a variety of crops – from fast-growing, single-season plants to willow coppiced every five years or so – is being used both for direct heating and as a fuel for electricity generation.

With food production now requiring far less agricultural land, the growing of crops for energy production seems an attractive alternative. The first step is, of course, to find the right crop or crops to suit the UK climatic and soil conditions. In considering the future for biomass, it is also vital that the whole life-cycle impacts of the growing and energy-generation processes are taken into account. For example, any crop that requires significant fertiliser inputs may well produce little net energy, as the manufacture of many fertilisers is energy intensive; issues such as the energy required to transport the crop to the power station also need to be considered.

BOX 4.1 Biomass for energy

The benefits of growing crops for energy production are not always as straightforward as they may appear. The French government has, for example, exempted diesel made from oilseed rape – rape methyl ester (RME) – from heavy fuel taxes until 1996 and plans to extend this indefinitely to encourage the switch from fossil-fuel-derived diesel to renewable resources. But scientists in France and Germany are at loggerheads over the environmental effects.

The French Environment and Energy Agency claims that growing, manufacturing and burning RME produces only one-fifth of the greenhouse gases compared with fossil fuels. But the German Federal Environment Office found that producing and burning RME causes the same or even more greenhouse gas emissions than fossil fuels and warned that its widespread introduction would increase the use of pesticides and fertilisers. Meanwhile, Britain's Department of Trade & Industry has published a study that concludes that a subsidy of approximately 15 pence per litre would be needed to make RME viable in the UK. The report also suggests that, if all the 630,000ha of land set aside for agricultural production in 1992 was used for RME production, it would only meet 6 per cent of the demand for the fuel.

Of course, RME is far from being the only potential bio-fuel. A pilot 100kW wood gasification reactor is soon to be built in Northern Ireland at a cost of £100,000 and is expected to convert at least a quarter of the energy of coppiced wood into useful energy. Miscanthus – a form of tall, fast-growing grass – is already being grown as a bio-fuel in Europe, although, as with RME, the use of substantial quantities of energy-intensive fertilisers is reducing the environmental benefit. Other suggested crops – especially such fast-growing trees as willow and poplar – may prove more beneficial, as they need little if any fertiliser.

Recommendation

The Government should negotiate with the European Commission an extension of the 1998 deadline for the NFFO, but for renewable energy sources only. In particular, this should be used to improve the viability of wind power outside National Parks, AONBs and other designated areas.

The government should, as soon as practicable, formulate a long-term strategy for renewable energy, looking ahead initially to 2025 and aiming to meet a minimum of 20 per cent of the UK's energy demand by that date.

The Department of the Environment should prepare national land-use guidance indicating broadly where particular types of renewable energy generation would be appropriate in order to assist planning authorities in preparing development plans and to ensure a consistency of approach and the meeting of national targets for renewable energy.

The government should fund research into both crops that may be suitable for growing in the UK as a source for energy and the technologies needed for biomass energy production and use.

UK ENERGY POLICY – THE PAST EXPERIENCE

Past UK energy policy has been largely conditioned by our abundant fossil fuel reserves, although there are signs now that production of oil and gas from the UK part of the North Sea fields may have peaked. Thus there has been less incentive than in many other countries to save energy and this has led the UK to concentrate on large coal- and oil-fired power stations which waste most of the energy they produce, rather than the usually smaller CHP plants for which we have already argued.

The other main strand of UK postwar energy policy, in addition to the exploitation of North Sea oil and gas – first discovered in the 1960s and significantly exploited from the mid-1970s, has been the nuclear power programme. Introduced in the 1950s as a practically limitless source of energy for the future, nuclear power, however, has failed to live up to the expectations of its promoters. In particular, the advanced gas-cooled reactors (AGRs) planned as the mainstay of the nuclear programme have been dogged by construction and technical problems, with the first plant, Dungeness B, commissioned only in 1984, fourteen years late[13]. With the wisdom of hindsight, it is difficult to argue that the British nuclear programme has been anything other than a financial failure. The opportunity cost, too, has been enormous, with promising alternative technologies starved of resources, or, in the case of wave power, even abandoned.

UK ENERGY POLICY AND THE 1989 ELECTRICITY ACT

The Electricity Act 1989 marked a profound turning point for UK energy policy with considerable consequences for the mix of energy supply and, as a result, for the environment. The Act paved the way for the privatisation and splitting up of the electricity supply industry in the interests of competition. As with the water industry, privatisation has coincided with an official recognition of the need to give much greater priority to the environment, as set out in the government's environment White Paper *This Common Inheritance*.[14] However, in the same way as with water, there is a clear conflict between the new environmental objectives and the interests of shareholders and it remains to be seen whether there will be any net benefit to the environment. The signs so far are mixed.

What has happened is that there has been a profound change in the type of plant being ordered by the generating companies. As recently as 1988, the Central Electricity Generating Board (CEGB) – supported by the government – was promoting a major programme of large new power stations. This programme was to consist of a 'small family' of pressurised water reactors (PWRs) together with some large coal-fired stations, amounting in total to some 12,000MW capacity.

In practice, just one of these PWRs, Sizewell B, was given the go-ahead; this is now under construction. The preparations for privatisation underlined, however, the high cost of nuclear power and, together with the tough commercial objectives of the Board's successors, led to the dropping of plans for further nuclear plants pending a review in 1994. Meanwhile, gas has replaced coal as the preferred fossil fuel for electricity generation.

The decision by the generating companies, National Power and Powergen, and a number of smaller companies who wished to sell electricity to the national grid, to look to gas rather than coal is based on two main factors.

First, the recently introduced combined cycle technology gives a generating efficiency of up to 50 per cent compared with the 30–35 per cent achieved in 'conventional' coal stations, making such plant significantly cheaper to run at current gas prices. Second, the very low sulphur content of gas makes it unnecessary to fit costly desulphurisation equipment. An added environmental benefit is that the combustion of gas generates perhaps 50 per cent less CO_2 than an equivalent amount of coal.

In *This Common Inheritance* the government argued that competition between the two new privatised electricity companies, together with the introduction of some smaller independent generators, would provide the incentive to develop energy-efficient technologies as well as encourage electricity generation from non-fossil fuels under the NFFO. Regrettably, however, the government had previously resisted an attempt to amend the Electricity Act to place a *duty* on suppliers to conserve energy in their operations and encourage conservation by their customers. This was despite firm evidence from many parts of the United States that, where utilities are required to show that they have considered all options including energy conservation when requesting permission to construct new generating plant, this has been to the advantage of all parties, improving the generators' profits by eliminating the need to invest in expensive plant and reducing costs to end-users.[15]

By contrast, in the United Kingdom the electricity supply industry has little incentive to produce less electricity (as distinct from producing it more efficiently). As with the gas industry, it is in the supplier's interest and the interest of its shareholders to maximise sales and profits by selling as much electricity as possible. Indeed, this is reinforced by tariff structures to the industrial sector which effectively encourage consumption – 'pile it high, sell it cheap'.

TOWARDS A SUSTAINABLE ENERGY PATH FOR BRITAIN

The TCPA welcomed one consequence of the electricity privatisation process: it exposed the true economics of nuclear power and gave a boost to the renewable energy industry. However, these steps forward are being tempered by the failure to build in conservation as a key objective for the privatised energy supply companies. This is a major lost opportunity.

We need now to re-examine and reframe our energy objectives and map out a new sustainable energy path which has the least possible effect on the environment and is compatible with our own global long-term interests.

We believe that the following principles should be at the heart of such a strategy:

- The use and pricing of individual fuels should be in accordance with an overall national energy strategy conceived in the context of sustainable development.
- Energy policy should have a proper regard for the environment both locally, in a European context, and globally. Indeed, environmental impact in its widest sense should be a primary factor in any energy planning decision.
- Energy policy should aim to meet real human needs. Everyone needs energy for warmth, cooking, light, power and transport. As the TCPA's report on the inner cities *Whose Responsibility*?[16] showed, this is not just a Third World issue: there are many instances in Britain where these basic needs are not being met because of acute poverty.
- Energy policy should recognise the finite nature of many of the fuels on which we now depend. While the continuous identification of new energy reserves has made the depletion of resources less of a worry than the environmental impacts of energy use, political and economic considerations make it unwise for any country to rely on long-term continuity of supply, particularly in relation to oil imports.

Adoption of these principles implies the following:

- a move towards much greater energy efficiency and conservation to minimise the quantity of energy that we need to generate, and thus help to safeguard the environment;
- the establishment of price regimes that reflect the need to economise on energy but that are socially responsible;

- action to reduce pollution from existing power stations and design measures to make their successors much more environmentally friendly;
- promoting improved coal combustion technologies;
- a long-term approach to energy policy which looks ahead to the second quarter of the twenty-first century, by which time it will be practicable – indeed, vital – for a substantial proportion of our energy needs to be met from renewable sources.

ENERGY CONSERVATION

A firm commitment to generating and using energy less wastefully and to energy conservation must be at the heart of Britain's future energy policy. Indeed, both the *This Common Inheritance* White Paper and the House of Commons Select Committee on Energy[17] have recognised their fundamental importance in strategies to counter global warming.

However, the United Kingdom's past record on energy efficiency has, to say the least, been poor. Overall, we have perhaps the worst insulated housing stock in Northern Europe. While this must in part reflect the high average age of our dwellings – with a significant proportion of homes being more than 100 years old – the energy performance of even our more modern housing trails well behind that of our Northern European neighbours. In 1990, the UK's building regulations were tightened but only to the point that Sweden reached in the 1930s, a standard that country has since improved upon. Amazingly, as recently as 1989 the British government cut back the financing of the Energy Efficiency Office (EEO) by half, reduced loft insulation grants to householders, and abandoned its support for energy surveys for the industry. (The opportunities for reducing substantially the quantity of energy consumed by buildings are examined in Chapter 6.)

We acknowledge that there is much in the government's White Paper that is potentially useful. In particular, we are encouraged by the proposal to co-operate with the Housing Corporation and the National Federation of Housing Associations to introduce an energy auditing scheme for their stock. We also welcome the government's apparent willingness to consider further strengthening the building regulations. But we would like to see the government go considerably further in promoting and securing energy efficiency and conservation: the White Paper's proposals are only the first stage.

In its Third Report on Energy Efficiency, published in 1991, the House of Commons Energy Committee expressed concern that the Government is failing to appreciate the scale of energy savings that could be readily achieved. The report cites ministers as indicating that the scope for further savings is some 20 per cent of current consumption. The Intergovernmental Panel on Climate Change, on the other hand, suggested that savings of 30 per cent would be quite feasible in economic terms alone, assuming a recovery of the full investment within five years. And this took no account either of the additional energy savings that could be justified as part of a programme to reduce CO_2 emissions nor of the shorter payback that will be an inevitable consequence of energy taxes and other moves to raise energy prices.

Bearing in mind the virtual certainty that the target for the stabilisation of CO_2 emissions by the year 2000 will need to be an interim one only, we believe that the government will have to be much more ambitious in its thinking. Much more attention needs to be given to the potential of possible changes in life-style to moderate demand and to the scope within all sectors to cut down usage. There has been an obsession with energy supply – the past presumption being that capacity has to be stepped up broadly in line with increases in GDP. But increasingly this approach is being challenged and a new question posed: 'For what actual uses is energy needed and how can those needs be most efficiently met?'

This 'end-use' approach underlies a range of alternative energy scenarios. The latest and most comprehensive – carried out by the international team of Goldemberg, Johansson, Reddy and Williams[18] – illustrates how the world's economy could grow, enabling those in developing countries to enjoy a living standard comparable to that of Western Europe today with a total energy use only 10 per cent higher than it was in 1987. In their global energy scenario for 2020, the authors suggest a per capita use in the industrialised countries of about half the level in 1980, despite the fact that material standards would be significantly higher than they are now.

The key to this approach, which effectively decouples GDP growth from growth in energy supply, is an evaluation from the bottom up of how energy is used, starting from the smallest electrical appliance, and at each stage investigating how savings could be made. In the case of lighting, for example, considerable savings can result from the substitution of the traditional incandescent light bulb by modern compact fluorescent lamps. Such lamps last at least eight times as long and cut energy consumption by up to 80 per cent: replacing a 100 watt incandescent bulb with a compact fluorescent can save up to a tonne of carbon dioxide from a coal-fired power station, as well as saving the consumer more than £30 over the life of the lamp. As a second example, further savings could be achieved through the introduction of condensing boilers for domestic heating systems: these burn gas with a thermal efficiency of more than 85 per cent compared with 65–70 per cent for conventional boilers. Third, there is much scope to improve the energy efficiency of such products as cookers, fridges and freezers: for example, the best-performing fridge and the best-performing washing machine on the British market today both use half the energy to do the same job as the worst performing machines. (See for example Table 4.2.)

Table 4.2 *Comparison of efficiency of refrigeration appliances*

Appliance type	Size (litres)	Annual consumption (kWh/yr)	Index
Refrigerators			
UK stock	144	350	100
UK average new	138	302	90
UK best new	153	160	43
World best	200	90	19
Chest freezer			
UK stock	277	760	100
UK average new	218	541	91
UK best new	221	240	39
World best	259	180	25
Fridge/freezer			
UK stock	285	730	100
UK average new	292	553	75
UK best new	237	280	46
World best	430	460	42

Source HMSO (1990) *Energy Efficiency in Domestic Electric Appliances*

In this we welcome the progress that is being made towards introducing systems of energy labelling that will assist the consumer in purchasing energy efficient appliances and recognise in the context of the Single European Market the desirability of an EC-wide system. We also agree that an energy efficiency rating and labelling system should be coupled with the establishment of minimum energy efficiency standards.

A recent development for the UK is for such energy efficiency standards to be applied to buildings (see Chapter 6). The newly established National Energy Foundation is pioneering the introduction of a building labelling system, the National Home Energy Rating. This measures the energy efficiency of houses on a scale of 1–10, full account being taken of size, construction, heating systems and so on. The TCPA would like to see the government take the lead in persuading owners to undertake energy audits of their properties with a view to upgrading them to higher energy ratings. The Labour party's concept of 'green mortgages' could be a further helpful move in this direction, encouraging the installation of energy insulation measures when a house is purchased.[19]

The Third Report of the House of Commons Energy Select Committee recommends that the Department of the Environment 'commence the work of revising the building regulations immediately and accelerate the present somewhat relaxed timescale'. The TCPA supports both this and the governments's intention as set out in its environment White Paper to incorporate energy labelling into the building regulations when these are next revised.

Experience from the Milton Keynes Energy Park has demonstrated that it is possible to achieve designs which are at least 30 per cent more energy efficient than is required under current building regulations with an increase in construction costs of just 1–2 per cent. What this scheme has also demonstrated, however, is that design for energy efficiency needs to encompass the estate layout as a whole, as well as just the design of the individual homes: because the Park's roads are aligned north–south and east–west to optimise the orientation for solar gain, the houses are all too often located askew to existing roads, reducing density and increasing the cost of services. The Milton Keynes Park also included shelter planting and special types of fencing to reduce windspeeds; these improve the microclimate and marginally reduce the loss of heat from the houses.

The TCPA believes that planning authorities should now be required to take energy considerations into account in their decision making, particularly in relation to development control matters.

Recommendations

The terms of operation of the privatised electricity and gas companies should be revised to require them to promote energy conservation wherever practicable.

The government should actively encourage the system of home energy rating and seek to persuade owners to undertake energy audits of their properties with a view to upgrading them to higher energy ratings.

The government should bring forward its commitment to upgrading the building regulations.

Energy labelling should be a requirement for all new buildings and should be extended in the future to cover all homes and other buildings that use a significant amount of energy.

Planning authorities should be required to take energy use into consideration in development control decisions as well as in the formulation of development plans.

ATMOSPHERIC POLLUTION

A stepped-up energy conservation and efficiency programme would reduce significantly the amount of fossil fuel that needs to be burnt and, as a consequence, cut emissions of carbon dioxide and other pollutants. Currently, Britain's power stations are responsible for some 39 per cent of our CO_2 emissions and 73 per cent of our sulphur dioxide and nitrogen oxide emissions respectively.[20] Outputs of sulphur dioxide can be reduced by 80–90 per cent through the installation of flue gas desulphurisation (FGD) equipment: but this process consumes sizeable quantities of limestone, the extraction of which can be a highly contentious local planning issue.

Other approaches include switching to fluidised bed technology (a technique that, as we have seen, burns coal more efficiently and can also remove SO_2 if limestone is included in the 'bed') or by switching to low sulphur coal. Low sulphur coal is not only often cheaper but its use has been seen by the government as a justification for not requiring the new generating companies to fit FGD equipment to many of the coal-fired stations inherited from the CEGB. It has, however, been argued that in allowing this to happen the UK is not acting within the spirit of EC legislation designed to combat acid rain by reducing sulphur dioxide emissions. Moreover, low-sulphur coal has to be imported, with implications for the balance of payments and with the same impact on the mining communities as abandoning the use of coal altogether.

Nitrogen oxide emissions can be reduced to moderate levels through the fitting of low NOx burners as is already happening with many coal-fired stations or, more effectively, through selective catalytic reduction (SCR). But both FGD and SCR reduce the overall efficiency of the plant, resulting in more fuel being burnt to generate the same amount of electricity. Thus these technologies may tackle acid rain but they also exacerbate CO_2 emissions. So, while they are appropriate for retrofitting to existing plant, new coal-fired stations should use different approaches, particularly fluidised bed combustion.

EQUITY

Given the background of the general age and disrepair of a substantial proportion of the UK's housing stock, it is not surprising that many homes are without central heating and lack even the most rudimentary insulation. Evidence presented to the House of Commons Energy Select Committee showed that some 1.7 million households had no loft insulation or less than 50mm of insulation and that 4.6 million had no draught-proofing. Evidence presented to the Committee by the National Right to Fuel Campaign (NRFC) indicated that about half of poor households were without central heating, with many households relying solely on electricity for heating. The NRFC indicated that 'to provide low income households with affordable warmth and other energy services while reducing the amount of carbon dioxide they emit' would entail capital expenditure averaging £2500 per household and a total annual cost of £1250 million.

Funds allocated by government departments for investment in energy efficiency fall far short of the total need. The Department of the Environment estimates that it will not be until 2005 that 90 per cent of local authority dwellings will have central heating and loft insulation and not until 2035 that 90 per cent will have cavity wall insulation and double glazing.

The obvious conclusion is that the resources available to local authorities and housing associations to repair and upgrade their stock must be expanded considerably. The TCPA believes that the achievement of higher energy efficiency standards must be an integral part of such programmes.

Recommendation

The government should increase the level of resources available through its Estate Action Programme and through local authorities to repair and refurbish both public sector housing and the older private stock through improvement grants, and ensure that the achievement of higher energy efficiency standards is an integral part of such programmes.

LOCAL ENERGY STRATEGIES

The TCPA believes in a national energy saving programme implemented in part at least by strategies formulated at the local level. One possible model would comprise local energy strategies prepared by consortia of local authorities, businesses and voluntary sector interests and the area electricity and gas boards and other fuel suppliers.

Such 'bottom up' strategies would be entirely consistent with the end-use approach advocated earlier in this report. With their considerable local knowledge, such consortia would be well placed to mastermind comprehensive local action. Borrowing from the experience of, say, the energy committees that operate within many Swedish and Danish local authorities, the consortia would be responsible for surveys of heat loss from local building stock and for providing detailed energy audits for business premises and for public and domestic buildings. They would also have a major role to play in devising and implementing strategies to improve the energy rating of the local housing stock, both public sector and private, and in providing general advice.

Within urban areas such consortia could also become involved in energy supply when, as we advocate, CHP comes into its own as a major energy supplier. They would then have a major responsibility both for supplying heat to homes and businesses and other customers within their area and for feeding electricity to the national grid. A number of local authorities, such as Sheffield and Newcastle-upon-Tyne, have already made a start with their own energy plans.

In certain counties, too, energy is becoming an important planning consideration: an example is Cornwall, where an impressive county-wide strategy for the development of renewable resources has been drawn up. The TCPA applauds such initiatives and hopes that they will lead to many others coming forward. We note, however, that such plans will require greater local autonomy over investment decisions if they are to be properly implemented.

Recommendations

Local authorities should be encouraged to set up energy consortia with representatives drawn from local government, business and voluntary sector interests and area energy utilities.

Local authorities should draw up energy plans for their areas showing how conservation measures and more use of renewable sources will be used to reduce pollution, including the impact of greenhouse gases.

Pollution and Waste –
A Sustainable Burden?
Andrew Blowers

A CRUCIAL ISSUE

Environmental pollution threatens health, amenity and, ultimately, the survival of life on the planet. Control of pollution is fundamental to the achievement of a sustainable future. Public concern about pollution is nothing new and efforts to escape or control pollution have been a feature of urban development for at least a century. But the scale and focus of the problem of pollution has shifted over time. History demonstrates that political action to control the effects of pollution has been motivated by the interests of the powerful and privileged groups in society. During the nineteenth century, pollution was a problem of public health. It was the squalor of the cities and the fear of cholera that prompted the development of the venous-arterial systems of water supply and sewerage.[1] In the twentieth century, communities protect their amenity by restricting access or preventing polluting activities. Environmental quality has become a desirable aspect of life-style and the consequence has been increasing segregation, social and spatial.

Another trend has become evident recently: pollution problems have grown in scale and there are now threats on a continental, even global, basis. Marine pollution, radioactive fall-out, ozone depletion and global warming are not socially discriminating; they engulf everything within their path. Of course, the richer groups or countries may be better able to defend themselves from the consequences, for a time at least but, unless avoiding action is taken the threats are ultimately inescapable. Such action requires co-operation and agreement on a global scale. For the first time in history, there is a mutual interest among rich and poor countries in acting to prevent environmental catastrophe.

There is, too, some evidence that action is being taken at all levels. At the local level, as Chapter 2 has shown, there is a range of initiatives, experiments, policies and actions by councils and local communities. Many of these make a small but locally significant contribution to pollution control. Industries, too, are co-operating with communities and councils in programmes of environmental enhancement.

However, one result of the success of some communities in resisting hazardous activities in its area can be the displacement of the hazard to a 'peripheral' community, often in a remote area that is economically marginal and relatively powerless (see the nuclear waste example in Box 1.1).

At national level, attention was drawn at the end of the 1980s to specific pollution and waste management problems by a series of parliamentary reports on such subjects as radioactive waste (1986), toxic waste (1989), nitrate in water (1989), the energy implications of the greenhouse effect (1989), and contaminated land (1990).[2] In 1990, the key White Paper *This Common Inheritance* provided a comprehensive analysis and action points for pollution control. A substantial part of the Environmental Protection

---

BOX 5.1 Working towards sustainability

Given the will, sufficient experience now exists at local authority level in the UK to introduce meaningful steps and mechanisms to promote a more sustainable environment. Picking from the examples of best practice across the country, a model authority would do most of the following:

- Devote a reasonable amount of its budget to addressing environmental issues.
- Give priority to energy efficiency measures and create self-perpetuating energy funds.
- Work towards integrated waste management where materials recovery and recycling are given highest priority.
- Put in place policies and programmes aimed at habitat creation and protection.
- Develop a planting programme with specific carbon dioxide reduction targets.
- Develop environmentally sound planning policies.
- Actively support public transport, cycling and walking and make budget choices that assist these.
- Adopt policies for environmentally aware new-build and repairs and make these mandatory for any capital works.
- Use its purchasing power in an environmentally sensitive fashion.
- Undertake an active environmental education programme.
- Promote the widest possible community involvement both in the formulation of environmental policy and in its implementation.
- Maintain an environmentally responsible investment strategy.
- Set up an active environmental monitoring system and carry out regular audits of its environmental performance.

Act (1990) was devoted to the introduction of Integrated Pollution Control. The proposed establishment of an Environment Agency bringing together air and water pollution control and responsibility for the handling and disposal of waste potentially provides institutional support for the principle of integration. But the abolition of any local government role in waste regulation and the complete absence of an effective and representative regional tier of government (as proposed in this report) is likely to limit effective implementation in practice.

The UK's pollution control practices are increasingly affected by European policies and initiatives. The EC has enacted over 300 regulations, standards and directives concerning such subjects as air and water pollution, toxic substances, landfill of waste, pollution of bathing beaches, and drinking water quality. It has developed five Environmental Action Programmes. The EC has taken an increasingly tough line on pollution control but there is concern as to whether all this activity is making a difference and whether the EC's environment policy is having any effect. For instance, the UK is unlikely fully to comply with the 1975 Bathing Water Directive until the end of the century. It was tardy in introducing targets to reduce sulphur dioxide (SO_2) emissions and intends to avoid expensive flue gas desulphurisation by switching into gas and low sulphur imported coal, thus leading to the virtual demise of the British deep-mined coal industry. Compliance with EC environmental requirements varies across the Community according to economic circumstances and political priorities. Resentment at EC interference in national environmental policy is one of the issues seized on by opponents of the Maastricht Treaty.

At the global level, as the problem of global warming becomes more apparent so the need to turn rhetoric into action becomes more paramount. The EC accounts for 13 per cent of global CO_2 emissions, the United States for 23 per cent, and much will depend on how far they are able to cut back and pay the poor countries to limit their output of emissions. Despite the conventions on climate change and biodiversity agreed at the Earth Summit in Rio de Janeiro in 1992, global action has not been backed effectively by funding, largely because the developed nations have cut back their promised commitments in the face of growing recession. Even the relatively tough protocols on ozone depletion could be undermined by a new generation of substitute chemicals which may not be phased out until 2020.

So there is evidence of action over pollution at every level, manifesting a combination of self-interest and common purpose. But the action is often unco-ordinated, inchoate and uneven. There are few signs yet that, despite the proof of the harmful effects of pollution, the need to take precautionary action is receiving the political priority and urgent attention that it deserves. But the common threat to environmental security provides both the cause and the opportunity for united action to achieve sustainable development.

In the rest of this chapter we identify the policies and commitments that will be necessary to achieve one of the five fundamental goals of sustainable development stated in chapter 1 – *to prevent or reduce processes that degrade or pollute the environment, to protect the regenerative capacity of ecosystems, and to prevent developments that are detrimental to human health or that diminish the quality of life.* We begin by clarifying what is meant by waste and pollution.

DEFINITIONS OF WASTE AND POLLUTION

Waste and pollution are the unwanted by-products of the production process. They are the back-end of the cycle of production whereby energy is applied to transform natural resources into food or into material products for human consumption. The production of waste and pollution is an integral part of the process. Both waste and pollution are environmental problems. Waste must be managed and pollution must be controlled. Sustainable development can only be achieved if energy and resources are conserved by reducing waste and if ecosystems are protected by the control and prevention of pollution. (The commercial benefits to individual companies of minimising waste and pollution are discussed in Chapter 8.) There are, however, certain distinguishing characteristics between waste and pollution.

Waste is the solid, liquid or, occasionally, gaseous by-product that must be accommodated in the environment in some way. Solid wastes may be recycled or treated and concentrated and disposed of in landfills or incinerated or dumped in the ocean. Liquid wastes can be piped into watercourses and gaseous wastes vented into the atmosphere. Waste management may include treatment before disposal to separate out certain waste streams or to compact the waste to reduce its volume. Since waste usually represents the unused part of non-renewable resources, recovery, reuse and recycling must be encouraged wherever possible.

But the critical environmental problem is the increasing volumes of wastes requiring some form of management. Waste treatment tackles the symptoms of the problem by reducing the volumes of waste that must be managed. It does not reduce the volume of waste being produced. So action must also focus on the prevention of the production of wastes in the first place.

Recommendation

The emphasis of waste management policy and industrial practice should be directed towards processes and measures that reduce the volumes of wastes arising from production processes. Environmental planning, at all levels, should include proposals for the reduction of waste arisings.

Wastes may contain substances which, if not effectively contained, can cause harmful pollution. One problem that arises is the inconsistencies in the classification of wastes. For example, radioactive wastes are classified in the UK and most European countries into low-, intermediate- and high level categories determined nowadays by reference to the half-lives and radioactivity of radionuclides. In the United States, low level wastes are divided into three categories and include most of those that would be classified as intermediate in the UK. High-level wastes include both spent fuel and the liquid wastes arising from reprocessing. There are similar problems in classifying hazardous wastes, although there has been an effort at international standardisation in some cases. Nevertheless, the lack of information, of common classification and of monitoring conceals the extent of the environmental problems and inhibits public knowledge.

There are formidable problems in attempting agreed classifications of the complex multitude of chemical wastes. A major problem is the definition and acceptability of risk, since perceptions vary widely. It will be necessary for definitions to be based on independent expert advice based on knowledge of the substances and on public consultation. It is most important that the evidence is carefully assessed, since the views of waste producers and environmentalists are likely to be far apart. Despite the difficulties, the following recommendation should be an aim of policy.

Recommendation

Where wastes contain materials that are harmful to health or the environment there should be an internationally-agreed system of classification based on the level of acceptable risk and the appropriate methods of management. Environmental planning should highlight the occurrence of such materials and indicate ways of dealing with them.

Waste may or may not be harmful. But pollution is always harmful in some way. Pollution has been defined as, 'The introduction by man into the environment of substances or energy liable to cause hazards to human health and harm to living resources and ecological systems, damage to structures or amenity, or interference with legitimate uses of the environment'.[3] Even noise is a pollutant that is ubiquitous and irritating and, at certain levels, harmful to health. Some forms of pollution are not apparent to the senses yet are very harmful. The production of nuclear energy or reprocessing creates radioactive substances that are dangerous through proximity and which may produce certain cancers or genetic disorders.[4] Likewise, certain heavy metals are highly dangerous if they enter the accessible environment.

Pollutants can also interact with environmental processes and transform environmental conditions. Oil slicks, acid rain, the greenhouse effect and the depletion of the ozone layer are each examples of polluting processes that threaten ecosystems from the local to the global scale. There is an increasing recognition that the costs of clean-up must be borne by those responsible for the damage. This is the 'polluter pays' principle. A Europe-wide Convention – Civil Liability for Damage Resulting From Activities Dangerous to the Environment – is intended to define the scope of dangerous activities, the types of damage for which compensation would be applicable and the extent of liability and its limitations.[5]

But there are often problems of evidence of relating cause and effect and consequently of identifying culprits. Even where blame can be clearly identified, the costs of clean-up and control may be way beyond the ability of individual companies or even countries to pay. In these cases, some form of international insurance scheme becomes necessary. Such a scheme faces formidable difficulties, especially since the insurance market is wary of providing cover where the magnitude of the payments is virtually unknown. Any scheme would have to be backed by international governmental agreements.

Recommendation

It is axiomatic that wherever possible the polluter pays principle should be invoked to deter environmental damage and to provide sufficient resources for environmental restoration. This should be supported by an international insurance scheme for the protection of the environment from major polluting incidents, such a scheme to be operated within an internationally agreed regulatory and financial framework.

SUSTAINABLE DEVELOPMENT AND THE PRECAUTIONARY PRINCIPLE

In terms of sustainability, the burden of waste and pollution must not exceed what the environment can cope with through its natural cleansing, decomposing and dispersing processes. These vital functions must be maintained for the future; human activity must respect the regenerative capacity of the earth's resources. There has been a tendency to interpret this as a need to conserve non-renewable resources while exploiting inexhaustible resources. It is now recognised that these supposedly inexhaustible resources of air, water or land can be degraded by pollution. Increasing population and greater consumption per head, combined with modern production processes, can severely deplete what were once abundant resources of clean water, pure air and fertile soil. Sustainable development is already threatened by the deterioration of regenerative capacity in many areas.

BOX 5.2 Unintended consequences

Actions to solve one problem sometimes have unintended consequences that can be as, or more, damaging than those of the original problem. For example, worries about the fire hazards of aerosols powered by butane gas led to the introduction of CFC propellants. At the time, this was hailed as a major advance, as CFCs are non-toxic as well as non-flammable. It was only some years later that it was discovered that CFCs in aerosols were contributing to the destruction of the earth's protective ozone layer in the stratosphere.

Preventing the exhaustion or overloading of the environment will only be achieved through application of the precautionary principle (Chapter 1). In the face of uncertainty, this means taking avoiding action now rather than waiting for the problem to materialise. Environmental planning will need to address this maxim in relation to proposed individual major projects. But the nature of the action must be carefully considered for two reasons. One is that actions taken to protect one aspect of the environment can sometimes themselves cause other damage elsewhere. This is the problem of *unintended consequences* (see Box 5.2). The other reason is that it might, in certain circumstances, be better not to act if the consequences of doing so are irreversible. This is the problem of *reversibility* (we gave the example of the deep disposal of radioactive waste in Chapter 1.) In general, however, it makes sense to anticipate problems before they arise rather than to react to them once their effects become obvious. But there are formidable technical and political problems that must be surmounted if action is to be effective.

Recommendation

The precautionary principle requires taking action now to avert future environmental deterioration and to avoid excessive costs; but action should be avoided in those cases where delay may be necessary to ensure that measures avoid irreversible harm to future generations.

A PROBLEM OF INTEGRATION

Pollution and waste are integral elements of production processes that transcend both natural and political frontiers. Environmental problems of pollution and waste must be tackled through an integrated approach. There are three aspects to this problem and each has specific political implications.

1. THE TRANS-MEDIA NATURE OF POLLUTION

The first such problem is the trans-media nature of pollution: pollution can adopt different natural states as solid, liquid or gas and pass through different environmental pathways. For example, sulphur and nitrogen oxides entering the atmosphere from tall chimneys are transformed into dilute sulphuric and nitric acids which are precipitated as 'acid rain' far from their original source. Other pollutants can retain their original state but be transported through different environmental pathways. Heavy metals can find their way through the air to sea or land. Nitrates released into the soil through farming practices may enter drinking water supplies. And, as was shown in the United States at the notorious Love Canal site, toxic chemicals released from chemical works can infiltrate the soil, contaminate the land and emerge in people's homes.

Radioactive nuclides from nuclear reprocessing may be discharged routinely into the atmosphere by chimney or by pipeline into the sea. Occasionally, accidental releases – such as that from Sellafield in 1983 when the local beaches were briefly closed to the public – can give rise to considerable public alarm. The discharge from the Chernobyl power reactor was, of course, catastrophic and the consequences will be experienced for generations in enhanced cancer rates, genetic malformations and contaminated countryside. The possibility that radionuclides from radioactive waste will be released into the accessible environment many centuries hence has provoked intense opposition by local communities wherever nuclear waste repositories are proposed.

This interaction between pollution and the different pathways of land, water and air is recognised in the concept of Integrated Pollution Control (IPC). By bringing together the different pollution control inspectorates (industrial air pollution, radioactive substances, hazardous wastes and water quality) under Her Majesty's Inspectorate of Pollution (HMIP), the UK government has adopted a cross-media approach. The incorporation of the National Rivers Authority (NRA) and the waste disposal functions of local authorities under the proposed Environment Agency takes this process a logical step further, ensuring that the multi-media functions of the NRA (pollution control, flood prevention, water supply and recreational management) are kept intact. There is recognition by government that 'the existence of some form of local or regional planning . . . is vital if local authorities are to plan effectively'.[6]

But, as we explained in Chapter 1, the TCPA believes that this process should go much further, bringing together land-use planning and environmental control functions under strategic elected regional authorities occupying a key position in the environmental planning process that we have proposed.[7]

In principle, it should be possible to anticipate and avoid unintended consequences, to ensure that control over pollution in one form does not result in more severe pollution in another form. However, we have two concerns. One is that sufficient resources of skilled inspectors and adequate research should be devoted to IPC so that it becomes fully effective in practice. A basic generic training for inspectors in multi-media approaches will be essential if IPC is to be realised in practice. Our other concern is that IPC may give too much emphasis to control instead of to prevention, which ought to be the priority.

Recommendation

Sufficient resources and powers must be applied to ensure the successful monitoring and enforcement of IPC to achieve agreed levels of pollution reduction. Wherever possible, IPC should place an emphasis on the prevention of pollution at source rather than on the control of emissions.

---

2. TRANS-BOUNDARY EFFECTS OF POLLUTION

The second problem of integration that we need to consider is the trans-boundary effects of pollution. Pollution and waste can cross political frontiers either through deliberate export or through environmental pathways shared by different countries. The problem has two dimensions – the physical export of polluting substances or processes and the trans-boundary effects of pollution itself.

Polluting industries or activities, prevented or unwanted in one country, can be exported to another country where pollution controls are weak and the need for industrial investment is strong. High rates of pollution are too often a measure of the developing economy. Polluting substances can also be exported as waste. The trade in toxic and other hazardous wastes became a notorious issue in the late 1980s as ships tried in vain to land their unwelcome cargoes.[8] Impoverished developing countries such as Guinea, Equatorial Guinea, Guinea-Bissau, Benin and Gabon in West and Central Africa became dumping grounds for wastes from Western countries. Reaction against this 'environmental racism' led twelve African countries to sign the Bamako Convention banning the import of hazardous and radioactive wastes into their territory (Box 5.3).

The high cost of disposal or lack of suitable disposal facilities has also generated a routine trans-frontier trade between rich countries. Occasionally this trade gives rise to protests, as when the attempted export of PCBs from Canada to Britain in Russian freighters was blocked in 1989. The trade in nuclear wastes between Germany and Belgium caused a major scandal in 1987–8 when widespread corruption, mismanagement and a possible trade in plutonium was revealed. The reprocessing of nuclear waste in the UK and France will give rise to an increasing trade in plutonium and plutonium contaminated wastes. This trade with its implications for nuclear proliferation and handling of dangerous materials is likely to prove deeply controversial.

BOX 5.3 Examples of Waste Shipments to Developing Countries

Benin. In late 1980s, shipments up to 5 million tons were proposed at $2.50 per ton with a total value of $12.5 million to the economy. Radioactive waste from the former USSR and France is thought to be dumped in the country.

Guinea. In 1988, 15,000 tons of toxic incinerator ash was received from the United States but returned after international protest.

Guinea-Bissau. A $120 million per year contract (more than the country's annual budget) to store industrial wastes from elsewhere was rescinded after public outcry. A deal to take wastes from the USA and some European countries worth $600 million over five years was also postponed.

Nigeria. Nearly 4000 tons of toxic wastes from Italy was illegally dumped at Koko in 1987–8 and leakage possibly caused deaths and illnesses. The Nigerian government sent the remaining wastes back to Italy.

Sources Asante-Duah et al (1992), Smith and Blowers, 1992

The export of toxic waste or pollution to the developing world is a direct result of inequality. This is reflected in the costs of disposal between developing and developed countries, with average savings estimated at $250 per tonne of wastes.[9] Trade in wastes between developed countries arises from the relative availability of disposal facilities. For example, the availability of relatively cheap landfill and waste treatment facilities in the UK has made it a target for exports from neighbouring European countries (Table 5.1). Eastern European countries, notably the former East Germany, have also been dumping grounds for Western hazardous wastes.

Table 1 *Imports of hazardous wastes into the UK 1990/91 (tonnes)*

Switzerland	13,550
Belgium	9229
Eire	3986
Netherlands	3949
Italy	3583
Austria	2912
Sweden	1595
Spain	1194
Portugal	1185
Germany	1010
Others	1762
Total	43,953

Source Environmental Data Services (June 1992)

In all these cases, the long-distance transport involved increases the hazards. Consequently, there has been international effort to regulate this trade. Under the Basel Convention (1989), 33 countries agreed global rules for the international waste trade requiring notification and consent before a country may export hazardous wastes. The EC has adopted the 'proximity principle', whereby wastes should be managed as close to their source as possible. But it is still possible to export wastes outside the EC and to exempt those wastes that are intended for reuse. The future of trade in wastes under the single free market in the EC is unclear. It is unlikely that policing of the various agreements will be able to eliminate the silent trade in illegal exports, facilitated by corruption that exploits the opportunities created by inequalities in environmental standards between countries. Nevertheless, the TCPA recommends that this issue must be tackled.

Recommendation

In principle, all wastes should be managed within their country of origin and as close to their source as practicable using the best environmental option.

3. TRANS-BOUNDARY TRANSFERS OF POLLUTION

The third problem of integration concerns trans-boundary transfers of pollution. It is self-evident that pollution knows no boundaries, travelling via different environmental media between countries which share air basins, rivers or oceans. Britain largely avoids pollution from elsewhere but exports acid rain to Nordic countries from tall stacks on its power stations and radioactivity from Sellafield through the Irish Sea. Downstream countries along the Rhine are at the other end of the scale, receiving considerable pollution from large chemical plants upstream. All countries surrounding the North Sea experience pollution from the rivers that feed into it and from the dumping of sewage at sea. Such transfers are cases of international negative externalities, that is costs imposed on one country by another.

The only defence against such invasion is international co-operation and agreement. Consequently, there have been considerable efforts within Europe either to eliminate such transfers – for example, through agreements on the North Sea and the Rhine – or to reduce pollution through the control of emissions (see Box 5.4). The problems of pollution from eastern Europe are likely to prove more intractable, requiring western aid and technology if dirty industrial practices are to be eliminated.

BOX 5.4 Examples of international agreements on trans-boundary pollution

There are many examples covering a wide variety of pollutants. Two examples are:

1. The UN Economic Commission for Europe Convention on Long-Range Trans-boundary Air Pollution came into force in 1983 and was signed by 35 countries in Europe and North America. A subsequent Protocol ratified by 18 countries committed them to a 30 per cent reduction in SO_2 from 1980 levels. This has been the major international agreement to reduce acid rain.

2. The Convention on the Prevention of Marine Pollution by Dumping of Wastes and Other Materials (usually known as the London Dumping Convention) was established in 1972 and sets the norms, guidelines and recommendations for the disposal of wastes at sea. It has been the legal basis for the prevention of dumping nuclear wastes in the ocean since 1983.

With the hole in the ozone layer and the prospect of global warming, the transfer of pollution has now reached global proportions. The scientific consensus is that there can be no escape from the disruptive effects. The impact may be gradual and uneven and some parts of the world will experience greater upheaval than others or will be less able to find the resources to combat the impacts. Global warming again reveals a pattern of economic inequality, with the wealthy countries making the major contributions: roughly half of all CO_2 emissions come from the OECD countries, with a quarter each from Eastern Europe and the rest of the world. The only conceivable solution is to impose cuts on Western emissions and to provide technology and aid so that emission levels can be controlled in the poor countries. With other Western countries, the UK has made commitments in principle to stabilising its CO_2 levels at 1990 levels by 2000 and to contributing to the ozone fund and the Global Environmental Facility established by the World Bank to fund the treaties on climate change and biodiversity signed at the Rio de Janeiro summit. At that summit, too, the majority of the world's nations subscribed to a Declaration on Environment and Development and supported the extensive agenda for action for a sustainable future known as Agenda 21 (See Box 5.5). Although these commitments may not be entirely fulfilled, certain principles have been achieved at the international level which will influence future policy making.

Recommendation

The principle of polluter pays should be applied to countries whose pollution levels threaten sustainable development in other countries. This principle should be related to levels of pollution and to ability to pay. Payments should be transferred to a fund to provide technology and aid to reduce pollution levels in developing countries.

BOX 5.5 Rio Declaration on Environment and Development

The following are some of the principles relating to pollution agreed at the 1992 Rio Summit:

- *Principle 14.* States should effectively co-operate to discourage or prevent the relocation and transfer to other states of any activities and substances that cause severe environmental degradation or are found to be harmful to human health.
- *Principle 15.* In order to protect the environment, the precautionary approach shall be widely applied by states according to their capabilities. Where there are threats of serious or irreversible damage, lack of full scientific certainty shall not be used as a reason for postponing cost-effective measures to prevent environmental degradation.
- *Principle 18.* States shall immediately notify other states of any natural disasters or other emergencies that are likely to produce sudden harmful effects on the environment of those states. Every effort shall be made by the international community to help states so afflicted.
- *Principle 19.* States shall provide prior and timely notification and relevant information to potentially affected states on activities that may have a significant adverse trans-boundary effect and shall consult with those states at an early stage and in good faith.

Source Rio Declaration on Environment and Development

Pollution and policy making

A third aspect of the integration of waste and pollution is its trans-sectoral nature. Waste and pollution arise at all stages in the production cycle – energy combustion, mining, farming, manufacturing, transportation and consumption. Waste and pollution can be routine and predictable, or unforeseen, accidental and incalculable.

In many sectors of policy making – transportation, energy and agriculture, for example – the environmental consequences have tended to be treated as incidental or residual. For example, in planning the roads programme to meet projected increases of 83–142 per cent in traffic by 2025, the Department of Transport treated such desirable environmental improvements as tree planting along motorways as mere desiderata. The environmental costs and benefits of building motorways as against policies for restraining traffic growth were not debated. Indeed, the programme was justified on environmental grounds in 1990 by the Transport Secretary's implausible sophism that 'stationary or slow moving traffic produces far more pollution than free-flowing traffic'.

What is required is a comprehensive and strategic approach to environmental policy making that ensures that environmentally sustainable policies are being pursued by all policy sectors. *This Common Inheritance* promised that the government would 'integrate environmental concerns more effectively into all policy areas'; ministers responsible for ensuring that environmental considerations were taken into account were identified for each department; and a guide was published explaining how environmental impacts of policies and programmes should be taken into account.[10] Annual monitoring statements are now being produced charting progress made towards the implementation of the environmental policies outlined in the White Paper.

While these are useful beginnings, the TCPA does not accept that they go anywhere near far enough. We believe that strategic planning for the environment at all levels – the process of environmental planning set out in Chapter 1 – must be given priority as an integral element in economic management and social development. Waste and pollution is a key component of this process.

Recommendation

There should be a strategic cross-sectoral approach to waste management and pollution control that draws together policies across all production sectors and sets out action plans for implementation.

WASTE AND THE CONSERVATION OF RESOURCES

We turn now to specific policies for sustainable development, first in the area of waste management and then for pollution prevention and control.

Waste represents a misuse of resources. Improved management of waste can make a major contribution to the achievement of the first goal for sustainable development stated in Chapter 1 – *'to ensure the supply of natural resources for present and future generations through the efficient use of land, less wasteful use of non-renewable resources, their substitution by renewable resources, and the maintenance of biodiversity'*. This can be achieved through three strategies – the efficient use of land; a reduction in the volume of wastes; and aftercare and restoration.

EFFICIENT USE OF LAND

In Chapter 3 we discussed the problem of derelict land in rural areas caused by mineral extraction and recommended that such land should be taxed, or in cases where ownership could not be determined, brought into public ownership. There are also in the cities large tracts of vacant, and often derelict, land lying idle for want of investment. One estimate puts the total area of vacant and derelict land in England alone at 210,000ha – an area the size of Nottinghamshire.[11]

Derelict and vacant land represents an inefficient use of resources. It can result from over-use or from under-use. The complex causes of vacant land have been much debated but essentially it is land without present value because it has no market. This may be brought about by lack of demand or by a failure to release supply. The potential or future value of such land is often unknown or unrealised.

Land sustains human activity and ecological variety and sustainable development requires that land on which a particular activity has ended should be left in a useful state. This does not mean that it must be developed. But it does mean that potentially useful land should not be abandoned in a useless state, as is the case with some vacant land and derelict land that has not been reclaimed. For instance, a wildlife sanctuary would be a sustainable use.

Land may be priced too high to attract demand. A tax on land values, set at appropriate levels, would act as an incentive, stimulating owners to improve it and release it rather than hold on to it. Where the market either causes or cannot prevent waste of land, intervention is justified. Where there is no value or even negative value or where owners cannot deal with clean-up it will be necessary to fund reclamation through grants from the taxpayer or to take the land into public ownership. Whilst the problems of ownership, value, responsibility and equity that arise in attempts to apply taxation to land values must be recognised, they should not place a barrier that inhibits attempts to deal with the problem of vacant and derelict land.

Recommendations

Land that serves no useful purpose and for which there is no market should be brought into a sustainable use by grants or by public ownership. Where possible, the funds for such intervention should be secured by a tax on marketable derelict land consistent with the polluter pays principle and intended to stimulate the release of the land.

Environmental plans should identify sustainable uses for such areas of land.

REDUCING THE VOLUME OF WASTE

Our second approach to conserving resources deals with the reduction of the volume of waste. The era of mass consumption and materialism has been marked by the generation of vast quantities of waste (see Box 5.6). Consumer durables such as washing machines and refrigerators have long since shifted from being luxuries to becoming necessities in the West. While there is an increasing emphasis on durability and quality, the volumes of production required to meet growing consumer demand intensify pressure on non-renewable resources and create large volumes of waste and pollution. The throw-away society has placed an emphasis on packaging as an integral part of marketing consumer goods. The packaging depletes resources and becomes waste which must be managed. A reduction in waste creation can only be brought about by changes in attitudes to waste, to packaging, and to technology.

BOX 5.6 Waste volumes in UK

The estimated total annual waste stream in the late 1980s was about 700 million tonnes broken down as follows:

Agriculture	37%
Industrial	11%
Dredged spoils	5%
Demolition	4%
Commercial	2%
Mining and quarrying	34%
Sewage sludge	4%
Household	3%

Source Matthew Gandy, derived from estimates in DoE Digest of Environmental Statistics (1991 and 1992)

Municipal waste, primarily household and commercial, accounts for a small proportion, around 20 million tonnes annually, of the total waste stream. Only about 20 per cent of the total stream (mainly industrial and municipal) is controlled waste under the Environmental Protection Act.

Controlled wastes are disposed of mainly in landfills (86 per cent), with only small proportions incinerated (4 per cent) or dumped at sea (4 per cent).

By far the biggest impact in reducing waste volumes will be achieved by changes in the nature of production itself. Here we focus on the need for sustainable industrial production. This involves three principles – minimising resource depletion; closing the production cycle; and waste volume reduction.

The minimisation of resource depletion can be achieved either through a reduction in the use of non-renewable resources or by using renewable resources or less wasteful substitutes for non-renewables or by greater emphasis on product durability. Such a shift would be fundamental in its implications. Product design, packaging and marketing would emphasise quality, durability and utility. There are, of course, many examples of such 'green' approaches to production and marketing emphasising environmentally benign characteristics. But there can also be unintended consequences. For example, it may sometimes be more sustainable to introduce new products that save energy or other resources than to maintain durable, polluting and wasteful products. This may be true for a range of consumer durables such as washing machines, refrigerators or cars. The resource costs over the lifetimes of products need to be carefully evaluated. (This is discussed further in Chapter 8.)

The fundamental principle of such evaluation is to value resources as environmental assets. Some resources are renewable and can be replaced either in situ or elsewhere. The relative costs of depleting such resources would be reflected in the price of products and so stimulate their replacement. But some resources are unique, so that once destroyed they are gone forever, or are critical in the sense that their depletion carries risks to health or even survival. Elsewhere we have urged the introduction of a carbon tax as a means of protecting the atmosphere and reducing pollution. But there are profound political difficulties in introducing such measures and, in any event, market criteria cannot be accurately applied to resources whose scarcity value might increase over time; neither can market criteria take into account different valuations placed by different societies over time. For these reasons, intervention may be necessary to ensure that resources are protected.

Minimising resource depletion will involve a reorientation of economic and political priorities and social values. A combination of market incentives and sanctions and greater intervention through environmental planning will be necessary to ensure a sustainable use of resources. Market-based policies alone are unlikely to lead to waste reduction, rather a shift to more profitable methods of waste management such as incineration with production of electricity. Environmental planning will be necessary to set and implement targets for waste reduction and to propose policies for achieving them.

Recommendation

Intervention should be directed towards ensuring that critical non-renewable resources are protected through pricing policies or through regulation in order to avoid the waste of resources.

Production processes tend to be linear: throughout the cycle, waste materials are produced which have to be managed in some way. The waste of resources and the cost of waste management can be avoided if the cycle of production is closed. In other words, the process should, as far as possible, become circular rather than linear. This can be achieved through the reuse, alternative use or recycling of materials otherwise unused during production, or, where feasible the use of waste products for energy or fertiliser or some other purpose.

Recovery and reuse of materials during production may be encouraged by the realistic pricing of resources suggested above. It can also be facilitated by the standardisation of such articles as containers and components and has the further advantage of reducing storage space, especially if combined with just-in-time methods of component supply. The use of standardised packaging products by consumers can be stimulated by incentives such as payment on return. Milk bottles are routinely used in this way and standard returnable glass bottles are making a strong reappearance in countries such as the Netherlands.

Recommendation

Reuse of resources both during production and consumption must be encouraged through product standardisation and incentives for return, including post-consumer waste.

Recycling – the reuse of materials transformed during production for the same or different purposes – has long been a feature of certain industrial processes, saving energy costs, reducing pollution and removing the need to find disposal sites. For instance, making a can from recycled aluminium requires only 5 per cent of the energy needed for one made from virgin material. Again, by using scrap metal, the steel industry can save two-thirds of the energy costs of using iron ore. A high percentage of certain metals is recovered by UK industry (around three-quarters of copper and two-thirds of lead). Recycled materials account for over half the input in the paper and board industry, and a third in aluminium, but less than 10 per cent in plastics.

A good example of the potential for recycling in minimising environmental damage is the use of aggregates for road building, which consumes about a third of all the aggregates used in the UK. The total demand for primary aggregates is forecast to double over twenty years, requiring excavation of 8.25 billion tonnes of sand, gravel and

---

BOX 5.7 Creative recycling

One project that well illustrates how the creativity of designers can short-circuit a problem has been carried out in the Design Research Centre attached to Brunel University in London. This tackled one of the most difficult of recycling problems – dealing with mixed plastics waste – and turns what are usually regarded as an obstacle into a positive advantage. One of the most interesting trials used discarded electric cabling complete with its mixed colours and copper wire. This was shredded and mixed and then heated and pressed to create decorative panels that exploit the colour variety and occasional glint of copper to produce a smooth decorative board suitable for such non-structural uses as interior claddings, shelving and so on. Several manufacturers have shown an interest in exploiting the technique, which produces a material that meets fire and safety standards.

---

crushed rock. This is estimated to be the equivalent of digging a hole 3 metres deep in an area the size of Berkshire. Sand and gravel extraction is an increasing source of local political conflict, especially in South-East England; and the use of imported crushed rock is an unsustainable practice, destroying the environment and creating long-distance transport costs. Yet, despite all these pressures and the proven feasibility of using recycled material for road building, only around half the total of aggregates used in road repairs is recycled and there is virtually no recycled material used in road construction.

BOX 5.8 Recycling of Household Wastes

About 1 million tonnes of municipal solid wastes are recycled annually, out of a total waste stream of 700 million. The average household recycling rate in England and Wales is 4.4 per cent.

Typically, well over half the household waste stream consists of paper (30 per cent of total) or putrescibles (25 per cent). Other components are: glass (11 per cent), dust and fines (9 per cent), plastics and metals (8 per cent each), and textiles (5 per cent). The proportions will vary according to such factors as the number of households with gardens, income levels, types of packaging and the existence of recycling programmes.

There are, broadly, three methods of waste recovery for recycling:

1. *Collect* systems include various types of kerbside collection such as wheeled bins and separation of wet and dry wastes. These systems are high cost and rely on public co-operation but can achieve a high level of recovery of a wide range of materials.

2. *Bring* systems provide on-street collection facilities or recycling centres. They are low cost but achieve low levels of recovery and have local environmental impacts.

3. *Centralised sorting plants* have the advantage of producing by-products such as energy recovery but are costly to develop and are often opposed on local environmental grounds.

Source Matthew Gandy

In terms of recycling domestic waste, the UK's performance is relatively poor. For instance, the UK's one bottle bank per 14,000 people compares unfavourably with Australia's one per 2000. It is estimated that around half the domestic waste stream is recyclable and a target has been set of recycling half of this (ie 25 per cent of the total) by the year 2000. This will involve considerable changes in behaviour depending on the methods used (see Box 5.8) and markets will have to be created where they do not exist today.

To achieve this target in less than ten years will require a strong lead by government, incentives and practical help. Experience in other countries shows that industry and the public can respond to such a challenge. The UK's overall recycling rate is around 2.2 per cent as against 9 per cent in Denmark; our record is also poor when compared with the Netherlands, where 53 per cent of glass and paper is recycled (compared with 9 per cent and 30 per cent respectively here); but the UK does perform well in scrap metals.

There are three principal obstacles to higher levels of recycling. First is the weakness of the secondary materials market which has repeatedly undermined recycling efforts over the postwar period, with materials such as waste paper being especially badly affected. Second, the doubling in size of the municipal waste stream since the 1960s can largely be attributed to the growth in packaging waste which can only be effectively tackled by national or EC government intervention. Lastly, the introduction of complex and expensive programmes involving kerbside collection and dual bin systems for the collection of putrescible wastes from households without gardens can only be tackled if local government is provided with the necessary administrative and financial resources.

Recycling is a means of reducing waste volumes; it is not a means of reducing waste production. Recycling is sometimes expensive and may have unforeseen consequences in that apparently sustainable practices may divert attention from alternative waste-reducing strategies. The costs and benefits of policies need to be carefully assessed. Although some caution is appropriate, action is required.

Recommendation

The recycling of materials must be encouraged wherever feasible and where harmful effects can be avoided. Measures should include:

- setting targets and monitoring progress;
- insisting on the separation of recyclable materials at the point of origin or at accessible collection centres;
- ensuring that markets for recycled products are created through the realistic pricing of resources.

Both reuse and recycling can be encouraged by the design of integrated waste management systems. For example, combined heat and power plants use waste heat. Similarly, an integrated waste recovery system would link the consumption and production processes. Household waste would be separated and collected either at the door or taken to a recovery facility (such as a bottle bank). Vegetable and garden wastes can be used directly for composting. The indiscriminate dumping of large items – cars, consumer durables, furniture etc – is obviously avoidable when there is an adequate recovery system or tidy tip. There are many local initiatives and innovatory ideas, incentives and innovations being introduced across the country. An integrated approach to waste management forms an integral part of a sustainable city system incorporating localised energy supply, food production and transportation systems.

Recommendation

Integrated waste recovery and recycling systems should be developed as an essential component of a settlement system designed to achieve sustainability.

REPROCESSING AND RADIOACTIVE WASTES

One area of recycling that presents particular difficulties is, of course, the reprocessing of radioactive wastes. Although recycling reduces the volume of high-level waste (but creates greater volumes of intermediate- and low-level wastes), it involves the production of plutonium which cannot be justified on military grounds and, with the abandonment of the fast-breeder reactor programmes, is no longer required as a fuel. Reprocessing remains in the UK and France primarily as a means of processing spent fuel and is in practice simply a method of waste management. With the opening of the Thermal Oxide Reprocessing Plant (THORP) at Sellafield, the process will become increasingly dependent on foreign contracts. The contracts signed since 1976 provide for all wastes to be sent back to the country of origin; but, given the high volumes of low-activity wastes involved, this is likely to prove impractical. Consequently, it is intended to substitute high-level wastes for an equivalent amount (in terms of radioactivity) of intermediate and low-level wastes. This will result in the UK becoming the *de facto* dump for foreign low- and intermediate-level waste.

Reprocessing has a number of serious implications. The transhipment of wastes and plutonium poses risks to populations on the transportation routes. There is also the risk of nuclear proliferation if cargoes are intercepted. The concentration of radioactive wastes in one location (Sellafield) increases the potential risks to people and the environment. And, if the proposed repository at Sellafield fails to meet the safety criteria imposed on it, the accumulated wastes will have to be transshipped elsewhere, thus further increasing the risks of exposure or accident during transportation.

Recommendation

The reprocessing of nuclear wastes should be abandoned: it serves no useful purpose, encourages the use of Sellafield as a dumping ground for foreign wastes, poses unacceptable risks to the local population and those living on transportation corridors, and carries the potential threat of nuclear proliferation.

As we saw in Chapter 1, efforts to find suitable sites for the disposal of radioactive wastes have met with stiff political resistance. As a result, NIREX was effectively forced to retreat to Sellafield in its search for a site where less public hostility might be expected. NIREX has now proposed the co-disposal of low and intermediate wastes in a geological repository between 200 and 1000 metres deep in the vicinity of the village of Gosforth. The hydrogeological characteristics of the site are being explored and the proposal for an underground laboratory to monitor rocks and groundwater will push back the date for completing the repository, even if it eventually achieves technical feasibility, radiological safety and public acceptability. In other countries, too, the search for deep repositories has slowed down for a variety of reasons. Given the unimaginable time-spans during which the integrity of the repository must be maintained, it makes good sense to undertake detailed research and to consider all possible options before constructing a repository.

Recommendation

No decision should be taken on the development of a deep geological repository until a measured programme of exploration, experiment and monitoring of different available options for the management of radioactive wastes has been completed.

WASTE VOLUME REDUCTION

Where the production of waste cannot be avoided, effort should normally be made to minimise the volumes that have to be managed. For example, putrescible wastes contain a large proportion of water, and an elementary composting process will substantially reduce the overall volume of that waste and this will dramatically reduce waste transportation costs. Space for disposal in landfills is at a premium, especially near to the large conurbations that generate the most waste.

As far as possible, the use of resources for the long-distance transport of useless material should be avoided. The most obvious solution is compaction of wastes to reduce volume. A major problem with compaction is that it slows down the rate of the degradation processes in landfills, making the control of gas and leachate production more difficult. Even inert wastes may contain leachate and gas-producing materials. Moving and turning waste encourages faster biodegradation and may consequently be a better environmental option.

Another option may be the incineration of a greater proportion of the waste stream. The UK incinerates much less than many other countries, with only just over 2 per cent of its municipal waste stream incinerated compared, for instance, with 9 per cent in Denmark. Incinerators pose a number of problems, including adding to greenhouse gases, creating toxic ash, traffic generation and local pollution problems.

Recommendation

Compaction of waste should be encouraged provided that it does not increase the risks from leachate or methane in landfills. Where feasible and not harmful, incineration should be used to reduce waste volumes and avoid transportation.

Again, incentives will be needed to achieve this, through charging systems which favour low volumes of compacted wastes and penalise high volumes of unconsolidated waste. The lower volumes will relieve the pressure on landfilling. The concept of paying the waste collecting authority credits for reductions in the waste stream has already been introduced, although its impact has been slight so far owing to administrative complexity and the problem of financial adjustments between the waste disposal authorities who pay the credits and the waste collecting authorities who receive them.

WASTE AND RESTORATION

Even residual wastes can have some environmental value. In areas where mineral extraction has gouged great voids or scars in the landscape, inert wastes can be used to restore or re-create environmental features. Restoration and aftercare are standard requirements in mineral planning applications. But, in some cases, the volumes of material extracted make restoration extremely difficult. For example, the voids created by extracting Oxford clay for fletton brickmaking in Bedfordshire can only be filled by importing waste for landfill from London and elsewhere.[12] In theory, London benefits from access to landfill space and the brickfield areas make an environmental gain. But the brickfields are 50 miles distant, requiring transfer stations and energy-consuming haulage systems. So this is an example where the environmental costs and benefits of different waste management options need to be evaluated. In addition, the strategic co-ordination of waste disposal has become more complicated with the abolition of the Greater London Council and the de-municipalisation of waste disposal functions, and the shift towards the private sector has added to the spatial fragmentation of the organisation of waste management.

Landfilling can bring environmental problems in the form of fly infestation, leachates, odour and the hazard of methane gas. Controls over landfilling have been tightened under the Environmental Protection Act and EC Directives. An integrated and strategic approach will be needed to ensure that the location and methods of landfilling are properly planned.

Recommendation

The best practicable environmental options of waste management should be evaluated, using sustainability criteria. Environmental benefits through restoration should be justified in strategic plans before landfilling of residual wastes is permitted.

POLLUTION AND SUSTAINABLE DEVELOPMENT

Since waste often contains pollutants, the methods already described for minimising wastes are likely also to contribute to the reduction of pollution. Pollution can be avoided by the adoption of three strategies, each applying to a stage in the production or consumption process. These are:

1. the *prevention* of the production of pollution at source;
2. the *control* of the discharge of pollution; and
3. the *reduction* of the impacts of pollution.

With regard to **pollution prevention**, the most effective method is, of course, the total elimination of polluting or hazardous processes. This requires an assessment of the costs and benefits of the process. Introducing sustainability criteria increases the costs of the polluting activities and hence strengthens the case for elimination. For instance, it has recently become clear that the benefits of CFCs are vastly outweighed by the global environmental damage they cause to the ozone layer. The fact that CFCs had limited uses and could be substituted made international agreement easier, although doubts remain about the acceptability of substitutes and the implementation of the ozone protocols.

Other cases are more difficult. In the case of energy production, both substitution and reduction of the rate of consumption will be essential. But the present methods of production are heavily dependent on fossil fuels, while conservation is inhibited by the view that increased energy use and the growth of motor vehicle numbers are both keys to economic development. The inherent conflicts between rich and poor countries make agreement extremely difficult to negotiate. Nuclear energy is unacceptable as a substitute on the grounds of cost, danger from accidents, and the risk to future generations from long-lived hazardous wastes.

Perhaps the major obstacle to achieving a sustainable future is the relatively short time-span in which we must accomplish a major transformation in technology to reduce the burden of pollution. Changes in energy production and conservation, in farming practices, building construction, manufacturing, employment and transportation are considered elsewhere in this report. The spatial pattern of development that should be encouraged to accommodate the technological changes are set out in Chapter 9. The means for achieving change, through intervention in the market and through planning, are discussed throughout the report. From the perspective of this chapter, it is vital that all these changes are effectively co-ordinated at local, national and international level. The following recommendation echoes the general principles urged throughout this report.

Recommendation

Wherever possible, pollution should be prevented by the elimination of polluting processes. Where this is not possible, technological changes in energy, agriculture, industry, construction and transportation should be encouraged which will ensure a reduction in the level of pollution in the longer term.

But some pollution is inevitable and **pollution control** is therefore important. Unlike waste, pollution has no potential reuse and therefore no market. The amount of pollution reflects a social choice between the benefits of increased production and the costs of pollution. As 'The tragedy of the global commons' (Box 1.4) makes clear, the optimal level of pollution for society is likely to be different from the optimal level for individual polluters. To make the situation more complex, the levels of pollution that will be tolerated vary over time and between different social groups and countries. On top of these differences, society is now having to grapple with the problem of defining the acceptable global level of pollution.

Another set of factors to consider arises from the methods used to control pollution. Pollution control must rely on intervention by the state at national or local level or through international agreements. Control can take various forms. One is the use of fiscal means in the form of sanctions, such as taxes or levies, a much advocated method on grounds of potential effectiveness. A carbon tax may well be the best approach to achieving emission reductions of CO_2 at national level (Chapter 4). But there are severe practical problems with using fiscal methods, including the attribution of costs, technical complexity, uncertainty of impact, insensitivity of distribution, and administrative expense. So, while fiscal methods are promising, they do require considerable investigation.

Fiscal methods can be used in conjunction with regulation. The regulation of pollution relies on the setting of standards and means of enforcement. Standards may be set generically in the form of environmental quality standards and they may be applied to individual polluters by fixing emission levels. Standards may be achieved in various ways. Polluters may be forced to introduce abatement technology or they may be able to offset polluting activity by reducing another source in the same area (as is practised in California) or they may be forced to relocate elsewhere. Box 5.9 gives an example how market incentives can be used by the state to achieve pollution standards.

There has been considerable convergence in the general approach towards pollution control. Integrated Pollution Control is now established in principle and is being introduced in practice. The traditional approach to control in the UK was 'best practicable means' (BPM). It had an inherent flexibility, weighing up the environmental benefits, thereby secured against the economic costs to the community and the polluter

BOX 5.9 An example of market based regulation – United States SO$_2$.

In order to comply with the 1990 Clean Air Act, sulphur dioxide emissions in the USA must be cut to 10 million tons – less than the 1980 level – by the end of the century.

The Environmental Protection Agency (EPA) has devised a scheme whereby each current producer receives a number of sulphur dioxide allowances depending on various factors, including current emission rates. Producers are able to trade their allowances in a free market. In addition, the EPA will offer some allowances at auction and some for direct sale, particularly to new companies, at a fixed price of $1500.

The market principle is intended to achieve environmental clean-up through economic incentives. Take the case of two plants, plant 'A' able to cut emissions to $1000 a ton, plant 'B' to only $2000 a ton. 'A' could cut its emissions by a ton and sell an allowance to 'B' for, say, $1500, thus making $500 on the deal while 'B' saves $500 over the cost of cutting its own emissions. In this case, the market ensures that emissions are cut at the lowest possible cost.

of imposing controls. The system attempted 'to satisfy the demands of the environmentalists, while achieving the quiescence of the business community'.[13] Much criticised as tending to favour industrial interests, BPM nevertheless had some advantages in being able to respond to local environmental circumstances and the economic and technical capacity of polluters to comply in the short term.

One of the problems with BPM is that it can result in environmental inequalities, as different standards are applied in different places. Under the standard-setting regimes now adopted to comply with practice elsewhere, the emphasis has shifted towards tougher controls. This is to be achieved through 'best available techniques not entailing excessive cost' (BATNEEC) which 'builds on the traditional British approach of 'best practicable means' in controlling pollution'. The choice of technology is also constrained by the use of 'best practicable environmental option' (BPEO), which emphasises regard to environmental impacts. In addition, major projects now require an Environmental Impact Assessment (EIA) which is intended to ensure that all effects have been considered prior to the project being given the go-ahead.

The adoption of BATNEEC, BPEOs and EIA within the context of IPC promises, in principle, to produce a coherent and consistent system of pollution control in the UK that converges with developments in the European Community. The TCPA welcomes this approach but would urge that adequate resources are devoted to its implementation. In particular, it is important that adequate research is undertaken into evaluating the best methods of pollution control. The concept of 'critical loads' now being adopted must be regarded as allowing a maximum rather than an acceptable level of pollution. The concept involves assessing the levels of a pollutant which local environments can tolerate without significant damage. At present, for many toxic substances there are no official guidelines on tolerable levels of contamination. In the case of pollution control, the strategic approach advocated throughout this report must incorporate a number of features.

Pollution has various **environmental impacts**. It may affect amenity through noise, loss of visibility or damage to the landscape. It can affect the health of living organisms, causing disease, decay or death. And it can threaten the survival of whole ecosystems. These impacts may be immediate or latent. For example, there are latent dangers lurking in abandoned toxic waste tips. A report in *The Observer* in 1990 drew attention to the 1300 sites in the UK from which toxic materials could be leaking into ground water and 59 sites from which there was a serious risk of contamination.[14] Radioactive waste is already leaking into the environment at sites in the United States and elsewhere and the potential impact on future generations is incalculable.

Recommendation

A strategic environmental planning framework should be established setting out the principles, policies and implementation programme of pollution control at local, regional and national level which is consistent with relevant developments at the international level. Essential features of such an approach include:

- Maximum acceptable levels of pollution should be defined, having regard to the impact on public health and ecosystems and the potential burden on future generations.
- Targets for the reduction of pollution below this maximum level should be set.
- Comprehensive and regular monitoring of critical pollutants should be carried out, with the results being made available to the public in an accessible form.
- Further investment in research should be undertaken to evaluate the effectiveness and consequences of different methods of pollution control.

Where pollution has already occurred or where it cannot be avoided, its effects must be ameliorated. Although some of the impacts can be tackled through health programmes, it is preferable to adopt preventive measures where possible. The TCPA believes that land use planning has a major part to play in this.

There are three ways in which planning can reduce the impact of pollution. The first is through environmental clean-up and restoration, a point already mentioned in connection with waste. Amenity damage can be mitigated by erecting barriers against noise, by landscaping derelict areas, or by insisting on the high-quality design of buildings.

Second, planning policies can encourage developments that counteract pollution damage. For example, the planting of forests can have both an amenity and a health value.

The third way that planning can minimise the impact of pollution is by influencing the pattern of location of polluting activities, thereby mitigating their impact. Polluting activities should be kept as free from settlements as possible. This can be done in various ways: by locating the activity in a remote area; by stand-off areas or emergency planning zones to defend communities from major hazardous activities; and by removing and dispersing pollutants by pipelines or tall chimneys.

Each of these locational strategies can have harmful consequences which must be recognised and minimised. Remote locations concentrating polluting activities can become 'pollution havens', imposing high levels of risk on local populations. Stand-off zones can induce a false sense of security, and experience has shown that people's actual behaviour in a real-life emergency is likely to be very different from the anticipated behaviour of predictive models. And pipelines and tall stacks simply move the pollution elsewhere, for instance from the UK to the Nordic countries. These unintended consequences raise problems of equity which we shall consider in a moment. First, we stress that pollution control must be regarded as an integral aspect of the environmental planning process that we have advocated throughout this report.

Recommendation

A major element in the environmental planning process is the setting out of strategies for the integration of pollution control, and land-use planning in the relevant national, regional and local environmental plans.

EQUITY AND COMPENSATION

In Chapter 1 we underlined the connection between social and environmental inequality. They are cause and effect, an outcome of the process of uneven development that leads to negative externalities in the form of pollution and waste being imposed by the rich on the poor. This happens at different spatial scales. Within nation-states in the developed world, opposition to locally unwanted land uses (LULUs) often results in such activities ending up in peripheral communities. These pollution havens have to accept environmental risks in order to ensure economic survival. Examples of such communities in the UK are the nuclear oasis of Sellafield and the pollution havens for hazardous chemical industries in Merseyside, Teesside and Canvey Island.

This process of uneven environmental development also operates at the international scale. As we have seen, poor countries become dumping grounds for toxic wastes. In addition, some areas have become the unwitting victims of trans-boundary pollution in the form of acid rain, radioactivity, marine pollution and other hazards. Principle 13 of the Rio Declaration addresses this issue:

> *States shall develop national law regarding liability and compensation for the victims of pollution and other environmental damage. States shall also co-operate in an expeditious and more determined manner to develop further international law regarding liability and compensation for adverse effects of environmental damage caused by activities within their jurisdiction or control to areas beyond their jurisdiction.*

Certain LULUs are inevitable and sites for them exist already or must be found. For example, there will be a need to find sites for the management of toxic or radioactive wastes that have already accumulated. Hazardous industrial sites already exist and cannot be shut down in the short term. Certain industrial processes may create local hazards but be justified for the wider social or environmental benefits that they bring. Wherever communities bear the burden of risk and pollution they should, on grounds of equity and increasingly of necessity, be compensated in some way. Unless this is done, it will become increasingly difficult to maintain existing locations, let alone secure new ones. Communities should be offered influence over the design and local impact of polluting and hazardous activities. Compensation in the form of tax concessions, provision of infrastructure, economic development and training may help to offset the negative impacts of such projects. Contingency plans including monitoring, emergency planning and liability coverage will also be necessary. Above all, communities must be enabled to participate as partners in decision making. Lack of any say in decisions has often driven local communities to oppose LULUs. In some countries – Czechoslovakia, for example – local communities can exercise a veto over unwanted activities. In Canada and some other countries, efforts have been made to achieve voluntary participation in the identification and selection of sites for activities such as radioactive waste disposal.

Resentment and resistance are hard to displace and too much emphasis on achieving locations that are publicly acceptable can lead to sites that are technically sub optimal, resulting in higher levels of risk or excessive and dangerous movements of hazardous materials over long distances. Safety considerations must remain paramount.

Recommendations

Communities that bear a disproportionate burden of pollution or risk should be compensated. Such compensation should depend on local needs and circumstances and include economic benefits, investment in infrastructure, and the provision of community facilities.

In order to secure locations for unavoidable but dangerous activities, host communities should be given an effective voice in decision making over the siting, operation and control of the activity.

The safety and long-term security of sites must take precedence over all other considerations.

Some activities impose burdens on future generations. For example, current levels of CO_2 production threaten global disaster within the space of two generations. Because this threat is so obvious, politicians are endeavouring to grapple with the problem, despite the manifest difficulties. But where the threat is more remote, there is less concern about the burdens from the present on the future. Nuclear waste is a case in point. The burden is already so great that it breaches the sustainability criterion of not imposing added costs or risks on succeeding generations. The risks from long-lived highly radioactive wastes are likely to increase over time as interest and knowledge of repositories fade and containment weakens. A similar situation occurs with toxic wastes in abandoned dumps. The claims of distant generations are exceedingly weak and are easily discounted or ignored.

Ultimately, some risk is inevitable and unavoidable but it must be minimised. Following the general principle argued earlier in this chapter, no irreversible decision should be taken until all available options have been evaluated and there is reasonable confidence of the effects of the action (or lack of it) on present and future generations.

CONCLUSION

Sustainable development means that the productive sectors of the economy must be so managed that resources are conserved, waste avoided and pollution eliminated as far as possible. In this chapter we have focused on the broader national and international context. While a wider framework for waste management and pollution control is vital, we do not have to wait for it to appear before taking action locally. The scope for local action is evident at many points in this report. Local pressure in favour of environmental clean-up, pollution reduction, the effective management of wastes, and the provision of proper compensation for communities hosting hazardous activities will be a powerful factor in ensuring action by a dilatory government and its agencies. Local action can be both practical and political.

Finally, we have emphasised the role of environmental planning in the achievement of sustainable policies for waste and pollution. A function of environmental planning is to examine sustainable levels of pollution and waste and to indicate the means by which they can be achieved. Environmental control and land-use planning must be brought together within appropriate and accountable levels of government, including regional authorities. A good way to begin would be with an experiment in environmental planning at local level, where people have a personal stake in the quality of their environment.

The author wishes to acknowledge the help of Matthew Gandy, Michael Clark, Elaine Lambert, David Lowry, Helmut Lusser, Ralph Rookwood and Denis Smith in the preparation of this chapter.

6

Building the Sustainable Environment

Brenda and Robert Vale

All construction work must, by definition, be more or less detrimental to the natural environment, since it replaces what is 'natural' by what is man made. A green field is a habitat for insects, birds and small mammals, a tarmac-covered car park is not. However, in terms of the current environmental debate, what is more usefully explored is the degree to which the environmental impact of construction work can be limited.

Before continuing the discussion of the role of buildings and construction in the creation of a sustainable society, it is essential to define the meaning of 'sustainable'. A sustainable society is one which can maintain its existence in the long term without threatening by its actions the existence of any other forms of life. Sustainability implies that there should be no irreversible pollution, no reliance on finite resources, and a stable population.

Current industrialised societies are anything but sustainable. They are fundamentally based on the use of energy sources – coal, oil, natural gas and uranium – without which they would cease to function; but these energy sources are also known to be finite. In the case of North Sea oil and gas, which together provide about 75 per cent of the energy delivered to the UK economy, the expected life of the resources is in the order of 30 years. If the entire world had the per capita energy demand of the industrialised nations, all the world's known and predicted fuel reserves would be used up in 200 years.

The depletion of the fuel reserves is not the only problem. The fossil fuels, when burned, add carbon dioxide to the atmosphere. As has already been discussed in earlier chapters, carbon dioxide is one of a number of greenhouse gases, the effect of which is to reduce the rate at which heat is lost from the earth into space. Carbon dioxide has been a constituent of the atmosphere for millions of years but historically it has been in balance, with trees and plants taking carbon from the atmosphere to build their structure; when they die and rot, the carbon returns to the atmosphere as part of a continuing cycle. The fossil fuels, formed from the remains of prehistoric animals and plants, contain carbon that did not return to the atmosphere but became trapped. When these fuels are burned the carbon is returned to the air, but there is no corresponding plant growth to absorb it. The net result is that the carbon dioxide content of the atmosphere, at present estimated at roughly 700 billion tonnes, is increasing annually by about 6 billion tonnes.

The Department of the Environment (DoE) predicts that the resulting rise in average world temperature over the next 100 years could be as high as 6°C if nothing is done to curb CO_2 emissions.[1] Six degrees may not sound very much, but the effects could be dramatic; the last time there was a temperature variation approaching this magnitude, although it was a lowering rather than a raising of temperature, one result was that southern England was covered by glaciers. The effects of such a rise are not easy or straightforward to predict. The DoE suggest that a sea level rise of up to a metre is possible, resulting in the inundation of some low-lying countries and increased flooding in many others. The rapidity of climate change may well have disastrous effects on agriculture and forestry, rendering the crops of many regions, such as the North American grain belt, no longer viable. Even more serious may be the impact on the remaining natural forest areas, which act as an absorber of atmospheric carbon. The rate of climate change will be too rapid for trees and other slow growing plants to adapt.

The estimated fossil fuel reserves of the world contain more than ten times as much carbon as is at present in the atmosphere. So not only are the fossil fuels a finite resource: they are a resource that the world cannot afford to use up without destroying itself. The figures quoted above, which show worrying rises in temperature and sea levels, assume only a doubling of atmospheric carbon. The effect of a tenfold increase would be catastrophic for all life on earth. If it were possible to rank environmental problems, the problem of global atmospheric change would probably be the most serious of all. In the search for the goal of environmental quality as outlined in Chapter 1, it is obvious that carbon dioxide production from the use of fossil fuels is, on a global scale, the priority pollution problem.

Many people, including those at the Department of the Environment, accept that global warming is happening and that its effects will be serious. But what is the relation of this to buildings and construction? In the United Kingdom, and probably in the whole of the developed world, the servicing of buildings accounts for 50 per cent of total fossil fuel consumption (see Fig 6.1).

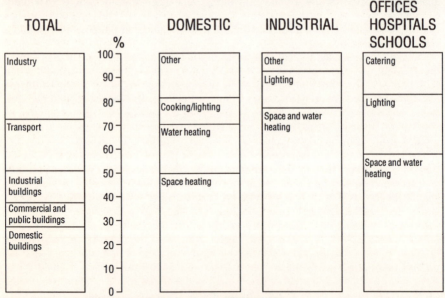

Source Building Research Energy Conservation Support Unit (BRECSU) (1985)

Fig 6.1 *UK energy use by sector*

If the energy used to make building materials and the energy used for travelling from home to employment and shopping are added into the equation, the design and planning of the built environment probably account for more than three-quarters of all fossil fuel use. Planners, architects and their clients have, therefore, an enormous responsibility for the continuing future of life on earth. Current attitudes and practices will have to change if the goal of conservation of energy and resources is to be met.

So, to achieve a sustainable future, the use of energy in the construction industry needs to be questioned under two headings. The first is *energy capital* – the energy that goes into the making of both buildings and infrastructure. The second is *energy revenue*

– the energy consumed by the operation of the built environment (heating, lighting, power, etc).

These critical energy issues are examined later in this chapter. However, there is another consideration that cannot be ignored in the search for a construction industry that can exist in a sustainable society: the effect that the extraction and processing of raw materials has on the ultimate finite resource, the land. Society has come a long way from the time when the materials for the creation of shelter were both close at hand and ultimately recyclable. But it is useful to remember that old technologies can still perform the function for which they were designed. The roofs of the great medieval cathedrals were built from timber – a material that can be grown, harvested and returned to the land without causing pollution – by manual labour with a minimal use of energy sources (the fire to forge the metal tools), yet they remained the longest span structures in England from the time of their construction until the Victorian development of cast and wrought iron. Similarly, the cob cottages of Devon and Dorset were built, again by manual labour, using as the base material the earth on which they stand mixed with straw and water: those cottages continue today to provide housing, unlike many of the postwar system-built flats that have been demolished before the end of their design life.

Some would view using such approaches as mere romanticism, suggesting that building with earth was hardly appropriate for a society that has seen a man walk on the moon and matter split into at least some of its constituent parts. Yet some advanced countries have maintained traditional methods and are, as a result, much closer to an environmentally sustainable building industry, at least for house construction. For example, half of Sweden is covered in forest and the usual method of house building in that country is timber frame: the raw material is grown in a landscape that is ultimately stable because it is managed; processing the timber requires some energy input and this input has the potential for replacement with renewable resources; and the material can, at the end of its life, be returned to the soil without causing pollution (provided, of course, that it has not been contaminated with chemical preservatives).

For a nation such as the UK with a domestic tradition of building in brick, the environmental consequences are more severe. Brick clay has to be extracted from the land, with resultant scars to the landscape. Although such scars can be 'repaired', the land is seldom returned to its former natural agricultural potential. Additionally, bricks have to be fired, a process that consumes energy and that is also polluting (the Oxford clays that run from Peterborough through Bedford to Milton Keynes produce sulphur dioxide, fluorides and mercaptans, all of which are pollutants with potentially harmful effects for crops, animals and, possibly, humans). At the end of their life, bricks can only be recycled for reuse if they have been laid in a soft mortar that can be cleaned off without damaging the brick. In practice, many bricks from demolished structures are broken up for hardcore. However, in the UK 95 per cent of timber for construction has to be imported, making its use a less obvious option.

This brief comparison demonstrates the complexity of trying to evaluate the environmental effects of the construction process. Nevertheless, without an understanding of exactly how the manufactured materials and components that form the built environment are supplied, it is impossible to suggest the use of the least environmentally harmful forms of construction. In an attempt to unravel some of these issues, the three aspects outlined in this introduction – energy capital, energy revenue, and environmental impact – are considered separately.

ENERGY CAPITAL

The construction industry is diverse: its products span the range from civil engineering projects such as road and bridge building and culminating in exploits such as the Channel tunnel, to the bathroom extension and replacement kitchen. Looking at the total value of contractors' output in 1990, approximately 40 per cent was in the commercial and public buildings sector, 25 per cent was in the housing sector, 14 per cent in the industrial, 7 per cent in infrastructure, energy supply and transportation, and 14 per cent in 'miscellaneous'.[2] From this it can be seen that, by cost, about three-quarters of all construction activity is concerned with buildings.

Most new buildings represent the putting together of components previously manufactured and transported to site. The process of assembly is labour intensive, a fact that is reflected in the way that the construction industry expands and contracts rapidly in response to changes in the economic situation through the employment and dismissal of labour. As a consequence, the energy used on sites is a small proportion of the capital energy costs of buildings. It has been computed that 70 per cent of the energy used in building construction is in the manufacture of materials and components; of the remaining 30 per cent, about half is used on site making the building and half in distribution and overheads.[3]

Energy use in the transport sector of the economy is growing faster than in any other sector, largely because energy is cheap because the users do not, at the moment, pay for consequences of the resulting pollution. So cost is no longer a barrier to the use of materials that are not produced locally. Prior to the industrial revolution and the exploitation of fossil fuels, it was the mark of the building of quality – and hence of high cost – that it was not just constructed from the locally available materials. Designers today expect to have a palette of materials that is unlimited, with a consequent loss of respect for the traditional materials and methods of construction that ensured that the materials would perform their best over the life of the building.

The energy used in transporting building materials can be a significant proportion of the total energy embodied in those materials. As a simple example, bricks delivered to site from a brickworks 20 miles distant will have a transport energy cost of 100kWh per 1000, whereas the same bricks travelling 250 miles will have a transport energy cost of 1250kWh per 1000. The manufacturing of 1000 bricks (extracting the clay, moulding it and firing the bricks) would require about 1400kWh, so transport over a long distance could double their energy intensiveness.[4] It is also always worth checking the origin of the clay for the bricks as some clays are imported from abroad for the manufacture of bricks in this country, further increasing their energy content.

Recommendation

Where there is a choice, material from the nearest source should always be specified.

The issue of transport energy costs also has a bearing on the use of timber frame construction in this country. Obviously, if managed forestry is extended in the UK to produce significant quantities of structural timber, the use of timber frame construction should be encouraged. At present, however, 95 per cent of UK timber used for building is imported, with the consequent transport energy penalty. (Moreover, for a timber frame system to have a low embodied energy content, then it needs to be constructed with timber cladding. The UK method of surrounding timber frame houses with fired brick cladding defeats the objective.[5])

However, by far the most important issue with regard to the use of capital energy in construction is that embodied in the materials and components and, therefore, the final building. Around 5–10 per cent of UK total annual energy consumption is used in the production of building materials and products.[6] There are two strands to the reduction of this figure: one is for manufacturers to conserve process energy; the other is for designers to specify only those materials with a low embodied energy content.

There is some room for continuing the improvements in the efficiency with which energy is used by manufacturers. Savings in the past have been significant: for example, there was a 34 per cent reduction in energy use by the building materials production industry between 1966 and 1976.[7] The cement industry is one industry where substantial savings could be made: the UK predominantly uses the energy intensive wet process, which uses twice the energy per tonne of cement as the dry process cement kilns used in Germany. This means that cement-based materials, such as concrete block and render, are considered low energy materials in Germany. Potential savings of about 30 per cent of current energy use have also been identified in the steel, glass and clay products industries.

BOX 6.1 Making the most of resources

A good example of such savings in action is a Yorkshire brickworks which, having dug out the clay to make the bricks, rents the holes left to Barnsley Council for filling with refuse. As the holes are filled, the brickworks lays collecting pipes and uses the landfill gas produced by the decomposition of the refuse to fire the brick kilns, halving the use of North Sea gas. The elegance of this example lies in its integrated approach to a series of problems: what to do with the holes; the need to find sites for refuse disposal; the dangerous nature of the inflammable gas given off from many refuse tips. As a result of this integrated approach, the land can be returned to agriculture when gas production has ceased; the explosive gas becomes a useful fuel; and the carbon in fossil fuels remains locked up (the carbon that enters the atmosphere from the waste is an inevitable by-product of the process of decomposition).

The carbon tax on fossil fuel energy generation proposed in Chapter 4 would, of course, encourage energy conservation in the building materials production industry.

For designers, the goal is to select low energy materials. For a new building, the capital energy embodied in its construction may represent between 5 and 30 times the revenue energy used to run it on an annual basis. Obviously the aim for all new buildings should be to reduce the embodied or capital energy content, but this may need qualifying in terms of the building type and its proposed life.

At present, houses with a design life of 60 years are built with some of the lower embodied energy materials (bricks; timber; concrete tiles). However, buildings in the commercial and retail sectors – designed with a relatively short life before major reconstruction and refurbishment – are often constructed of materials with a relatively high embodied energy content (steel; aluminium; glass). For some commercial buildings, the embodied energy may be as high as the revenue energy over the relatively short life-cycle (ten or fifteen years). Such a situation is untenable in a sustainable future.

It is imperative, therefore, to question the intended life-span of new buildings. Buildings that are to have a relatively short life should either be made of materials with a low embodied energy content – for example, timber *if* a managed timber industry were to be established in this country – or they should be made in such a way that all materials can be recycled at the end of the short life of the building. Where buildings have a high embodied energy cost, then they should be designed to be adaptable so that their life can be extended; this means designing them so that they are capable of accepting changing uses without recourse to energy-expensive rebuilding or alteration. However, the location of the building may also be critical. If the change of use leads to significant transport energy being expended by those who use or work in the building, then there may be no overall saving. (The travel-to-work issue is dealt with fully in Chapter 7.)

The picture, therefore, begins to emerge of buildings with a high embodied energy content being situated in compact neighbourhoods or other units where they can be accessed easily on foot or by bicycle. The prestige out-of-town business park, often constructed of high energy materials, is not compatible with the goal of conservation of energy and resources.

In practice, these goals may have interesting repercussions on what is designed and where. If a building is to have only a short life, then it will need to be designed in such a way that the components can be assembled and taken to pieces more than once. Such an approach suggests a frame structure with cladding rather than a load-bearing masonry structure. This kit-of-parts approach may point towards the use of materials such as timber or possibly steel, the latter having a relatively high embodied energy content but possessing the robustness to be recycled in this way.

This kit-of-parts approach may also demand a changed outlook from those who commission and design commercial and retail buildings. Such buildings currently tend to strive for individual expression in order to promote the product or company through the visual identity of its outlets or headquarters. In future, such expression will have to be limited to a system that will not affect the ultimate goal of recycling the structure: perhaps schemes of painting or planting to establish company colours and identity will take over from the design of the structure itself.

In a sustainable world, the short life buildings will not be heedlessly thrown away. Design skills will be devoted to adapting and reusing existing components in a creative way rather than constantly seeking for the new and unique.

Recommendation

Before development is permitted, some assessment of embodied energy should be made to determine the suitability of the design to its purpose, intended length of life, and location.

Another issue related to embodied energy and the life of the building concerns, paradoxically, the revenue energy which it consumes on an annual basis. To reduce the demand for revenue energy and meet the goal of conservation of resources, buildings need to be insulated, as will be discussed later. However, as revenue energy is thus reduced the embodied energy content of the structure rises relative to it, possibly to as much as 30 times that used annually in the building's operation.

In terms of the insulation materials themselves, the amounts of energy consumed in their extraction and manufacture are such that for mineral fibre insulation in roofs, a thickness of up to 900mm will save more energy than it embodies over the nominal 60-year life of the building and for mineral fibre insulation in walls, the limiting thickness is 700mm.[8] For buildings in Europe and North America that have been designed not to require any fossil fuels for space heating, the thicknesses of insulation materials used in the building envelope tends to be between 250mm and 500mm.

Recommendation

Building specifiers and designers should ensure a balance between the design life of a building and the amount of insulation, to achieve the maximum net energy saving.

However, the rate at which the existing building stock is replaced is extremely slow – about 1 per cent a year – and about 40 per cent of annual construction output is used on the repair, maintenance and improvement of the existing building stock. So, with such a vast investment in embodied energy being made in existing buildings, it makes sense to ensure a balance between the embodied energy put into refurbishment and the reduction of revenue energy. This means simply that thermal upgrading of all buildings should be required in proportion to the scope and type of alterations carried out. This subject is dealt with in more detail in the section on revenue energy.

Recommendation

All buildings that are converted or upgraded should be designed to reduce their energy in use in proportion to the embodied energy of their new components.

Such an approach to existing buildings does no more than recognise the enormous embodied energy contained in the built environment and points to a national programme of thermal upgrading of existing buildings, although care needs to be taken in establishing priorities. These depend on whether society is looking for short-, medium- or long-term goals in approaching sustainability through carbon dioxide reduction.

In the short term, because materials are currently used for building without any linked programme of thermal upgrading, the maximum return will probably come from concentrating on energy conservation measures related to the production process. In the medium term, the optimum benefit will come from upgrading the existing building stock, as large savings in energy revenue can be made for a limited embodied energy investment.

However, in the very long term and looking to the future when all energy will have to come from renewable resources (because of the need to minimise carbon dioxide emissions), it might make most sense to start investing in buildings with very low energy use as, despite the embodied energy cost, the long-term savings will be very much greater.

An entirely different approach would be to link all new development with the planting of trees so that they will take up the carbon dioxide emitted during the manufacture of the materials used in the development. A typical three-bedroom house has materials with a capital energy content equivalent to the generation of 20 tonnes of carbon dioxide[9] and would need about 20 trees to offset this over a 60-year period. This could be the fastest route to the re-establishment of a home timber industry, as well as offsetting the global warming implications of construction.

Recommendation

All new development should have its embodied energy content offset with the planting of trees to take up the carbon dioxide involved in the manufacture of the materials.

In order to achieve the maximum reduction in the energy embodied in construction, all the approaches outlined above need to be addressed.

REVENUE ENERGY

In terms of the energy used during the life of a building – the revenue energy – it is useful to think separately about new and existing buildings, with an emphasis on the domestic sector, as this alone accounts for more than a quarter of the UK's total energy consumption.[10]

For new buildings at a domestic scale of detailing (much commercial development fits into this category, as well as purely residential accommodation), it is perfectly possible to build to standards recognised as superinsulation without incurring any additional costs.[11] These standards are explained in Box 6.2.

BOX 6.2 Standards for superinsulation

Superinsulation requires levels of insulation within the building fabric much higher than demanded by the current UK building regulations, typically 150mm in full-filled masonry cavity walls, 300 – 400mm in the roof and 150mm under the whole area of the floor slab, since for domestic scale buildings the ground floor area is generally small compared with the length of the perimeter. In addition, the building should be constructed to be as airtight as possible: typical UK masonry construction with plastered brickwork gives good levels of air-tightness providing certain practices are avoided, such as building the joists of upper floors into the inner leaf of the external wall. Airtightness can be achieved in the roof, normally of timber frame construction, through the use of well-sealed air-vapour barriers. Glazing should be upgraded using triple, or at least double, glazed units with low-emissivity coatings to the inner surfaces and argon or krypton gas in the glazing units. All windows and external doors should be draught sealed, with lobby spaces being provided to all external doors. Ventilation air can be provided either through the use of mechanical units with heat recovery or through humidity-sensing passive stack ventilation drawing the outside air through conservatory or similar spaces to provide pre warming.

The superinsulation techniques described above would meet the Swedish building regulations (probably the most stringent in Europe) and are achievable in the UK now without the need for the development of any new technologies. However, it is doubtful if designers or builders will really start moving towards these standards without some external coercion.

Recommendation

The current building regulations on thermal performance in buildings must be upgraded as soon as possible in line with current Danish or Swedish practice.

Superinsulation (to the standards outlined in Box 6.2) would give an 80 per cent reduction in energy usage for space heating (and a similar reduction in carbon dioxide production) in domestic scale buildings. These results are being achieved regularly in Scandinavian and other European countries such as Germany, Switzerland and the Netherlands. With such low levels of heat loss it is possible to look towards solar gain through south-facing windows to supplement the missing space heating energy, as passive solar energy can provide up to 20 per cent of the annual space heating energy required for a well insulated building.

Utilising solar energy affects building orientation as the potential for a solar contribution is maximised if the collecting surface, in this case the window, faces optimally south or at least within 30 degrees east or west of south (although windows facing up to 45 degrees west of south can still be helpful, as the afternoon and evening sun can be quite warming). A double glazed window with low emissivity coatings will show a net energy gain over a full year, although the majority of this energy will be collected in the spring and autumn when heating may not be required due to the high degree of insulation. (In practice, this serves to reduce the apparent heating season.) Using triple glazing and internal insulated shutters closed during the hours of darkness, the thermal performance of the window can be improved so that the net gain is augmented by reducing night time losses.

Recommendation

Planning authorities should favour buildings oriented to maximise passive solar heating.

However, any designer who attempts to increase the area of south-facing windows to increase passive solar gain should proceed with caution. A large south facing window draped in net curtains is not a significant energy gainer, as was discovered in Milton Keynes.[12] There are other considerations too: too much glazing can decrease the sense of security and privacy.

In more public buildings, such as schools and offices where the intimacy required in housing is not a problem, it may make more sense to use an enhanced passive solar solution. Similarly, it may be easier to provide an optimum orientation for a sizeable complex on a larger site, such as a school, rather than trying to impose a total south-facing orientation on a housing scheme where the designers may need to respond to other patterns, such as the 'privacy gradient' running through from the public street to the private outdoor space at the rear of the house.

For houses at urban densities the simplest solution may be a careful planning of the interior spaces to optimise the solar gain from the south and minimise glazing on the north or exposed sides of the dwelling but without interfering with traditional expectations for low-rise housing forms. (See Box 6.3).

But however carefully buildings are designed to reduce energy in use, the way in which people live and work in buildings can have a dramatic effect on energy performance and production of carbon dioxide. Just as car drivers can – through different driving styles – have a significant effect on the miles per gallon achieved by the same car, so similar buildings can be used in either an energy wasteful or an energy conserving manner. In pursuit of the goal of social equity, as outlined in Chapter 1, some measure of the behaviour of people within buildings needs to be taken into account. Two aspects of this problem are of immediate interest.

The first concerns the way in which energy is currently priced. While proposals such as energy and carbon taxes are likely to increase energy costs and therefore make most people more careful in their use of energy, there will still be the dilemma that wealthier people are less likely to be interested in energy conservation, since they can buy their way out of the problem. It has been argued that a sustainable society is basically incompatible with capitalism since the latter depends on the exploitation of resources in an effort to create a constant growth in wealth; it is certainly likely that a sustainable society will be one in which wealth is distributed more equably, with each individual having a basic right to the same resources.

BOX 6.3 Conservatories

A potential passive solar measure that has found its way into the domestic market is the conservatory. If correctly designed, these can form buffer spaces around the building, reducing heat loss, and providing a path for prewarmed ventilation air. However, if sun-spaces or conservatories are used they must be decoupled from the spaces inside the main building. Without such measures, the sun-space will be a cause of overheating in summer and excessive heat loss in winter.

Such sun-spaces should not be seen as an inexpensive way of providing additional floor space by designers, but rather as a 'rain free' outdoor space. On no account should conservatories be heated; this is just an alternative way of having a radiator in the garden. The current building regulations allow for the erection of domestic conservatories without any controls. This has produced a situation where firms suggest that such sun-spaces can be used as additional rooms and erect them with heating. This is a practice which should be stopped.

At present, however, tariff structures are so arranged that energy is costed to encourage greater use, with the price falling as the quantity increases. This is not only unfair on the poorer families, who may use less energy than those who are better off, but is the reverse of what is needed if energy conservation is to be the objective. The simplest solution would be to set recognised targets for energy use in specific situations – such as domestic, commercial, and different types of industry – and then to reward those who use less than the target figure by charging them less per unit.

There is a second strand to encouraging people to behave in an energy-conscious way: the involvement of the end-users in the design of their buildings. The present structure of the construction industry in the UK does not favour the involvement of the user in any part of the design process. In other parts of Europe, where speculative office development does not exist to the extent that it does in Britain, commercial firms commission buildings for their own use and normally ensure that their employees form part of the team that develops the brief. In this way the employees have a stake in the building: they feel a responsibility for it and have an interest in its final performance.

Such participation could, in an ideal world, spread into the domestic sector. There exist people without jobs and without houses. Rather than having housing provided through the well-meaning but centralised housing corporation, an alternative approach would be to design houses so that those who are going to live in them could construct them. In so doing, the occupant has a far larger stake in the project and is far more likely to have an interest in the performance of the house.

Where measures such as superinsulation and solar gain are insufficient to maintain comfortable conditions within the building, energy will be needed. So, to minimise the environmental damage of the additional energy demand, the first step should be to use sources of renewable energy. But where conventional fuels have to be used, then the most efficient use of fossil fuels should be the aim. This means, for example, using gas condensing boilers to replace a standard boiler, which show up to a 20 per cent reduction in the fuel used.

As we have shown in Chapter 4, CHP schemes can show more effective use of conventional energy sources in urban situations and for large building complexes such as hospitals and universities. But, again, human behaviour has to be taken into account and such schemes must include metering of heat so that users are encouraged to be as energy conserving as possible. Early CHP schemes without such metering showed that users left windows open with the heating on because they were only paying a flat fee for energy.

Ultimately, however, if a sustainable future is the goal then all additional energies for space heating need to come from renewable sources, such as wind and wave power, or possibly in a less concentrated way through the use of photovoltaic panels. Since all these technologies produce energy in the form of electricity, it may be that the form in which energy is used in buildings will eventually have to change to respond to this. The more efficient use of fossil fuels can only be a medium term measure in an effort to reduce but not eliminate carbon dioxide production.

As the energy used for space heating is reduced in houses, other forms of energy use become more critical, including the demand for hot water and for lighting (see Figure 6.1). Again, technologies exist to reduce energy demand. Solar-assisted hot water systems can reduce demand where there is a suitable space for mounting collectors – which need to face south and be inclined at 30 – 45 degrees to the horizontal – and where water can be stored in insulated calorifiers. The demand of a typical house would require a minimum area of 5 square metres of panel to provide solar preheating of the water, the balance coming from conventional fossil fuel use or, ultimately, electricity generated from renewables.

Lighting is a significant energy use where major savings can be made: electronically-ballasted compact fluorescent lamps can cut lighting energy use by 80 per cent compared with tungsten light bulbs. Appliances in buildings are also important users of energy and are also susceptible to improved design to give considerable energy savings. Many appliances in use on the Continent are far more efficient in their use of energy than UK counterparts. The average larder-type refrigerator sold in the UK uses 270kWh/annum whereas the best European model (Danish) uses 85kWh/annum,[13] a reduction in energy consumption and therefore of pollution, of nearly 70 per cent for exactly the same performance.

The recommendations in Chapter 4 for energy efficiency standards to be set for products such as domestic appliances and for the energy labelling of such products would, of course, encourage a considerable improvement in energy performance. However, the current UK energy labelling schemes for buildings do not yet incorporate the sort of standards that are common on the Continent. For example, one of the home energy labelling schemes only gives allowances for double glazed windows with low emissivity coatings, with no allowances for similar triple glazed windows or for windows with shutters. If such labels are to be taken seriously, they need to incorporate the best products and technologies that are already available rather than merely the lowest common denominator.

To summarise the measures necessary for the reduction of revenue energy use in small-scale buildings:

- All new buildings should incorporate levels of insulation comparable with those found in Scandinavia.
- Buildings should be orientated and detailed to make use of passive solar gain wherever possible.
- Fossil fuels should only be consumed in the most efficient way possible.
- Fuel tariffs should be structured to encourage energy conservation.
- Investment should be made in renewable energy generation rather than fossil fuel consumption.

LARGER, NON-DOMESTIC BUILDINGS

For buildings other than those of a domestic type the starting point should always be to identify what are the scales of the differing energy uses that the building generates. For example, many office buildings have a far higher energy use related to computer demands or lighting demands than is associated with simple space heating.[14]

The first consideration for new commercial buildings should, however, be access. The so-called 'green' office building sitting in the middle of a business park which can only be accessed by car is a folly in energy terms. All buildings in which people work should be placed so that access is possible from those forms of transport that use less energy. This means that pedestrian or bicycle access, or access from public transport, should provide the major means of reaching the building. The least convenient access should be for private car users.

Such a rule applies equally to the domestic sector where access should be seen primarily for pedestrians and only secondarily for cars. As such, the norm would be for children to play in the streets and for visibility splays to disappear, so that drivers were forced to slow down. Such measures could be reinforced by road surfaces, such as cobbles, which slow traffic, interspersed by planting, exactly as is found in the Dutch *woonerven*, where priority has been given to pedestrians in the normal street in housing developments.

Recommendation

For all building types the priority for access should be given to the least energy-intensive form of transport.

The design of all developments should respond to energy conserving priorities. For example, the aim might be to provide as much natural daylight as possible to reduce the energy demand for lighting. Thus designs should move away from the deep plan fully air-conditioned office building towards a thinner section. A plan depth of up to 13 metres allows for natural daylight and ventilation from windows in both sides. Such an approach can still produce unusual building forms, as is shown in the NMB Bank Headquarters in Amsterdam, proclaimed at the time it was built as the most energy efficient building in the world.[15]

Alternatively, glazed courtyards, streets and light wells (atria) can be used to bring more daylight into the plan form. However, such spaces should not become fully heated during the winter season, as they will then consume more energy than they provide. The glazed courtyard can also be used to induce a stack ventilation effect to draw fresh air in across the building section, thereby possibly eliminating the need for mechanical ventilation. In a temperate climate such as that enjoyed by Great Britain, air-conditioning should not be required except in exceptional circumstances (such as document preservation).

What is required is a looser code for dress and behaviour at work. Far wider swings in temperature are accepted in the domestic sector, where it is assumed that people insulate themselves at times with a thick jumper, than happens in the commercial sector where the blouse or suit do not offer the best standards of personal insulation.

Such issues suggest a strategic approach to new buildings for work. Where these occur in dense settlements they may take new forms to allow for natural daylight and ventilation strategies. In other instances, much smaller work spaces may be produced, more domestic in scale, in order to bring work closer to people's homes in the suburban and rural situations, where these new buildings can achieve low energy use through the methods described earlier.

EXISTING BUILDINGS

To some extent, all the issues discussed above in reference to new buildings apply equally to the existing building stock. Because of the energy capital tied up both in existing buildings and infrastructure, it is important to consider what future life these have and how revenue energy can be reduced, even though the long-term savings may be greater for new build.

Looking first at the domestic sector, the problems of improving building performance become obvious. Approximately half of all houses are solid wall construction. To improve the insulation value of such houses demands either major disruption to the inhabitants or a total change in the appearance of the exterior, a dilemma which has not yet been tackled on any scale. Obviously the simple measures of improving loft insulation, draught stripping doors and windows and insulating hot water tanks have no overall visual effect. However, the levels of energy conservation required for a sustainable future need more serious measures to bring the performance of existing houses into the 'superinsulated' category. In fact, unless such drastic measures are undertaken, the nominal increases in energy conservation achieved through draught stripping and loft insulation are likely to be used to allow houses to be heated to a level of comfort which hitherto people could not afford, with no overall gain in energy conservation at the national scale.

To achieve high levels of insulation and airtightness comparable with the levels previously suggested for new buildings, the insulation needs ideally to be placed on the external skin of the existing building and covered with a waterproofing layer, such as render or timber cladding. Placing insulation on the inside of existing buildings is problematic, as it is difficult to achieve an unbroken skin through intermediate floors, under the ground floor and so on. Moreover, internal insulation produces a building that is thermally light in that it heats up and cools down quickly with little thermal mass to store any solar gain coming through the windows. Because of this, external insulation is the route favoured in Continental countries such as Germany (where cavity walls are uncommon), where a study group in Darmstadt concluded that to effect a reduction in carbon dioxide emissions of 80–90 per cent in 50 years the minimum thickness of insulation applied to the walls should be 120mm.[16] Improving houses with less insulation was not thought worth while since future upgrading would still be required.

Recommendation

All existing buildings should be inspected to decide which are worth upgrading properly for an extended life so that the capital available for energy conservation work is used in the most effective way.

Nevertheless, for short-term gains it is still worth while performing the simple insulation methods outlined above, especially since loose-laid insulation materials could be reclaimed in the future. What mitigates against such simple measures are the current values placed on them by the government through taxation. Although the government has now announced that VAT is to be charged on domestic fuel, it has done nothing to encourage investment in conservation by, for example, removing the tax on insulation materials.

Recommendation

Insulation materials should be zero rated for VAT.

Not surprisingly, the German study cited above concluded that listed buildings should not be externally insulated, as external insulation would radically alter their appearance. However, this does raise the question of what should be done in conservation areas, where the merit is both in some individual buildings and in the quality of the overall environment. One choice might be for just the historic brick buildings to be retained unchanged, other buildings being upgraded with a consequent visual change. Or the fact that even non-important brick buildings add a consistent background to those of real historic merit may lead to the decision to leave all the buildings untouched, perhaps offsetting the energy effects with increased investment in renewable energy generation elsewhere to provide power for the unaltered building.

Perhaps what is required is a change to the current attitude that historic buildings are inviolable. The joy of the medieval era, where what existed was all too often replaced or extended by rebuilding that was higher, more finely worked, or simply more fashionable has been replaced by a feeling that nothing new is any good when juxtaposed with what already exists. Were true sustainability to be the goal, it might be that attitudes to history would themselves change and all buildings that were worth preserving would be seen as candidates for thermal upgrading. Alternatively, since many buildings of historical merit that are presently preserved without alteration were never designed to be heated in any comprehensive way, perhaps conservation should mean retaining not just their appearance but also the levels of comfort for which they were designed. For example, the clothing of an Edwardian middle-class lady allowed her to be comfortable sitting in a room at only 12°C, while the present inhabitants of the same room expect it to be at a minimum of 20°C.

Generally, however, it should be recognised that the appearance of the built environment will change in response to the demands of sustainability. The predominantly brick appearance of the current UK building stock may well be in question because of the need for upgrading with externally applied insulation. Even houses with cavity walls would not be immune, for the cavities are normally only 50mm wide and, as has been shown above, much higher levels of insulation are required for the goal of sustainability and these would have to be applied to the outside of the building.

Such issues also apply when considering buildings in the non-domestic sector. What needs to be decided is the ultimate energy goals for such buildings. It is then necessary to decide whether a refurbished building would best meet these goals, taking into account both capital and revenue energies, or whether it would be better to demolish and rebuild.

Unlike the domestic sector, where there may be merit in upgrading less suitable buildings to maintain stable communities and prevent people having to move, the non-domestic sector could be subject to a more rigorous energy analysis. If the goal for sustainability is also to move the workplace nearer to where people live to reduce the energy costs of commuting, it may well be that upgrading is concentrated in the domestic sector and new build in the non-domestic.

What is inescapable if society is to achieve sustainability is the massive capital investment needed to improve the built environment. Clearly, sustainable policies will require reallocation of resources from consumption to conservation. In the case of buildings, the anticipated savings on energy consumption should be taken into account in ensuring financial resources for energy conservation. The first step should be to ensure that, from now on, all investment in construction should be made on a basis that will lead to a sustainable future.

The model in the capitalist United States is interesting in this context. American utilities are investing in the thermal upgrading of existing buildings at no cost to the consumer as this is cheaper than constructing new power supply equipment and generating stations to replace worn-out plant. This illustrates the point that any form of building to conserve energy, whether new build or refurbishment, is cheaper on a national scale by a factor of three than the generation of energy through burning fossil fuels, even under present economic conditions.[17] So, to achieve sustainability, all investment in power generation would be much more effective if switched to programmes of energy conservation. What is required is a recognition that selling fuels is not the aim; rather, the objective should be to ensure that everyone has a satisfactory access to the energy they need.

Recommendation

All proposals for new power plant should only be approved if, over their total life (including construction and demolition costs), the net economic and environmental result is better than putting the same investment into energy conservation.

ENVIRONMENTAL IMPACT OF CONSTRUCTION

In a sustainable future the goal should be to limit the environmental impact of all building activity, whether refurbishment, new build or the provision of infrastructure. While there is a general acceptance of the 'polluter pays' principle, the mechanisms for identifying and charging polluters are, as yet, far from effective. So the cost of rectifying environmental damage from the extraction of resources has not yet been properly recognised as part of the cost of those resources to society and is therefore not included in the price paid by those using the product. Indeed, the reverse is quite often the case. For example, many land reclamation schemes benefit from extraordinary grants from the taxpayer so that the cost of the minerals extracted in no way reflects the true costs to the environment. The impact of the construction industry needs to be considered at a number of levels from the macro-effect on the planet right through to the building site.

The obvious starting point in making the construction industry sustainable is to develop a far greater recycling of building materials, either as components or as potential reprocessed materials. (Recycled aggregates can, for instance, be used in concrete or as roadbase, as has already been mentioned in Chapter 5.) Certain manufacturers are beginning to realise that responsibility for their product does not end at the point of sale: they are not selling the product as such but the performance that the product gives over the life of the construction itself. As an example, a concrete firm in Nottingham is experimenting with reprocessing prefabricated cladding panels of its own making, taking back the panels when the building is demolished and re-forming them. This approach in turn demands an approach to detailing buildings to enable the constituent parts to be separated out at the end of the building life and reused, as is beginning to happen in the motor industry.

Limited recycling of materials already happens in the domestic sector of the industry. Bricks which have been laid in a soft lime mortar can be cleaned and reused; many Victorian slate roofs are failing not because the materials have deteriorated but because of fixing failures and it is often possible to reuse a high proportion of the slate when re-roofing occurs. However, the recycling industry is still small and this constrains those wishing to build in recycled materials in order to lower embodied energy costs. Conservation officers prefer to make the limited supply of recycled materials available for the repair of historic buildings rather than seeing them put into new build.

Recommendation

There should be more encouragement to extend the use of recycled materials in the building industry, including zero rating such materials for VAT.

Materials that have a global impact, such as CFCs and other ozone-depleting gases, should be avoided in construction. At present, CFCs are used in the refrigeration systems used for air-conditioning, in fire extinguishers, and for foaming some of the plastic insulating materials. As discussed earlier, air-conditioning should not be necessary in a temperate climate. However, designers and specifiers need more information to be able to choose materials such as insulation that minimise environmental damage. An acceptable labelling system must outlaw such current practices as stating that CFCs are not used when the materials are still foamed with chemicals that deplete the ozone layer (although to a lesser extent than CFCs).

The use of some materials in construction should also be questioned because of their effect on those who extract and process them, as well as for their effect on building users and constructors. One material which must be so questioned is lead, which is toxic to produce and process, as well as being a mineral that has to be extracted from the ground. This might mean much simpler buildings with roofs designed to avoid the use of lead flashings: perhaps, to paraphrase Voysey, all spaces within the envelope should be drawn together under a simple roof shape.[18] This in turn may have an effect on building forms.

Many other specifications within the building industry require contractors to use materials, such as wood preservatives, that are potentially hazardous: the common preservative creosote, sold over the counter to householders, is a powerful carcinogen. Designers must re-learn the traditional techniques of detailing timber so that it remains at the correct moisture content to avoid rot. Much timber is also needlessly treated just because the insurance industry expects that designers should take precautions whether these are needed or not in order not to be shown as negligent. If environmental impact became an accepted component of professional competence, then this situation should change overnight.

Recommendation

Where two materials do the same job for a similar cost, the designer should always choose the material which is less toxic to produce or use.

Apart from an increasing use of recycled materials, the other approach to minimise environmental impact is to use as few resources as possible to achieve the given aim – shelter – and for these materials to have a low embodied energy content. At present, however, designers find themselves being encouraged to 'waste' resources because of the way that fee scales are arranged. No-one is ever rewarded for time spent in saving their clients money because fees have been traditionally paid as a percentage of the final contract sum. To encourage the least use of resources this needs to be changed, if possible by rewarding the designer in line with the amount of revenue saved for the client through minimising environmental impact. This has happened in North America, where the builders of superinsulated houses guarantee the householder a fixed fuel cost for space heating and the builders agree to pay the difference if this cost is exceeded.

Recommendation

The fee structure for designers and constructors should be altered from the current cost-based system to relate instead to building performance both at the completion of the project (capital energy) and over a specified period (revenue energy).

The environmental costs of the services that people expect to find in buildings should also be examined. It is already cost effective[19] to collect rainwater, screen for debris, and to use it for flushing WCs. Such an approach could have an effect on large-scale water collection and on the cost of purification, a process that is energy and chemical intensive. The cost of water, although rising, does not yet include the environmental impact of collection, although the metering of water supplies may help to encourage conservation methods for the building user. However, as yet the only low flush toilet (3.75 litres per flush in place of the normal 9 litres) has to be imported from Sweden. Perhaps UK manufacturers should be encouraged to improve the technology of their products in this field.

Another example where fewer resources could do the same job is the possible use of permeable surfaces on forecourts and similar spaces, allowing rainwater to soak away through the ground to the underlying strata rather than being drained off artificially. The current practice of covering the ground with concrete or tarmac and providing pipes to collect and channel water to the crumbling sewers uses more materials to do the same job, and hence has a greater environmental impact. This is just one example of the need to examine each design decision for its ultimate environmental impact.

At the scale of the site it is also possible to view the building not as a sterile replacement for growing things but as a potential habitat for animals and plants. It is possible to design buildings to provide roosts and nesting sites for birds insects and mammals, such as bats,[20] even without going so far as literally to green buildings with a turf roof.

CONCLUSION

To bring all the strands mentioned above together is difficult, for the construction industry covers such a diversity of scales and types. All construction projects need to be subjected to life-cycle cost analysis so that their true environmental impact can be assessed: but who would carry this out and how it would be regulated is difficult to picture.

One possible route is for development to be linked in any particular region or district to a carbon budget. This budget would be set as part of the environmental planning process outlined elsewhere in this report and would be part of a programme aimed at stabilising the production of carbon dioxide emissions at some preset level. Any new development would, therefore, have to be so designed that it had zero carbon dioxide production through such measures as energy conservation, the use of renewable energy supplies on site, the planting of trees to lock up carbon, together with other measures. If the new development could not meet zero carbon dioxide production within its own terms, further investment would have to be made to other buildings within the area holding the carbon budget to reduce carbon dioxide production in this way. The method of counting carbon dioxide output should include that used for transportation, a situation that would heavily penalise developments that could only be reached by private vehicles, such as the out-of-town shopping centre. The carbon budget might have other ramifications: for example, historic centres could be preserved and heated if the carbon dioxide produced was offset, perhaps by restricting vehicular access or by investment in large scale renewable supplies.

A measure such as linking development to a carbon budget might seem extreme and difficult to manage. It would probably require control at the district and neighbourhood level rather than by regional or central governments. Carbon budgets would need to be set with regard to local conditions and in a way that could be policed by monitoring the small rather than the large situation. The problem is global but the solution may be much more realistically handled at a small scale.

The problem of creating a sustainable future is immense. What is required is a new way of viewing the processes by which society lives, with a move from consumer to custodian. Perhaps it is time to dismantle the 'bookshop' approach and think about the creation of the 'lending library'. In such a scenario those controlling the production of the built environment have an important part to play.

Getting Around: Public and Private Transport

Chris Gossop and Adrian Webb

INTRODUCTION

As an instrument of death and mayhem, the car knocks war into a cocked hat. As a source of pollution and environmental degradation it offends on every level – in the extraction of minerals for its manufacture, in the emissions it produces in its use, in the laying waste of land to accommodate it. The car dictates the planning and layout of our communities in spite of the fact that a majority of people still don't possess cars – notably, women, children, the elderly, the infirm and the poor, all of whose needs for public transport go more and more unmet.

The above was written by Ian Breach in *The Guardian* in 1989.[1] Current trends in the transport sector – particularly the increase in car dependence and use, and the growth in road freight – pose a major obstacle to achieving sustainability. These trends, about to be reinforced by a substantial road building and improvement programme, imply increasing consumption of energy and other resources, and more pollution, threatening to swamp the gains that can be achieved through, for example, the improved energy conservation in buildings and less polluting industrial processes. Transport is the only sector where the output of greenhouse gases is rising; the sector already accounts for more than 20 per cent of the total greenhouse gas emissions in the UK.

The government's White Paper on the Environment *This Common Inheritance*[2] had few answers on how to tackle these crucial issues beyond commitments to research studies, which have since laid a basis for possible policy changes. Recently, there has been some switch of political emphasis from road to rail; but there is little sign as yet of the resources and changes in procedures needed to achieve this on any significant scale. Indeed, uncertainties caused by the prospect of privatisation appear to be driving some freight back on to the roads, while much-needed investment is being held back too.

Politically, the government's failure to address the growing impacts of transport is understandable, for effective policies to restrain road traffic growth may prove electorally unpopular. However, on environmental and social grounds, inaction is unacceptable.

In this chapter we set out what we believe should be done to reframe the United Kingdom's transport policies in line with the sustainability objectives that we established in Chapter 1, with a particular emphasis on the role of environmental planning. The chapter concentrates on four main modes of transport – road, rail, the bicycle and foot. Other modes – such as water – are ignored, largely for reasons of space. With regard to air transport, the problem of noise has long been recognised; the TCPA would also draw attention both to the need for better public transport links to airports and to the problem of the growing contribution made by aircraft to greenhouse gas emissions, an issue highlighted in a recent report for the Worldwide Fund for Nature.[3]

We will first set the scene with brief analyses of current trends and the impact of transport and existing policies.

RECENT TRENDS

Transport growth is, of course, a world-wide phenomenon, with transport accounting for an increasing share of global energy consumption and pollution. World wide, there are now over 400 million cars, a total that has been growing at about 3 per cent per year[4] with a commensurate increase in CO_2 and other pollutants.

By the year 2000, car numbers in the industrialised countries are forecast to increase by some 55 per cent compared with 1984. (The British Department of Transport is forecasting a 129 per cent increase on 1988 levels by 2025.) However, this projection is far outstripped by forecasts for the developing countries of some 150 per cent. Of course, such countries start from a low base: China, India, Pakistan and Bangladesh put together probably have only half the car population of Greater Los Angeles.[5] But such comparisons only highlight the enormous unmet demand for personal transport in the developing world. As these countries industrialise, their citizens will almost inevitably crave the material benefits enjoyed by the richer nations, including private transport. This Third World perspective reinforces the need for urgent international agreement on controlling CO_2 and other pollutants and for the major vehicle-owning countries – the United Kingdom included – to demonstrate through bold environmental transport strategies just what can be achieved. This chapter sets out the possible components for such strategies, based on the United Kingdom.

There are now some 18 million cars in the UK (plus a further 5 million 'other' vehicles, ie goods vehicles, buses, coaches and motor bikes), an increase of 10 million or 125 per cent since 1965. In 1965, 41 per cent of households had the use of a car, a figure which had grown to 62 per cent by 1985.[6]

Even with present traffic levels, Britain has some of the most congested roads in Europe. Comparatively recent motorways such as the M25 already handle traffic densities well in excess of their design capacities. And the roads in our cities and towns are often grossly overloaded, with journey times increasingly unpredictable as snarl-ups mount. Although car ownership levels remain lower than in Germany, France and Italy, levels of use are higher, largely because public transport in the UK has a lower social status.

A recent analysis by Transport and Environment Studies (TEST) showed that, between 1952 and 1988, passenger kilometres travelled in Britain decreased for cycling, bus and train; expanded substantially for air; and increased tenfold for the car.[7] Three main reasons were suggested for the huge growth in car use: the increasingly availability of the car has made more attractive journeys that were previously slow or difficult; the 'because it's there' factor – having made the heavy outlay to buy a car, owners perceive the apparent low running costs as justifying journeys that would be expensive or impossible by other means; and land-use changes which have increased the separation between homes, jobs and services.

A second recent study has shown that, over the two decades 1965 – 1985, the largest single cause of traffic growth was not in the number of journeys made by people but in the length of journeys, with people travelling further to carry out the same activities.[8] This was particularly marked for journeys to work, where the average length increased by 50 per cent. Given the greater length of journey and the increasing dispersal of centres of employment, this growth has been accompanied by an ever-greater dependence on the car.

Increasing mobility has gone hand in hand with land-use changes. The facilities that people need have become more dispersed, with much new development – especially for employment and retail uses – built at a substantially lower density, often in an edge-of-town business park. In employment density and accessibility terms, such development is a far cry from the Victorian multistorey factory still commonplace within many urban cores. Added to this, the twentieth-century development and planning practice of securing a greater segregation between uses for operational and environmental reasons is in marked contrast to the older parts of towns, where workplaces and housing tend to exist cheek by jowl. A further land-use trend has been towards replacing local – and generally small – shopping, health and education services with larger, more dispersed units. The impact of these changes is examined further in Chapter 8.

Turning to freight, at the end of 1988 there were some 650,000 goods vehicles of all types in the United Kingdom. In terms of absolute numbers, this is a decline from the peak years of the 1960s; however, in terms of tonnes of freight moved per kilometre, the figure has doubled since the 1960s. The growth in heavy articulated lorries has been particularly marked.[9]

Of course, not all freight within the UK is moved by road. For certain products – including petroleum and coal, oils and metal waste – most transport is by water or rail (although pre-privatisation price increases are driving some traditional rail traffic, such as cement, on to the roads). However, whereas rail carried more freight overall than road in the early 1950s, the proportion had fallen to only 11.2 per cent by 1989,[10] a figure that will reduce substantially as the coal pit closures decided in 1993 take place. That percentage may be compared with the French figure of almost 25 per cent.

The connection of the UK rail system to that of the Continent that will follow the opening of the Channel tunnel could enable rail to increase its market share for both international and domestic freight. However, this will depend on firm action at both UK government and EC level to ensure that the necessary infrastructure is provided and that systems and operating practices are made compatible.[11] Without such action, the completion of the Single European Market and the accompanying liberalisation of international road haulage seems destined to increase cross-border lorry traffic, to the severe detriment of the environment.[12] Switzerland has responded to this threat by approving the construction of new Gotthard and Lotschberg rail tunnels costing some \$6–9 billion, so as to maintain the national ban on heavy lorry transit traffic.

ENVIRONMENTAL AND SOCIAL IMPACTS

The transport sector's contribution to air pollution, both locally and globally, is well documented.[13] The principal pollutants involved are:

- *Nitrogen oxides (NOx)*. Transport is responsible for 50 per cent of the United Kingdom's emissions of NOx, a major cause of acid rain. Road vehicles account for almost all of this, with more than 80 per cent of the total coming from road vehicles within urban areas.
- *Volatile organic compounds (VOCs)*. The hydrocarbons emitted from road vehicles are responsible for 37 per cent of VOCs. In the presence of sunlight, VOCs react with NOx to form tropospheric (low-level) ozone which, beyond certain concentrations, can exacerbate some respiratory problems and cause damage to sensitive vegetation, including some food crops.
- *Carbon monoxide (CO)*. Road vehicles generate 88 per cent of the UK's CO emissions. Harmful to health in confined spaces, CO oxidises rapidly to carbon dioxide.
- *Carbon dioxide (CO_2)*. CO_2 is by volume the most important greenhouse gas. Transport is responsible for about 19 per cent of the UK's emissions and is solely responsible for the increases in recent years.

- *Particulates*. Resulting largely from the burning of diesel fuel, these make buildings dirty and, at high concentrations, may be carcinogenic.
- *Other pollutants*. These include sulphur dioxide (2 per cent of emissions, chiefly from the burning of diesel fuel), benzene (which is carcinogenic) and lead (which can damage the brain, especially in young children). Lead emissions have fallen considerably since the introduction of lead-free petrol, which now accounts for more than 40 per cent of current sales.

There is a growing consensus about the wider national and international impacts of vehicle emissions, such as their contribution to acid rain and global warming. However, in Britain there has been less attention on the more local effects – particularly within towns and cities – and on the direct impact of emissions on human health and amenity.

Given the dominance of road transport, it is not surprising that the vast bulk of transport sector pollution derives from road vehicles. Accurate comparisons between modes are complex, particularly between road and rail where motive power may be either direct, through diesel traction, or indirect by means of electricity. However, the available data, taking into account emissions produced in the generation of electricity, suggests that, per passenger-kilometre, rail is much less polluting than the car in terms of CO, NOx and hydrocarbon emissions and significantly so in terms of CO_2. The picture is similar for freight, where rail produces several times less CO_2 than road in terms of grammes per tonne kilometre and far less CO, NOx and hydrocarbons. Table 7.1 gives a convincing demonstration of the benefits which could be derived from a switch from private to public transport, and in particular, from road to rail (and also illustrates the heavy environmental impact made by air travel).

Table 7.1 *Energy consumption for different transport modes Megajoules primary energy/passenger-kilometre)*

Mode	Occupancy rate			
	25%	50%	75%	100%
Petrol car (< 1.4 litres)	2.61	1.31	0.87	0.62
Petrol car (> 2 litres)	4.65	2.33	1.55	1.16
Diesel car (< 1.4 litres)	2.26	1.13	0.75	0.57
Diesel care (> 2 litres)	3.65	1.83	1.22	0.91
Rail (Intercity)	1.14	0.57	0.38	0.29
Rail (suburban electric)	1.05	0.59	0.35	0.26
Bus (double decker)	0.7	0.35	0.23	0.17
Minibus	1.42	0.71	0.47	0.35
Air (Boeing 727)	5.78	2.89	1.94	1.45
Cycling				0.06
Walking				0.16

Source European Commission (1992) *The Impact of Transport on the Environment*

The impact that transport makes on the environment extends beyond vehicle use. As a recent Transnet report pointed out, vehicle manufacture and maintenance and infrastructure provision increase the total energy used by transport by another 50 per cent, implying that the official figures on CO_2 and other emissions by this sector understate the total levels involved.[14]

Road and rail construction projects can also have damaging effects on landscape, on established plant and animal communities, and on historic sites. The extension of the M3 motorway through Twyford Down in Hampshire is a notorious example, destroying or damaging an AONB, two SSSIs and two Ancient Monuments. Even the planning of new roads or railways can have a blighting effect on communities. While compensation codes have in some respects improved, there is still much room for greater sensitivity in the handling of projects deemed vital in the national interest but which nevertheless have a considerable human impact.

Clearly, the transport needs of society must be reassessed in the light of sustainability criteria. It is all too apparent that attempts to provide the mobility and freedom offered by the car have had immense consequences; in particular, the rights of the non-car user have been largely ignored. There is also no doubt that the steady decline in the environmental quality of many towns and cities – caused in no small part by the impact of traffic – is one factor in the decision by many to move out to the suburbs or to more rural areas, often fuelling car commuting and the spiral of urban environmental decline.

LAND-USE CHANGES

Of course, the trend for urban settlements to become more spread out has contributed directly to increased travel distances and heightened car dependence. This, in turn, has led to more energy intensive land use and activity patterns.

Certain types of land-use change can be especially significant in this respect. For example, the last two decades have seen local planning authorities placed under considerable pressure to permit substantial out-of-town or edge-of-town shopping centres to exploit increasing affluence and mobility. Fundamentally, such centres are based around the use of the car – a 1987 survey by TEST showing that whereas only 27 per cent of shoppers in Newcastle city centre had travelled there by car, 80 per cent of those using the Gateshead Metro Centre had come by car.[15] It is quite clear that the trip generation implications of such schemes can be considerable. To quote what is admittedly an extreme example, it was estimated that the Wraysbury Regional Shopping Centre – one of a number of such proposals centred on the M25 – would have generated 23,000 vehicle trips per day and that, during peak periods, one car a second would be leaving the centre via junction 13.[16]

The Wraysbury Centre was ultimately refused on appeal on local traffic grounds. But smaller schemes also have major environmental implications and the very fact that they depend on large numbers of people driving substantial distances makes them unacceptable on sustainability grounds. Even developments with excellent public transport connections – such as South Yorkshire's Meadowhall development on the M1 between Sheffield and Rotherham – may have deleterious effects on existing centres.

Another decentralisation trend of recent years has been the development of the business park, generally located on the edge of towns with ready access to a motorway or other major highway. Such parks – which may combine office, manufacturing, distribution and, occasionally, research activities – tend to be low in density and accessible only by car; as with the out-of-town shopping centre, business parks exacerbate car dependence and this factor clearly needs to be set against their possible advantages in business location terms.

Sustainability is also impeded by the trend towards larger, centralised health and, in certain instances, higher educational facilities. These are justified, at least in part, by claims that such facilities can provide a wider range of specialisms, services and courses than is possible with locally based centres. However, possible gains in operational efficiency have often been at the expense of user accessibility and have reinforced dependence on the car.

Research from the Netherlands provides a striking example of the influence of location on car use: the relocation of two Amsterdam inner city hospitals to a new site outside the city led to an increase of 116 per cent in the total number of car kilometres travelled. Another Dutch research finding is that, in general, the transfer of offices from the city to the perimeter raises car use by 10–40 per cent and reduces travel by public transport and bicycle by 4–8 per cent.[17]

TRANSPORT AND THE ENVIRONMENT – CURRENT POLICIES

The Environment White Paper *This Common Inheritance* was at its most inadequate when dealing with transport. In particular, it failed to confront the dilemma of how forecasts of rising car usage – with predictions of an 83–140 per cent increase in vehicle mileage by 2025 – can be reconciled with the government's objective of stabilising CO_2 emissions at 1990 levels by 2005 (a target since brought forward to 2000).

The paper stated that 'reducing CO_2 emissions means using less fossil fuel...the best results will come if people choose the most efficient form of transport available and use it as economically as they can.' But no real incentive was suggested to stimulate people to adopt such behaviour, to encourage a switch to more fuel-efficient vehicles, or to make public transport more effective and acceptable. Efficiency has, anyway, continued to be defined in narrow financial terms with little regard to environmental, social and longer-term economic costs. One consequence has been that revenue support for public transport has steadily reduced.

Indeed, it seems likely that recent decisions by the Department of Transport (DTp) will exacerbate the growth trends in road transport. The TCPA cannot support the recent expansion of the road building and widening programme that, the DTp claims, will reduce congestion on inter-urban roads. We fear that the schemes planned will at best provide only temporary relief from congestion and that the extra road space will, as has happened in the past, rapidly generate new traffic to fill the enlarged capacity. Any such growth is likely to exacerbate congestion in the towns linked by the new roads, in turn adding to the demands of business to decentralise and thus fostering yet further car dependence. An examination of the American experience shows that, ultimately, attempts to solve congestion through road building are self-defeating: the eventual outcome is suburban gridlock.

We referred earlier to the fact that UK car ownership is lower than our major Continental neighbours, but usage is higher (Table 7.2).

Table 7.2   *Car ownership and use (1986)*

Country	Kms per car per year	Cars per 1000 people
Italy	18,400	393
West Germany	18,900	441
France	23,800	386
United Kingdom	24,800	323
Holland	29,200	346

One possible explanation for the high usage rate of British cars may lie in the higher proportion of company cars in the UK: in 1988, more than half of all new car registrations were for company cars. Evidence suggests that company cars do roughly double the mileage of privately purchased vehicles. Another possible cause may lie with the greater Continental acceptance of public transport as a genuine alternative for much travel within cities. Many Continental cities have developed highly integrated transport policies that combine high-quality public transport – often using a mix of traditional and light rail, metros, trams and buses – with restrictions on car parking, comprehensive provision for cycling, and large-scale pedestrianisation. By contrast, British cities have lagged behind.

BOX 7.1 Greater Lyon: enhancing public transport

The local authorities for Greater Lyon have launched a plan to increase the public transport share of all journeys from 22 per cent to 32 per cent. The Rhône department and the Lyons authorities have agreed to increase their public transport spending by 20 per cent annually between 1991 and 1995. During the same period, investment will total FFr6 billion, of which two-thirds will be devoted to the metro and a fifth to suburban rail lines.

The first two metro lines were opened in 1978, with a third following in 1984 and a fourth in 1992; the system is used by some 200,000 passengers daily. There are two major interchanges with the bus and SNCF suburban rail networks, and other stations are fed by bus too.

In general, the UK government has done little to promote actively the strengthening of public transport in our cities and towns. Indeed, it can be argued that government action has had the reverse effect, with its concentration on the privatisation of bus services having very mixed results and probably accelerating the decline in bus transport patronage. The combination of privatisation and deregulation has undermined any local strategies on Continental lines.

Turning to the railways, the last few years have seen a considerable increase in capital investment in terms of new trains and the electrification and upgrading of certain inter city routes. This is welcome, and in part led to some increase in passenger journeys during the latter half of the 1980s (although the recession reversed this trend).[18] Nevertheless, a significant proportion of British Rail's capital investment was funded from its own resources, particularly from the sale of property, and did not represent new public investment in any real sense. Furthermore, revenue support in the form of the Public Service Obligation Grant was steadily reduced, although initial plans to eliminate it completely in certain sectors were later abandoned. There have also been many lost opportunities to open or reopen cross-country passenger routes which could prove attractive alternatives to heavily congested roads (for example, the key strategic passenger link between Swindon and Peterborough).

An obvious failure has been to plan properly to exploit the Channel Tunnel. In particular, using the tunnel to link the UK network into the Continental rail network could transform the economics of rail freight, whose development within the UK has been limited by the relative shortness of most hauls. The tunnel will open up prospects for a vast expansion of inter-modal working, with goods being transported increasingly by rail at least for the majority of a journey. However, the signs are that, by 1993–1994 when the tunnel opens, only some of the necessary road–rail depots will be in place and that the growth in international rail freight will be far less than its potential. Rail privatisation is introducing such uncertainty that the actual level of railway working may suffer for some time.

At the heart of the failure to develop rail transport in a way that could help to stem the environmental damage caused by road transport are the financial rules by which investment in road and rail is decided by government. These rules judge the case for a rail project on a different, and usually less favourable, basis from that used for road schemes. Rail schemes are expected to generate a financial return of 8 per cent of the capital invested, with no allowance for the wider environmental and social benefits or even the indirect financial ones. Channel Tunnel-related projects have the additional straitjacket of Section 42 of the Channel Tunnel Act which precludes any public subsidy.

The effects of the rail privatisation that the government has now embarked upon are the matter of much speculation. The government claims that it will bring much-needed new investment, greater efficiency, and services that are more sensitive to consumer demands. Critics – who span the political spectrum and include most transport experts – forecast chaos as the network is fragmented between different operators, destroying integrated timetables and fare structures and undermining non-profitable routes. If the critics are right and more freight and passengers switch from rail to road, the environmental consequences will be serious and are likely to undermine any hope that the government has of reducing carbon dioxide emissions to 1990 levels by 2000.

TOWARDS AN ENVIRONMENTAL TRANSPORT STRATEGY FOR THE UNITED KINGDOM

Concern about the effects of unrestrained traffic growth is, of course, far from new. As long ago as 1963, Colin Buchanan drew attention to the 'national emergency' represented by the growth in car ownership, and the need for integrated transport plans if the environment of towns and cities was not to suffer unacceptable damage. But the great majority of people aspire to own a car, and, as many have fulfilled their dream and as new roads have been built to accommodate the increased usage, so politicians have fought shy of action to tackle the social and environmental impacts of unrestrained vehicle use. The freedoms offered by the car have been judged largely sacrosanct.

Arguments about the rights of those without a car, about the true costs of road accidents and about local pollution and other immediate impacts have failed to do much to influence official policy. However, growing evidence of the reality of global warming and of transport's contribution to this will be harder to ignore.

The evidence of global warming presents us with an over-riding reason to adopt a fresh approach to transport which attempts to reconcile the need for transport with the new environmental imperatives. The TCPA believes that the time is right for the United Kingdom, in concert with its European neighbours and, where possible, with other industrialised countries, to develop an Environmental Transport Strategy which should be fully integrated into the comprehensive environmental planning system proposed in this report.

As is widely recognised, there is no one solution to the securing of a more sustainable transport path for the United Kingdom. Co-ordinated action is required on several fronts and at a range of levels if current trends are to be reversed. The underlying theme must be the precautionary principle, recognising that the risks of not taking action to respond to the greenhouse threat are unacceptably high. Even if the threat proves to be less serious than currently anticipated, society would still benefit from a switch to environmental transport policies through reduced energy costs, fewer accidents, and a higher quality of life for many millions.

The Environmental Transport Strategy should embody four principal types of mechanism:

1. Regulatory mechanisms aimed in particular at restricting pollution levels to prescribed limits.

118

2. Financial mechanisms through taxes and incentives, notably energy taxes, whereby each travel mode accounts for its true overall cost (including the environmental cost), thereby favouring modes which consume less energy and which produce the least pollution.
3. Inducements to encourage research and development into more fuel-efficient vehicles and alternative transport technologies.
4. Planning – a greater emphasis on the integration of land use and transportation planning, key aims being to minimise travel distances, to encourage the use of modes other than the car and to improve accessibility to facilities.

The strategy would apply at a range of levels and be both top down and bottom up, combining action at the UK government (and, increasingly, the EC) level with policies relevant to the regional and local scales. The assumption here is that effective action at the local level can contribute significantly to achieving strategic goals set in London or Brussels. Indeed, part of the rationale of the recent EC Green Paper on the urban environment was that the solution of local environmental problems through urban strategies – including strategies for transport – also plays a part in achieving global goals.[19]

With reference to transport, what might these wider goals be? The TCPA believes that the UK government should borrow from the example set by the Dutch in their National Environmental Policy Plan. The NEPP places firm limits on the build-up of traffic growth in line with a prescribed ceiling on CO_2 emissions from the transport sector. This target implies a 48 per cent reduction in the anticipated growth in car use between 1986 and 2010.[20] In Chapter 4, we have called on the Government to reduce UK CO_2 emissions overall. We believe that, as in the Netherlands, this goal needs to be reinforced by specific targets for transport and other sectors: the government needs to spell out the contribution expected of each sector if the overall goal is to be attained.

Recommendation

The government should set targets for the contribution that the transport sector will be required to make as part of an overall strategy to stabilise and subsequently reduce the UK's CO_2 emissions.

REGULATION

Regulation is the first mechanism available to assist the fulfilment of any Environmental Transport Strategy. Progress is being made, primarily at the EC level, in tightening emission limits on other pollutants which has led – in the case of petrol-engined cars – to all new vehicles being fitted with three way catalytic converters. Tight regulatory emission limits are necessary for all types of vehicle, including those that are diesel powered, and must be accompanied by stringent enforcement.

FINANCIAL MECHANISMS

Financial mechanisms are the second type to be embodied in an Environmental Transport Strategy. There are two main categories of financial mechanism: those designed to increase the cost of motoring generally, and those intended primarily to apply to congested urban areas.

In the first category, proposals made range, for example, from increasing fuel taxes – perhaps in association with the phasing out of Vehicle Excise Duty (VED) – to banding VED and company car taxes according to fuel efficiency or even phasing out company car tax breaks altogether. The government can claim that it has taken some action on these fronts: tax advantages on company cars were reduced in the 1991 Budget and there has been some switch in the balance of taxation from VED to petrol duties. This means that those driving longer distances or less fuel-efficient cars pay a greater share of overall taxes than those who drive fewer miles or use more economical vehicles.

However, these actions must be seen as a first step only, for there is little evidence yet of any switch to higher miles per gallon (mpg) models or of people driving more economically, let alone transferring to public transport. The TCPA believes that the government should work closely with its EC partners to devise financial mechanisms to ensure that drivers pay something closer to the true costs, including the environmental costs, of motoring.

So we support in principle the EC proposal for a $10 per barrel tax on oil or its equivalent as a first step in this direction. However, this would not come fully into force until the year 2000 and even at that stage would be likely to amount to a comparatively modest 30 pence on a gallon of petrol.[21] Thus the price of fuel will remain a relatively minor proportion of the overall cost of running a car and the EC measure will not, of itself, lead to any big reductions in the energy used in transport. The TCPA wants the fuel tax to be introduced at a faster rate than now planned, with the tax being increased beyond the $10 a barrel level if, as we expect, the planned level proves ineffective. We would also like to see the revenue raised used to support the development of public transport and other measures aimed at providing alternatives to the car.

Recommendations

The EC proposal for an additional $10 per barrel tax on oil or its equivalent should be introduced earlier than the current target of the year 2000; it should be seen as only a first step towards making the cost of motoring reflect its true overall cost.

The UK government should undertake to use the revenue from the proposed EC fuel tax to bolster public transport, provision for cycling and walking, and measures designed to reduce the impact of the car.

Current road pricing schemes are relatively crude in that they are 'all or nothing', the charges bearing no relationship to the time spent within the urban cordon or the distance driven. In Singapore, motorists have to purchase a daily permit; the Milan system requires motorists to pay for a peak period entry licence; the Bergen and Oslo systems rely on tolls. The likelihood is that the next generation of schemes will employ electronic road pricing (ERP), enabling graduated charges to be made. The Chartered Institute of Transport (CIT) advocates the introduction of ERP in London and estimates that the setting up of a system extending out to the M25 would cost some £100 million, with annual running costs of £80 million. The London Planning Advisory Committee has suggested that annual revenue could exceed £600 million with resulting economic benefits amounting to an additional £400 million.

A possible adverse consequence of road pricing is that it could encourage companies to move outside the road-pricing cordon boundaries, such dispersal leading to the generation of additional traffic. Much is likely to depend on the level of the levies and the degree of benefit experienced by businesses through reduced road congestion, a better environment, and better accessibility by public transport. Such questions could most readily be tested through the operation of pilot schemes.

Recommendation

The government should help fund the introduction of electronic road pricing into one or two British cities to enable practical evaluations to be carried out.

TECHNOLOGICAL SOLUTIONS

The oil crises of 1973 and 1979 encouraged car manufacturers to develop more fuel-efficient vehicles: in the last fifteen years, the energy efficiency of comparable cars has improved by 50 per cent. However, in Britain the benefits have been dissipated, as drivers have used the technical improvements to acquire larger and more powerful cars rather than more economical ones. The net result is that the amount of fuel used per car has dropped by a mere 7 per cent. This compares with a 25 per cent reduction in France and Belgium and 40 per cent in Italy.[22] The fact that fuel prices are relatively low, having lagged well behind the cost of inflation over the past few years, has done little to foster a demand for more economical cars or encourage more careful driving behaviour.

In terms of reducing pollution, the introduction of three-way catalytic converters – now mandatory in the EC for all new petrol-engined cars – will temporarily reduce acidifying emissions from road vehicles, although the forecast growth in vehicle numbers would wipe out these gains early in the next century. Carbon dioxide emissions cannot, of course, be eliminated through this 'end of pipe' technology; indeed, the fitting of catalytic converters leads to a worsening of fuel efficiency. With fossil-fuel-powered cars the only technological way to reduce CO_2 emissions is to develop models offering better fuel economy. There would appear to be some net benefit in promoting the purchase of diesel- rather than petrol-engined cars as a typical diesel-powered car consumes 25 per cent less fuel than petrol vehicles and consequently emits less CO_2. However, more needs to be done to minimise the particulates in diesel exhausts, which are believed to be a risk to human health, particularly in urban areas.

An intensive government-sponsored drive towards more fuel- efficient vehicles – supported through tax incentives favouring economical models – could reduce the projected rate of increase in CO_2 emissions from road vehicles. Action on these lines, coupled with an effective public information campaign highlighting the most economical models and the savings that can result from proper maintenance and more careful driving behaviour, should form an essential part of any Environmental Transport Strategy.

In the longer term, a number of technologies are now at the prototype stage that may offer alternative ways of meeting people's transport needs. For example, there has been much discussion of the merits of the electric car, particularly in the wake of the decision by the South California authorities to support the introduction of such vehicles as part of a strategy to tackle the area's notorious traffic smog. However, while this represents a bold response to a local problem, current designs of electric vehicles are restricted to a relatively short range and, more seriously, emissions are simply transferred to central power stations, at least while the bulk of these remain fossil-fuel powered. A key to future progress is the development of new kinds of battery to improve power/weight ratio and so improve efficiency and range. Another option in terms of tackling local pollution caused by high densities of traffic in towns is the hybrid car, in which electric power is used for slow-moving, in-town trips and petrol or diesel elsewhere.

Such technologies are likely to prove helpful in tackling the particular environmental problems of areas such as Los Angeles. But there are major doubts about the applicability of electric vehicles on any large scale world wide. A technology that merely substitutes pollution from the power station for emissions from the vehicle offers no real solution, as a study carried out by the Institute for Environmental Protection and Energy Technology in Germany showed. This found that replacing the million or so internal combustion-engined vehicles in Cologne with electric-engined alternatives would lead to a 20 per cent rise in net carbon dioxide emissions and an increase in sulphur dioxide, if current electricity generating methods were used.

Other solutions for the future are being researched, including the possibility of using hydrogen as a fuel. But it is obvious that it will be some years before any one technological fix could significantly reduce the environmental impact of the motor vehicle. Even if some radically new non-CO_2 producing alternative were to come on to the scene, it would, given the life-span of the existing vehicle fleet, take time before it would make any significant impact.

Recommendations

The government should actively promote the development of more fuel-efficient cars both through tax incentives and through a public awareness campaign highlighting the most economical vehicles.

The European Community, together with individual member states, should support research into less polluting forms of transport for both private and public travel and, where appropriate, support the introduction of these through tax and other financial incentives.

PLANNING AND INTEGRATION

The final mechanism in any Environmental Transport Strategy is a much more integrated approach to the way in which transport and movement needs are planned. Currently, there are few signs of any such integration at any level in the UK; the frequent result is a traffic system in which the car and lorry dominate, in which serious congestion is rife, and in which the environment is degraded for everyone. What planning there is proceeds in narrow compartments and lacks the unifying vision needed to address the new environmental imperatives.

Thus, transport planning within the Department of Transport is heavily dominated by planning for roads and the needs of private transport. At the same time, while British Rail (BR) has recently stepped up its investment in new trains and other infrastructure, this has largely been planned independently of the road network. This lack of an integrated approach means that, despite train and bus travel having considerably less impact on the environment than the car, there is no unifying strategy which seeking to shift usage away from the car.

This failure to integrate extends to the relationship between land use and transport planning. While development control decisions normally take into account the local traffic and highway implications, structure and local plans have tended to pay relatively little regard to the links between land use form and the overall demand for movement. In line with government advice, such planning has tended to fall in with the demands of the market rather than make any real attempt to steer demand to areas most readily accessible by public transport or, at the local level, by foot or bicycle. Some planning authorities have recognised the need to plan land uses so as to minimise the need to travel.

The failure to plan properly, bringing together transport and land use, is particularly apparent at the level of the city. In such areas, the dominance of the car is at its most pronounced and the result is, all too often, an unhealthy and unsafe environment for everyone. Many urban authorities have created car-free pedestrian havens in their central core areas. Outside these, however, the needs of the pedestrian have often been ignored and walking has become an unpleasant and occasionally dangerous experience; cyclists suffer from being ignored too, with many having been driven off the streets.

The trends which have led to this situation will be difficult to stem, let alone reverse, and there may be a considerable time-lag before any new land-use policies could have an effect. Nevertheless, it is important that a start is made in reframing the planning system, for it is abundantly clear that current trends are unsustainable, implying increasing CO_2 and other emissions, worsening road congestion, and a reduced quality of life for a large proportion, if not the majority, of the population.

In the following section, we spell out the sorts of planning steps that need to be considered as part of an effective sustainable transport strategy.

LONG-DISTANCE TRAVEL

Increasing congestion in the skies over Europe and on many strategic road links has led to a revival of interest in rail both by national governments and at EC level, where plans are being developed for a comprehensive network of high speed rail services. Of the various national plans, those in France are the most advanced. In 1990, SNCF opened the first stretch of the TGV 'Atlantique' linking Paris to the west of the country at speeds of up to 186mph; at the same time, a £20 billion plan for the building of thirteen new TGV lines over the next twenty years was unveiled.

National projects of this type are an integral part of the European Community of Railways plan to create a comprehensive network of high speed routes by the year 2010. In parallel, the European Commission is hoping to establish a substantial European Transport Infrastructure Fund to help cover the cost of providing the links needed to connect national networks, thereby facilitating international journeys between European capitals and other cities. The Commission is also advancing measures to secure a greater harmonisation of the individual rail systems and is seeking agreement on a network of high speed rail services to facilitate a much higher proportion of international freight being carried by rail for at least the greater part of its journey. Of course, this European programme depends on the new strategic links being co-ordinated at state level with the necessary investment in national and local rail services. There is also a strong case for the extension of more rail connections to major national and regional airports.

In a *Financial Times* conference speech in May 1991, the Secretary of State for Transport declared himself an enthusiast for seeing 'far more traffic, both passengers and freight, travelling by the railways'. Little has been done, however, to realise that ambition, partly because of arguments over privatisation. Such action as has been taken is a very pale reflection of the commitment already made in France. The fact remains that while there has been some increase in passenger kilometres since 1984, the 1990 figure of some 34 billion passenger kilometres stands at roughly half that recorded in 1952. The trend for freight has been similar. In the same period, there has been a tenfold increase in car journeys (again, in terms of passenger kilometres) and a massive increase in road congestion.

What is needed is a long term expansion plan with the initial target of achieving a doubling in passenger kilometres carried to restore levels to the position in the early 1950s. In some areas, track and station capacity is sufficient to allow such an increase; in others, it would require further tracks and platforms at railway termini.

For freight, British Rail is planning substantial expansion. Once the Channel Tunnel opens, it intends to triple the 2 million tonnes per year currently carried by rail on international journeys. However, while this would mean a transfer of 400,000 lorry trunk hauls to rail, BR's target represents only a small proportion of total international freight.

The TCPA would like to see a much more ambitious plan incorporating a network of high-standard freight routes to the tunnel with road/rail transfer depots convenient for business around the country and further investment in rail links to major ports, particularly those in East Anglia. Whenever possible, such infrastructure should be planned with a view also to serving domestic needs, enabling rail potentially to take a greater share of the medium- and long-haul freight market within the UK and so relieving road congestion.

The case for further investment in new rail infrastructure should be considered on a comparable basis to that of roads, taking into account the full environmental costs and benefits. Taking this further, the TCPA believes that no major road project should proceed without an analysis of the relative costs and benefits of an alternative strategy of investing in rail being made at the conceptual stage. It is likely that analyses of this type, taking into account the likely additional CO_2 and other emissions, would throw into question the wisdom of proceeding with much new road investment. As has been pointed out, a major justification of the £12 billion investment announced in the 1989 White Paper *Roads for Prosperity* was the potential that this spending offered for creating bypasses for towns and villages. However, 85 per cent of the total expenditure is to go on increasing motorway and trunk road capacity, with just 15 per cent on building bypasses. Spending priorities on national transport schemes ought to shift towards rail schemes and road projects which provide a genuine environmental and social benefit.

Recommendations

In conjunction with the Department of Transport, British Rail should be given the remit to develop a long term expansion plan to attract a major growth in passenger usage and increasing substantially rail's share of freight transport both internationally and domestically.

There should be a change of emphasis in national transport spending to give higher priority to rail schemes and road bypasses which provide a genuine net environmental benefit and with much lower priority for motorway and trunk road schemes whose main justification is to increase capacity for inter-urban journeys.

The requirement that rail schemes must achieve an 8 per cent rate of return on investment should be replaced by a new formula whereby they are evaluated on a strictly comparable basis to road projects, taking full account of environmental costs and benefits and including the factor of CO_2 emissions.

TRAVEL AT THE REGIONAL/COUNTY LEVEL

It is at the level of the region and below that land use planning can begin to play a useful role in reducing car dependence. In arguing the case for new settlements as a means of accommodating projected growth, the TCPA has stressed that these need to be balanced communities having a good range of services and job opportunities to minimise their enforced dependence on other employment centres and thus minimise travel needs. (This is explained further in Chapter 9.) Another highly desirable element would be to locate new settlements and other major developments in railway corridors to cater for inevitable mobility needs, providing from the outset an environmentally superior alternative to the car for many journeys.

Of course, simply keeping employment and housing in balance in any one place does not guarantee that a resident in any particular town will necessarily take a job there, especially if he or she has a car. In practice, there are two factors which could reinforce greater self-containment. First, there is a strong likelihood that mounting congestion on inter-urban roads will increasingly become a deterrent to long-distance car commuting inter-urban roads will increasingly become a deterrent to long-distance car commuting where those involved have any genuine choice of job. Second, there is the prospect that increasing the cost of energy to encourage its more frugal use, as discussed elsewhere in this chapter, will swing the balance in favour of local jobs where the right opportunities exist, by making long distance commuting more expensive. So there is a case for applying self-containment policies much more widely – for example, in existing developments as well as new settlements – as a necessary part of any CO_2 control strategy.

The TCPA has three proposals in this area. First, public transport at the intra-regional level should be strengthened to reduce dependence on the car; the current twenty-year plan for the West Midlands gives some idea of the scale of commitment that is required. Second, environmental strategic plans at both the regional and local levels should to be strengthened to ensure that jobs and homes are brought broadly into balance within identified catchment areas. Third, active steps should be taken to secure as broad a base and choice of jobs as is practicable, minimising the need for individuals to seek work much beyond their home areas.

Clearly, changes of this kind are long term and the strategies to be followed – whether through land provision, new training initiatives or other means – will differ greatly between areas. But, overall, the target would be to cut car commuting and reduce the total distance travelled to work.

Recommendations

Environmental strategic plans at the regional and local level, backed up by local authority employment strategies, should aim to provide an appropriate balance of homes and employment to secure local job opportunities and reduce average commuting distances.

Wherever practicable, new settlements and other major urban developments should be located along railway or bus or coach corridors to secure the best possible public transport access to other major centres.

Long-term strategies for the development of public transport, including a major switch in investment away from new roads, should be formulated.

NEW BUSINESS DEVELOPMENTS

Structure and Local Plans have a key role in defining locations for new businesses. As discussed earlier, there has been a tendency in recent years for many such developments to be in the form of a business park – a development of the industrial estate but which typically mixes offices, manufacturing, storage and, occasionally, research at a considerably lower density. Such parks tend to be located on the urban edge, often on the town bypass, thus offering easy access to the strategic road network. Visually, they can be very attractive, with buildings of some architectural quality set in well-landscaped surroundings. At the same time, a considerable proportion of the land is set aside for car parking. While these developments may well represent successful locations in business and image terms, they are unacceptable in sustainability terms because of their very heavy reliance on accessibility by car. They are excessive generators of traffic.

The whole question of business location requires a fresh approach, borrowing perhaps from the experience of the Dutch and their newly defined policy of 'The Right Business in the Right Place'.[23] The aim of this policy is to match locations and businesses. Thus firms with many employees and visitors (Mobility Profile A) are appropriately located near a major public transport node, typically a railway station. At the other extreme, transport companies (Mobility Profile C) belong in the vicinity of a motorway access (Accessibility Profile C). The profiles are coupled with suggested parking standards. The A-B-C policy integrates parking norms with the use of the profiles and is now a central pillar of the Dutch government's planning policies. Efforts are currently being made to implement this policy through local and provincial land use plans, as well as through regional transport plans to be drawn up by the local authorities in collaboration with the railway and bus companies. The aim is to ensure that, if parking is restricted through the policy, companies can be adequately served by public transport.

EXISTING BUSINESSES AND INSTITUTIONS

As a separate but equally important exercise, there is a need to examine the scope for limiting commuting flows to existing businesses and institutions. Here, the obvious precedent is the scheme being developed in the Los Angeles area to encourage businesses to establish car sharing schemes and introduce communal transport.

Recent surveys in the United Kingdom have shown that, while some businesses have gone to considerable lengths to recycle waste, to develop more energy-efficient products and processes, and to take other action to minimise impact on the environment, little has been done to cut car use by individual employees. Indeed, encouraged by a favourable tax regime, many have offered extremely attractive company car schemes which have served to discourage the use public transport, regardless of journey length. There are exceptions: the Body Shop, for example, runs shuttle buses from local stations to its head office and offers subsidised bicycles to its staff. Government has been no better at encouraging its employees to use public transport than most of the private sector.

There is much that the government could do to encourage companies to develop their own 'mileage reduction' plans. At least initially, these would need to be supported with tax rebates and other financial incentives. There is a major role for central and local government and other public agencies to set an example through the establishment of car sharing schemes and, where demand warrants it, the provision of special bus services. The ultimate aim should be for every company or organisation having, say, 100 employees or more to operate such a scheme. Collectively, the savings that would result in terms of less congestion on the roads would amply repay the initial expenditure.

Recommendations

The Department of the Environment should develop new policies for the location of businesses and associated parking standards on the lines of the Dutch 'The Right Business in the Right Place' scheme, with the aim of minimising commuting mileage.

The government should encourage and, after an initial period, require existing businesses and public organisations to develop mileage reduction plans and should introduce suitable financial incentives to speed the introduction of such schemes.

MAJOR SHOPPING DEVELOPMENTS

Journeys undertaken in the course of work, including travel to and from work, represent only part of the total mileage covered by cars – just over half for company purchased cars and only a third for privately purchased vehicles. Of the remainder, shopping trips form one of the main components, with recent increases stimulated by the new emphasis on edge of town/out of town developments which, through their very scale and turnover needs, depend on wide catchments.[24]

Such trends towards large dispersed shopping centres are difficult, if not impossible, to square with sustainability criteria. While a number of operators have provided their own bus services for those without a car, these tend to cater for a small minority of shopping trips; as with the new business parks, these developments generate substantial total vehicle mileage.

Sustainability as well as equity objectives would be best served by continued support for town centre shopping, with new developments reinforcing the old, not least because the town centre is likely to be the part of the built-up area most accessible by public transport. Outside the established centres, we believe that planning authorities should seek to ensure that their policies are at least compatible with the retention of the remaining 'corner shops' and local shopping parades and that within new residential developments of any size some provision is made for local shops to meet day-to-day needs.

The present *laissez faire* market-driven approach must give way to a more planned approach both at the development plan level – where the overall land-use decisions are made – and at the level of the individual project. There may also be scope for enhanced satisfaction of regional needs from within the area. If new shopping capacity is genuinely needed and cannot readily be accommodated within existing centres, planners, in discussion with retailers, should actively seek locations which are – or can – be well served by public transport. This should be an essential prerequisite for any new shopping development.

Second, we believe that it will often make sense to cluster off-centre facilities both to help justify a fast and frequent public transport service and to enable 'one stop' car-borne shopping; isolated 'stand alone' facilities should be avoided. This will help minimise the number of shopping trips and the overall mileage driven.

Third, efforts should be made to relate retail developments to housing areas, both existing and proposed, in the interests of providing some local catchment for new shops.

In all cases where new major developments are proposed, we believe that these should be subject to a full shopping impact analysis. This should include an assessment of the full environmental impact, including traffic generation. The information considered should comprise not only the numbers of vehicles visiting the new shops but also some assessment of the total vehicle mileage likely to be generated. Where appropriate, the data assembled should include an assessment of the amount and impact of the traffic likely to be generated by a comparable scale of development within or adjacent to nearby established shopping centres, together with an analysis of the comparative costs and benefits of investing in the two locations, taking full account of environmental factors.

Recommendation

In the interests of sustainability and equity objectives, there should be continued strong support for city and town centre shopping, with new developments being planned to reinforce existing provision.

Many of the principles and recommendations outlined above are of relevance to the planning of other public facilities. The planning of hospitals is a case in point. The replacement of the cottage hospital with large, often campus-style, hospital complexes may have created centres of medical excellence but it has been at the expense of ready accessibility for many and has reinforced car dependence. In future, those planning all such facilities must have far greater regard to the travel needs of the people they are intended to serve.

Recommendation

In the planning of all public facilities, much more regard must be paid to access needs. Generally, such facilities should be readily accessible by public transport and, preferably, foot and bicycle.

LOCAL ACCESSIBILITY TO FACILITIES AND LESSONS FOR URBAN FORM

Far too many recent housing and business developments have been built without proper regard to the need for readily accessible facilities. All too often this has come about as a result of piecemeal schemes with no one developer charged with putting in the local shops or a small park or other facilities that a broader, long-term plan would require. Such facilities may simply not have been 'part of the brief' or they may have been ruled out because of high land prices. The extreme is the single-use 'formless' suburb so heavily criticised by the European Commission in its *Green Paper on the Urban Environment*.[25]

Given the right circumstances, good local facilities can be provided in residential areas, as has been demonstrated in the New Town programme. To take one example, Redditch: the layout of many of the residential areas is centred on a bus-only or bus-priority spine along which community facilities are clustered. Densities vary from 185 persons per hectare (pp ha) near the bus stop to 62pp ha at the periphery averaging 124pp ha (equivalent to about 20 dwellings to the acre).

Such schemes demonstrate that it is possible to achieve good access to public facilities without recourse to high densities – the maximum walking distance to a local centre in Redditch is about a third of a mile. At these moderate densities, which allow the predominant dwelling type to be a two-storey terrace house with a garden, it is possible to support a fast and frequent public transport service to take people to work and to the central area shops.

The British New Towns experience provides a number of lessons. both good and bad, which may well prove helpful in the planning of future major developments. New Town neighbourhood planning – the identification of communities of, say, up to 6000 people based on local accessibility criteria – is one largely successful example. Pursued essentially for social reasons, this concept seems entirely compatible with the new environmental objectives.

The New Towns have also been important 'test beds' for transport planning: among them can be found strongly contrasting approaches to land-use/transport structures.[26] At one extreme are designs such as at Milton Keynes, with a transport system and dispersed land use structure optimised around the car; at the other are Redditch and Runcorn, whose design is centred around a dedicated public transport corridor. It is this second approach – building in excellent public transport from the outset – which may well be of particular relevance to the design of future neighbourhoods, whether within a further generation of new towns or elsewhere.

A study of the possible scope for the introduction of a light rapid transit (LRT) scheme in Bristol came to the same conclusion: the LRT would only become viable as an alternative to the car if there was some increase in residential densities within the outermost parts of the rapid transit corridors with 'a switch from an undiluted diet of family houses to a mixed development including a much higher proportion of flats and small terraced houses to reflect overall housing demand'.[27] This is very much the pattern that has been developed in many of the New Towns to cater for demographic and social mix and which, when planned around a high-quality public transport corridor, represents at least one model of urban development, combining a concern for sustainability with social objectives.

Recommendations

In the planning and design of new residential areas and – where possible and necessary – in the restructuring of older ones, priority should be given to securing a full range of local facilities readily accessible by foot or bicycle.

Future substantial residential areas should be built around high-quality public transport routes with homes generally no more than five minutes' walking distance from a bus or light rail stop.

THE URBAN ENVIRONMENT

Solving the problems of the city would make a major contribution to solving the most pressing global environmental problems, notably the greenhouse effect and acid rain. For it is in the cities that we find the greatest concentration of population and economic activity – and hence of emissions. And it is the cities which make the crucial, long term and often irreversible decisions on infrastructure investments in energy supply, waste and water treatment and transport.

The EC's 1990 *Green Paper on the Urban Environment*, quoted above and much criticised for its attempt to define universal remedies for Europe's urban problems, has nevertheless played a vital role in identifying the cities as focal points for action on the environment. Cities are, simultaneously, the cause of much of the present problem and potentially a major part of the solution. There is no doubt that, in any environmental transport strategy for the United Kingdom, considerable emphasis will need to be given to measures to tackle both the transport needs of cities and towns and the problems created by current patterns of use.

Cities require attention to all of the aspects discussed in earlier sections of this chapter; in some respects, it is necessary to go much further. In particular, current, very piecemeal, planning will have to be replaced by a new fully integrated approach giving proper weight to the rights of the pedestrian and cyclist and, indeed, inner city resident for a clean, safe environment with high-quality public transport.

The TCPA envisages new integrated plans incorporating ambitious targets on modal split – the aim being to shift the balance towards far greater use of public transport and far less of the car. Such targets should, crucially, also deal with emissions and noise. The plans would establish priority routes for public transport – including light rail systems where appropriate – linked at the urban periphery to 'park and ride'; safe routes for cyclists; and major extensions to pedestrian areas. At the same time, they would aim to limit access by car through strict parking controls, particularly to limit all-day use, and/ or through-road pricing. And many of the streets in inner residential areas could become traffic-calmed pedestrian priority zones developed on the lines of the Dutch *woonerven*. On all these fronts there is much that can be learned from Continental practice and from the experiences of a range of cities which have already begun to put such policies into practice.

Recommendation

As part of an overall Environmental Transport Strategy, the authorities respons- ible for land use and transport planning within major cities should be required to prepare integrated transport strategies which would aim to secure significant reductions in vehicle emissions and a general major improvement in the environment.

CONCLUSIONS

This chapter has outlined a range of actions that might be taken to reduce the environmental impact of transport, many of which would also have immense social benefits. As has been stressed, the various measures would need to be implemented in concert to have any significant effect. Simply to boost public transport within urban areas, for example, would be unlikely to lead to lasting improvements in the environment without complementary car restraint. Neither would the proposed energy tax have any major effect on car dependency if applied in isolation without action on other fronts, including the provision of acceptable alternatives. As with current transport planning which concentrates overwhelmingly on planning for roads with other modes an afterthought, there is an acute danger that the response to present problems will be piecemeal action when what is required is a firm overall strategy cutting across many current responsibilities at local, national and EC level.

The Environmental Transport Strategy would lead to significant progress; but, in the longer term, more action would probably be required. It represents a package of action that might be realistic over the next five to ten years and which is capable of securing public support. Coupled with action in other European countries, it would represent a move in the right direction, with potentially immense benefits for society even if current worries over global warming and other environmental problems prove to be exaggerated.

This chapter has concentrated on the short and medium term. If, as seems likely, scientific evidence confirms the need to go much further, the strategy set out above would be a useful interim stage, a springboard for a replacement programme embodying even more ambitious aims.

A Sustainable Economy
Michael Clark, Paul Burall and Peter Roberts

Achieving sustainable economic development is at the heart of any consideration of how the aims of the Brundtland Report may be implemented. At the outset, it is vital to distinguish development from growth and to relate the achievement of economic development to broader notions of social equity. Developing a sustainable economy implies altering the way in which an economy is managed and relating this to the need for changed perceptions, life-styles and livelihoods. This chapter outlines recent progress on the greening of the economy as it affects both consumers and industry and explores the potential for further progress. We also look at the role of environmental planning in improving the economy, especially the continuing need for an effective regional industrial policy and the desirability of incorporating within that policy a strong environmental dimension. At a more local scale, we discuss the environmental issues raised by the tendency for households to depend on an increasingly remote and large-scale provision of the goods and services that they need.

While it is tempting to concentrate on the impact which decision makers can have on the location and nature of work, there are advantages in going beyond employment issues to address the question of how our life-styles might meet sustainability objectives and how planning and other forms of governmental intervention might assist this process.

The adoption of the principle of sustainable development in the future management of the economy implies that we need to go beyond the conventional definition of what constitutes a successful policy and incorporate a number of associated actions and activities. Among the most obvious are the effects of paid work in industries and commercial services. Such activity consumes resources, changes or damages the natural environment, and influences the behaviour of individuals. It also has a direct effect on journeys to work, on residential location and on leisure activity, and helps determine the availability and quality of non-market services, including the bulk of education, health care and crime prevention in the UK.

Activity within the money economy is paralleled and supported by what may be seen as a domestic and informal economy, hereafter referred to as the 'self-support' economy. Action by individuals, households and communities makes a direct contribution to people's quality of life and must be incorporated in any attempt to understand how employment and other forms of economic activity might contribute to the objectives of sustainable development.

Sustainable economic development can be related to the five goals of sustainable development identified in Chapter 1.

The first is the conservation of resources. This key sustainability objective has benefits for industry, for the efficient use of resources contributes to commercial viability. It also helps protect businesses from future risks, ensuring a realistic approach to natural resource limits and other environmental constraints. Conservation can also involve resource substitution and other changes in consumption patterns well in advance of problems of degradation or depletion, again helping decision makers who take a longer-term view. It should also give proper weight to such intangible or non-monetary factors as aesthetic or amenity value, ecological diversity, and heritage.

Balanced development is another key sustainability objective, enabling all areas to realise their potential, rural as well as urban. The aim should be to minimise the waste of resources and damage to communities that occurs when some areas experience excessive development pressure while others suffer the trauma of business closures and lost jobs. Strategic planning and the progressive upgrading of environmental standards can counter the tendency for new investment to be located away from places that have experienced industrial decline. Strategic planning should also recognise the needs, opportunities and special characteristics of all parts of the country, including areas whose economic potential is limited by population size or by their remote location.

The third objective is environmental quality. This requires reducing or altering manufacturing processes that pollute or degrade the environment, with consequent benefits all round. For example, the adoption of more environmentally-responsible methods of packaging can generate cost savings, while reducing pollution in older industrial areas both improves the quality of life for residents and workers and makes it more likely that these areas will be able to attract business investment.

A fourth area relates to the reduction of wasted human resources. Social equity is crucial in achieving sustainability. Effective economic management requires measures to deal with the causes of unemployment and other lost economic opportunities. Effective environmental management requires that the damage and waste associated with poverty are addressed, alongside the more obvious – and more easily regulated – problems of affluence and over-consumption.

The final area is participation We are optimistic about the concern of individual people for their immediate environment and for their children's future. Popular involvement is necessary to achieve many of the improvements that are now possible and that are a qualitative advance on the decades of material progress that has traditionally been seen as the essence of economic development. The principle of subsidiarity should apply here if it reflects local circumstances or priorities and if it helps achieve full participation. But it should not excuse a local authority or national government from allowing its citizens environmental benefits achieved elsewhere. Lax environmental controls must not be used to promote the economy. Even if the ethical debate about unequal distribution of risk can be resolved, it is still necessary to cope with the inter-generational and trans-boundary nature of most forms of pollution.

The TCPA's emphasis on what is currently practicable favours changes that are incremental or that may be achieved through new policies or priorities. This should not be taken as an uncritical endorsement of the status quo, or as a rejection of the possibility of more utopian alternatives, or of a need for more drastic remedies. The sustainability concept is stretched to the limit to envisage how our industrially based way of life can be maintained in the long term within the constraints of the earth's resources and with a fair distribution of opportunity for all the world's population.

The remainder of this chapter considers three key aspects of sustainable economic development: first, it examines the 'greening' of business; then it reviews the adoption of sustainable development and the practice of planning and economic development; and finally it looks at the wider issue of sustainable livelihood.

THE 'GREENING' OF BUSINESS

The 'greening' of business represents both the greatest challenge and the best hope for sustainable development. Together, industry and commerce comprise the bulk of economic activity within the money economy. They include most activity that produces and supplies goods and services and represent the linkage between resources of various types and the satisfaction of the consumer. In the industrialised world, it is business that accounts for most of humanity's impact on the environment.

Of course, the threat of increased pressure on resources through unsustainable activity (for example, by exceeding the ecosystem's capacity to assimilate waste products) is intensified by growth in consumption. This has been somewhat offset by increases in the efficiency with which business operates and by firms switching to technologies that reduce the pressure on scarce or vulnerable resources.

Most importantly, many firms have now recognised the need to consider the 'ecological environment' alongside the 'competitive environment'. Such a fundamental shift in the culture and activities of a firm implies considerable investment in terms of technology and training in order to return benefits to the corporation and to the environment.[1]

One recent study[2] has identified ten key themes in the business and environment relationship:

1. environmental auditing and the development of corporate environmental policy;
2. the development of environmentally conscious accounting procedures;
3. the creation and operation of environmental funds and policies in the financial sector;
4. greater concern for environmental issues in legislation and in the insurance industries;
5. green packaging and product design;
6. the development of environmentally sensitive marketing and public relations;
7. greater emphasis on the provision of environmental awareness training and education;
8. the growth of green consumerism;
9. a greater concern for the effective management of pollution;
10. the development of the pollution control industry.

The shift that has occurred in business thinking and action affects many aspects of company behaviour. One helpful way of illustrating the need for a total approach to business methods and products is through life-cycle analysis (see Box 8.1).

Recommendation

The Department of Trade and Industry should assist companies with information and advice about the practical use of life-cycle analysis and other tools necessary to develop and design green products.

Can such gains overcome the tendency for industrial production to expand beyond environmental or resource limits? It is evident that most businesses have to meet strict commercial criteria. Loans must be repaid and profit made in the short term, and firms owe a primary legal obligation to shareholders. However, many banks and other financial institutions now offer preferential terms to firms that operate at enhanced environmental standards. It is therefore possible for the legal duties of the firm to be consistent with the desire of a firm to implement environmental objectives.

To blame industry for tactics which favour consumerism, especially advertising and short-life products, misses the extent to which business is part of contemporary society. We may be the unwitting target of an all-pervading industrial marketing machine, but the life-styles this promotes reinforce established behaviour and build on, rather than impose, our wants and material aspirations. Consumers' environmental sensitivity has

BOX 8.1 Life-cycle Analysis, or Cradle to Grave Assessment

Life-cycle analysis is a way of identifying the environmental impacts that occur over the whole life-cycle of a product, from the winning of raw materials to the product's eventual disposal as waste. An example is the European Community's eco-labelling scheme, which uses an 'indicative assessment matrix' to identify the different types of environmental impact resulting from a product's manufacture, distribution, use and disposal. (See Table 8.1)

The use of life-cycle analysis and other techniques to identify the prime targets for improving the environmental performance of products is demonstrating both the extent to which environmental performance can be improved and the importance of making decisions based on facts rather than preconceptions. The need for this kind of analysis is demonstrated by the belief by many commentators that the major cause of environmental damage is at the resource acquisition (mining and processing materials, for example) and manufacture stages of product life, with damage from disposal also featuring as a significant cause of pollution. Yet, for many products, this is entirely wrong.

One study[3] that proved how wrong such preconceptions can be was carried out as part of the European eco-labelling scheme by PA Consulting to determine what were the key criteria in deciding which washing machines best minimise environmental damage. The study split the life of a washing machine into four stages: production (including materials); distribution; use; and disposal. It then examined the environmental impact made at each stage on energy consumption, air pollution, water pollution, solid waste, and water consumption.

The results surprised many people, for the overwhelming impacts came from the use stage of the machine's life, not from manufacture or disposal. Well over 90 per cent of the solid wastes and air and water pollution produced during the life of a washing machine come from its use, with energy and water consumption being similarly concentrated in this phase of the machine's life. In environmental terms, the materials and processes used to make a washing machine, how it is packaged and transported, and whether it is recycled or not are almost irrelevant compared to how it performs in use.

Just as significant were the variations in performance of different washing machines in use, with the best using half the water and energy of the worst. And when it came to the efficiency with which the machines used detergent, the differences were even more notable, with the worst wasting 30 times more than the best: this is significant, as detergents are damaging both in the quantity of energy needed to make them and in the harm that they can cause on disposal to rivers and lakes.

This study has two important lessons. First, there is huge scope for making everyday products less environmentally damaging. Second, many preconceptions about what is green and what is not are proved wrong once the facts are known. For example, the difference between the best-performing and the worst washing machine on the market in Britain today is such that, if you bought the worst today, dumped it tomorrow and bought the best, there would be an environmental benefit within a year. Surprisingly, long product life is not necessarily 'green'. (See Box 8.2.)

Table 8.1 *The matrix used for the life-cycle assessment of washing machines for the European eco-label*

Product Life-cycle Impact	Supply (Materials etc)	Production	Distribution	Use	Disposal
Air Contamination					
Water Contamination					
Soil Contamination					
Waste					
Energy Consumption					
Local Habitat					

BOX 8.2 The path to a green product

Designing a product to minimise pollution and the use of materials and energy during manufacture is only a small part of the task of developing a 'green' product.

Other questions that need consideration include:

- What is the ideal life for the product? There is no point in wasting resources on a super-strong product that will be overtaken by new technology or become out of date rapidly.
- Has energy consumption and other environmental damage caused by the use of the product been minimised?
- Has the design been reviewed and tested to eliminate weaknesses? Premature failure wastes resources.
- Can the product be easily maintained and repaired? Can its life be extended by designing for the updating of components or systems?
- Once its prime use is ended, has the product a second purpose?
- Has the product been designed to simplify disassembly for recycling and the recovery of components for reuse?
- Does the combination of materials create difficulties for recycling?

---

an influence on product design and business behaviour, even if this may also lead to cynical and superficial marketing ploys that do little to change damaging and unsustainable industrial practices or alter profligate consumer behaviour.

Fortunately, commercial competition does not necessarily mean that environmental sensitivity or long-term thinking will expose a firm to the risk of takeover or bankruptcy. In many cases, the opposite applies. Business prospects, and the economic vitality of any locality depend on a firm's ability to innovate: to exploit new opportunities, adapt and improve technology, and generally to anticipate, exploit and, in some cases, influence the future business environment. (See Box 8.3). There are a number of reasons for arguing that sustainability objectives can actually improve business prospects, although some will believe that such optimism is misplaced. The pessimists suggest that the combination of market forces and the exploitative power of capital will suppress any environmentally sensitive or longer-term thinking and that businesses aiming for a quick profit will be able to circumvent, restrict or take advantage of any attempt at intervention to control their environmental impacts.

The optimistic perspective relies on a number of facts:

- Conservation of resources and reduction of pollution, waste and other undesirable 'externalities' usually contribute to better business performance. They are associated with more efficient technologies that reduce the inputs needed to achieve a unit of output.
- Companies that have a policy of minimising environmental damage also benefit indirectly. Responsible management is more effective, presents a better image to customers and clients, and has less risk of damaging confrontation with its workforce.
- The workers in any firm share popular values which are sensitive to 'green' issues. They will contribute to environmental initiatives that also benefit the firm, often resulting in cost cuts. Such initiatives frequently come from workers rather than management. Employee dissatisfaction can oblige management to seek less damaging processes. A 'clean' image helps staff recruitment and retention.

BOX 8.3 Pollution prevention pays

One major international company that has long understood the cost-saving benefits of minimising pollution is 3M, which has world-wide sales of $14 billion, employs 88,000 people, and makes some 60,000 different products ranging from transparent adhesive tape and abrasive paper to medical products and computer diskettes. 3M launched its now-famous 'Pollution prevention pays' project in 1975. The project is based on the belief that pollution and inefficiency are two sides of the same coin: after all, if a production process turns all the energy and materials inputs into useful products, there is, by definition, nothing left to create pollution or waste.

The 3M scheme relies largely on individual and team suggestions for cutting waste, and rewards successful ideas. The results have been staggering: some 3000 suggestions have been accepted, resulting in the elimination of 134,000 tonnes of air pollutants, 17,000 tonnes of solid waste, and 1.7 billion gallons of waste water. In the process, 3M have made first-year savings in excess of $500 million.

Recommendation

Companies should be required to include in their annual reports a summary of any contribution to profits made by reducing the use of energy and materials and by minimising waste and pollution.

One particular area of opportunity that requires co-operation between local authorities and local businesses is recycling. We described in Chapter 5 the importance of recovering and reusing waste materials and products and the government and many local authorities are now beginning to translate broad support for recycling into action. Over the next decade or so, this will lead to a huge growth in the quantities of recycled materials available to manufacturing industry. Yet little thought is going into how such materials will actually be used: this applies particularly to plastics, where the recycled material usually has different qualities from virgin material. This situation provides opportunities for new products and new businesses based on recycled materials, preferably sited close to the recycling centres in order to minimise the costs of transporting the materials.

Recommendation

Environmental plans should encourage partnership between local industrialists and the authorities responsible for recycling in order to ensure a high added-value outlet for recycled materials.

Recycling is one area of 'green consumerism' that regularly proves its popularity. But green consumerism goes much further and customers are making increasingly rigorous demands, both about the products they buy and about the effects of industrial processes. (See Box 8.4.) To meet these demands, firms must understand the new consumer preferences and be able to deliver an acceptable product. Companies that restrict the provision of 'environmentally sound' goods to higher priced 'niche marketing' are likely to be caught out by more general shifts in consumer behaviour.

BOX 8.4 Green consumerism

Compared with some other European countries, green consumerism is at an early stage of development in Britain. A 1991 survey of shoppers showed that the majority claimed to be green but that, if buying green increased the price by more than 5 per cent, few would actually spend the extra money. The survey also showed that most shoppers suspected that they were being conned about green claims or that manufacturers were using green issues as an excuse to raise prices. These results were supported by the government's 1992 *British Social Attitudes* survey, which summed up the position by saying that: 'It is almost beyond dispute that Britain is now experiencing a cultural shift with respect to environmental values. But the process seems to be one of wider permeation rather than one of deeper commitment.'

Increasingly strict laws and regulations will penalise companies that fail to change their products and processes in time. This will give the competitive edge to those that can anticipate future requirements. Firms will be obliged to adopt the 'best available techniques not entailing excessive cost' (BATNEEC) approach. We can expect regulators to demand more speedy compliance and be less sympathetic to the notion of excessive costs. As we have seen in the discussion of waste disposal in Chapter 5, firms and their directors and managers are increasingly being held accountable for the consequences of their actions.

Some argue that governments will be inhibited from too drastic action by commercial lobbies. In fact, the evidence is sometimes the reverse. After all, if one company invests in a cleaner product or process, it may wish to exploit this by forcing its competitors to adopt similarly high standards, probably at considerable cost. Politicians find it very difficult to resist the pressure to introduce higher environmental standards when one company is already achieving those standards. Thus some of Europe's major car manufacturers were caught out by the speed with which the European Community adopted catalytic converters (Box 8.5).

BOX 8.5 Car manufacturers caught out

There have been many approaches to cutting emissions from small cars. In Britain during the 1980s, Austin Rover and Ford invested many hundreds of millions of pounds in developing lean-burn engines: by increasing the air-to-petrol ratio, the engine burns fuel more efficiently, reducing both petrol consumption and polluting emissions.

But other countries and manufacturers had taken a different route: fitting catalytic converters to existing engines to convert noxious emissions into relatively harmless gases. At the end of the decade, the European Community opted for catalytic converters and set a standard that effectively outlawed the lean-burn solution.

Roland Bertodo, Austin Rover's Director of Strategic Planning, believed at the time that his company had been led up the garden path by European politicians failing to make up their minds as to which standard to go for:

If you collect together a group of five politicians, they'll never agree on anything and the kind of situation we have been in is that there have been collections of politicians stitching together some compromise that has fallen apart three weeks later. They have then got together again six months later and stitched together a different compromise.

Meanwhile, the Japanese simply adopted the world's most stringent emission standards – those in the USA – and began to apply them to every car sold anywhere.

Source Burall, Paul (1991) *Green Design*, Design Council

Market forces will favour companies that can respond easily to price and supply instability in such crucial inputs as energy, water and materials and in the availability of waste disposal facilities. Price rises are likely because of resource depletion and environmental degradation. For example, the energy taxes now being considered by the European Community are forecast to increase the price of energy generated from fossil fuels by the equivalent of $10 for a barrel of oil within ten years. Again, the costs of waste disposal have already begun to soar. The most severe shocks in materials' price and availability have been associated with wars and government intervention, sometimes linked to competition for scarce or 'strategic' resources.

Reuse, recycling and waste elimination all help protect a firm from external shocks and so may be commercially expedient even where there is no obvious danger of problems with the supply or cost of materials.

There is a great, and growing, market for environmental products and services. The Centre for the Exploitation of Science and Technology has suggested that almost £50 billion will be spent in this decade in the UK to tackle global warming alone. And that figure will be doubled by spending on products and processes to deal with other environmental problems.[4] Firms which acknowledge sustainability objectives are more likely to recognise and exploit related business opportunities.

One of the major commercial hazards which faces British industry comes from the country's relatively poorly developed domestic market for energy saving and pollution control products and equipment compared with those of countries such as Sweden, Japan and the United States. Despite the technological leadership of some UK firms in the design and manufacture of environmental control equipment, their competitive position is hindered by a relatively poorly developed home market and by the risk that UK pollution control requirements will be imported from countries where more rigorous standards are already established.

Raising UK environmental standards will, therefore, have more general macro-economic benefits, and would ensure British industry a share of the growing market for processes, goods and services created by the competitive international business environment.

There are other pressures for companies to green their activities. The European Community's economic audit scheme (see Box 8.6) and voluntary initiatives such as the British Standards Institute's BS7750 specification for environmental management systems point to increasingly rigorous appraisal of the environmental policies of companies and other organisations. These demand comprehensive management systems to ensure the implementation of coherent, explicit and practical environmental policies backed up by effective monitoring.

BOX 8.6 Proposal for EC Eco-audit scheme

The proposed eco-audit scheme will include the following elements: an environmental policy, environmental objectives, an environmental programme and an environmental management system, including an audit programme.

The environmental policy will include technical and organisational measures and procedures aimed at generating the information and data necessary to evaluate the environmental performance of activities at the site, with reference to the company's environmental policies, objectives and programmes. Issues to be covered by the scheme include:

- the activity's impact: its assessment, control and prevention;
- energy management, savings and choice;
- raw materials and water;
- waste avoidance, recycling, reuse, transportation and disposal;
- selection of production processes;
- product planning (design, packaging, transportation, use and disposal);
- accident prevention;
- staff information, training and participation;
- informing the public and dealing with complaints.

Assessment under the scheme will relate to a comprehensive list of 'good management practices' and environmental auditing will give particular attention to current environmental management systems.

Although voluntary, the pressure to meet such standards may grow rapidly, not least because of the growing tendency to chain green responsibility from one company to another. Companies in the front line of green accountability are increasingly demanding that their suppliers operate in a green way too, knowing that their reputation can be damaged by the activities of the businesses they deal with as well as by their own actions. This chaining of green responsibility is especially important in a country such as Britain, where the big retail groups wield enormous power. Not only are they extremely sensitive to criticisms from the environmental pressure groups, but they are increasingly dictating green terms to their suppliers, including very major manufacturers. (See Box 8.8.)

BOX 8.7 British Standard on Environmental Management Systems

The British Standard has been prepared in response to increasing concerns about environmental protection and environmental performance. It contains a specification for an environmental management system for ensuring and demonstrating compliance with stated environmental policies and objectives. It also provides guidance on the specification and its implementation within the overall management system of an organisation.

The standard is designed to enable any organisation to establish an effective management system, as a foundation for both sound environmental performance and participation in 'environmental auditing' schemes.

(See Figure 8.1.)

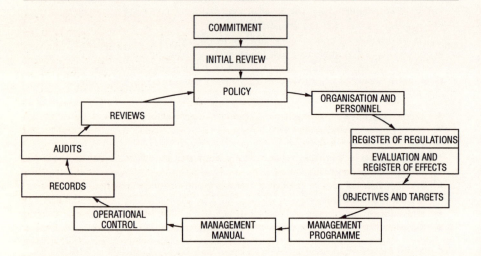

Source British Standards Institution (1992), BS 7750

Figure 8.1 *Schematic diagram of the stages in the implementation of an environmental management system*

BOX 8.8 Chaining green responsibility

B&Q – one of Britain's largest do-it-yourself retailers – sells 40 per cent of all garden peat supplied in the UK. In 1992, the company sent a detailed questionnaire about environmental performance to all its 450 suppliers. One of B&Q's major suppliers of garden peat, Fisons, was subsequently dropped as a supplier after failing to give assurances on its environmental performance.

Commitment to a genuine environmental policy, implemented throughout a company and based on standards which are set and validated externally, will give firms the understanding necessary to achieve greater flexibility in their operations, products and approach to the market. It will also, of course, contribute to wider environmental objectives.

The greening of business must, of course, be matched by the adoption of the principle of sustainable development in the design and operation of planning and economic development polices and it is to this issue that we now turn.

PLANNING AND ECONOMIC DEVELOPMENT

Recent employment trends have been paradoxical. The total number of people in work is historically high, with female activity rates, in particular, having risen greatly in the last few decades. However, since the late 1970s, unemployment has also been at a very high level. Much of the increase in employment has been through the expansion of part-time work, sometimes casual and generally lacking the levels of pay, employment benefits or security of full-time posts. The geography of employment has tended to reinforce established patterns of advantage and disadvantage, with the residents of some areas experiencing extremely high levels of unemployment and limited work opportunities while other locations have been characterised, until the most recent recession, by severe skill shortages.

Planners and local authorities have a long association with attempts to adjust the geography of employment so that jobs are retained or created at those locations where there is a particular shortage of employment opportunities and where unemployment levels are high. These forms of regional industrial planning have also sought to minimise the congestion and inflationary effects of excessive levels of economic growth in areas of labour shortage which have often resulted in localised housing shortages, further aggravating companies' recruitment problems. However, the period since 1979 has seen fewer resources and less priority given to this sort of intervention.

Recommendation

Planning powers should be used to encourage changes in the location of economic activity which match infrastructure and housing resources and which contribute to an equitable spread of employment opportunities.

The national picture repeats the picture of advantage and disadvantage. Of course, the most severe changes in fortune have occurred in those areas that were dependent on such industries as mining and heavy engineering. Fifty years ago, the heavy industrial areas of Britain were still smogbound for much of each winter and pollution hung over many major cities. That the smog has largely gone is in part due to 'clean' air legislation and the wholesale changes in the types of fuel used for domestic heating and rail transport. But much of the improvement is due to the dramatic decline in mining, ship building, heavy engineering and textiles.

The decline in the traditional manufacturing base is well recorded but the offsetting increases in production in chemicals, electronics, and for many years, in vehicles seem less well appreciated. Between 1973 and 1988, net output of all manufacturing industries increased by about 17 per cent. But the changes in different major manufacturing sectors varied greatly, as the examples in Table 8.2 show.

Table 8.1   *Changes in manufacturing output 1973–1988*

Food, drink and tobacco	+19.1%
Chemicals and allied industries	+157.1%
Metal manufacture	−33.6%
Engineering (other than transport)	+30.0%
Transport engineering manufacture	+5.3%
Textiles and clothing	−22.7%
Timber and furniture	+2.0%
Printing, publishing and paper	+54.9%

Source Central Statistical Office, Census of Production

Of still greater significance is the fact that some areas continued to enjoy prosperity in manufacturing industries while others suffered sharp decline. For example, Cheshire, Teesside and the Midlands sustained a higher level of prosperity than, say, Clydeside or Tyneside. The defence industry maintained its momentum but favoured the M4 corridor proportionately more than its traditional locations in Northern Britain. Such growth is often seen only as dispersal from London but the restructuring of industry has played a major part in creating the new pattern of lower-density living.

These changes in the economic geography of Britain not only reflect changes in the structure and competitiveness of industry but also indicate the increasing importance attached to an enhanced life-style and the broader quality of life. European studies echo the desire of firms to locate in 'good places'. Environmental quality and the adoption of policies and plans to transform poor environments are essential both for the retention of existing jobs and the attraction of new industries.

Older industrial districts and many inner city areas are not attractive to decision makers who want to ensure a good life-style for themselves and their workers. These areas are perceived to be associated with such difficulties as high rates of crime, union militancy, congestion and parking problems, poor-quality and inappropriate buildings, difficulty in finding accommodation for key staff, long and difficult journeys to work, and a poor working environment.

Initiatives such as docklands redevelopment schemes and urban development corporations have attempted to address these problems head on. But the economic geography of the UK remains starkly segregated. Smaller country towns throughout England show remarkably low levels of unemployment, only in part due to a lack of low-cost housing and a predominance of service employment. Such areas as the City of London (financial services, the information economy and global markets), Aberdeen (oil industry led), around Reading (high tech industry and proximity to Heathrow) and Cambridge (science led) have experienced boom conditions during the 1980s; but sharp downturns have now occurred, with major cuts in income and job opportunities in some of these areas and drastic repercussions for domestic and commercial property markets.

The consequences of localised economic growth in the 1980s included congestion and excessive development pressure leading to over-intensive redevelopment of town centres and residential areas ('town cramming') and to unsympathetic peripheral development, especially at motorway junctions in Southern England. Local communities have organised to fight unwelcome change: while this may have protected some environmental assets and parts of our heritage, its effect was to accentuate the problems of unbalanced growth and to deny opportunities for investment aimed at redressing social, environmental and economic problems. Many of these problems were themselves exacerbated by unregulated growth, ranging from homelessness and poor-quality housing to inadequate infrastructure and little effective diversion of high-quality job opportunities to poor communities (even when, as in London's Docklands, such communities were immediately adjacent to a major investment scheme).

Failure to deflect investment pressure was reinforced by the relative unattractiveness of areas still experiencing decline. While local businesses were encouraged to relocate in enterprise zones, and the tradition of advance factories and of office relocation has continued and been encouraged by locally based enterprise units and development agencies, the weaker areas still receive too small a share of total economic activity to realise their full economic potential. They also remain vulnerable to changing markets and business opportunities and in many cases have an insecure and over-dependent small firms sector.

These factors affect sustainability objectives in a number of ways. First, they have adverse equity implications, tending to favour relatively well-off individuals and areas and denying opportunities to people who are disadvantaged. They also lead to a waste of potential and to an opportunity cost: economic assets and potentiality are under-used in some areas and are over-exploited to damaging effect elsewhere. Adverse environmental consequences can be overcome or avoided by an integrated approach so that economic development does not result in the loss of areas of high amenity and ecological interest but is instead redirected to reviving areas suffering from economic decline and a lack of investment.

Environmental problems can be self-sustaining: areas with economic problems generally have a poor environment and this discourages the better-quality forms of economic activity from locating there, thus tending to encourage the continuation of low-quality environments and polluting activities. While regional industrial policy has been out of favour in the UK for many years – with considerable scepticism about its effectiveness and implications, not least for the environment – it is evident that the economy is continuing to be reorganised in ways that tend to accentuate rather than reduce patterns of economic polarisation and disadvantage. This process affects sustainability objectives, and so deserves attention and treatment.

Recommendation ·

A vigorous regional economic policy should be an integral part of the environmental planning process. It should give particular attention to the quality of employment, aiming to provide a full range of employment and investment opportunities and seek the highest possible environmental standards.

At local level, economic development and planning activities should seek to incorporate environmental objectives in a number of ways: first, in the design of policies; second, in the development of plans and objectives; and, third, in the specification of projects.

The development of policies which incorporate environmental objectives means placing the environment first in the order of consideration. There are many opportunities to do this and some towns and cities have now developed an interlocking series of policy statements – for land, for transport, for economic development and for social and leisure facilities – which are framed in such a way as to allow for the elaboration of a broader corporate green strategy. Placing the environment first is a tangible expression of the call to 'think globally – act locally'.

There is an overwhelming case for the adoption of an environmental theme in all aspects of planning and development policy. This case rests on both the desirability and necessity of local authorities playing their role in the creation and activation of local environmental partnerships. A case in point is the creation in Leeds of the Leeds

Environment City Initiative, a partnership between the local authority, the business sector, voluntary agencies and the local community that is designed to develop and implement environmental polices in all aspects of the city's life (see Figure 8.2).

Figure 8.2 *The example of Leeds*

The realisation of the Leeds partnership has been achieved through the establishment of a raft of green policies in the Green Strategy, the priority given to environmental concerns in the Unitary Development plan, and through a series of sectoral and subject policies.

The second stage is the implementation of green policies through plans and other programmes. Such plans cover many subjects and sectors, including economic development, housing, refuse collection and recycling, transport, leisure and purchasing. In green plans and programmes the emphasis is on introducing environmental screening and assessment. The British Standard on environmental management systems or the European eco-audit approach are equally applicable to the development of environmental policies and programmes as they are to the development of corporate environmental strategies.

The third component of local economic and planning activity is the generation of environmentally sound project specifications. These can take the form of guidance notes and best practice guides for intending inward investors, for existing firms wishing to move towards better environmental practice, and for a variety of businesses that simply wish to develop their activities in a more sustainable manner. Such guides to best practice often provide simple checklists of key environmental considerations. This might cover such aspects as:

- ensure optimum heat insulation;
- minimise waste production;
- maximise recycling;
- use 'grey' water, don't waste it;
- avoid hazardous processes and materials;
- build for long life.

Many firms currently lack the technical expertise to develop their own environmental specifications, but this offers an opportunity for local authorities and environmental business organisations to act as opinion formers and providers of guidance. Once the process has been stimulated, experience shows that the messages of good environmental practice are soon transmitted throughout the business community. Furthermore, firms will realise that cost savings are associated with many environmental improvements.

Why are these options important and what effect will they have? They are important because economic development policies, plans and actions which assume that environmental priorities can be ignored run the risk of further eroding environmental standards and the quality of life. Such an approach is likely to make the area less attractive to potential investors and could drive away existing firms who are seeking to improve their own environmental standards. They are also important because higher environmental standards are likely to generate new activities: waste recycling is an obvious example.

Finally, there is the issue of the need for firms to think in terms of their own standard of environmental achievement as a precondition for future trading. Supplier firms will have to comply with the environmental standards that are set by their customers. This implies that business success could depend on achieving an acceptable level of environmental performance. The Body Shop, for example, is hardly likely to purchase materials from a supplier which indulges in cruelty to animals, while the instance given earlier of B&Q's attitude to suppliers who fail to provide assurances on their environmental performance provides a salutary lesson.

Recommendations

Local economic development and planning policies should be reviewed for their environmental performance and green policies and strategies developed.

Plans and programmes should give priority to environmental considerations.

Guidance should be provided for existing firms and potential new businesses on how to achieve acceptable environmental standards.

Local partnership arrangements should be encouraged, including the formation of environmental business organisations.

SUSTAINABLE LIFE-STYLES AND LIVELIHOODS

There are many other aspects of economic activity, both formal and informal, that need to be incorporated in the development of a sustainable approach to the economy. The location, form and operation of retailing is one such aspects; other examples include the self-support economy and the generation of alternative modes of working, such as home-working.

RETAILING

An increasingly large proportion of routine daily purchases in the UK are through the outlets of a few major retail chains. These are strongly placed to influence consumer behaviour and to set the conditions for manufacturers and other suppliers. One major impact from this influence results from the preference of the big retail chains for urban fringe locations, with huge stores that can meet a large part of most families' day-to-day requirements and that are now also beginning to compete for the lucrative 'comparison shopping' business which still dominates most UK high streets. Competition to build hypermarkets and large shopping complexes, such as Sheffield's Meadowhall and the Metro-Centre on Tyneside, threatens to increase still further the number of shopping trips involving lengthy journeys by private car.

The paradox of this situation is that, while it generates greatly increased car journeys, out-of-town retailing does offer a solution to the problem of the growing numbers of private cars in traditional shopping centres. Out-of-town shops can meet the operational and commercial requirements of modern retailing without destroying what is left of the character and physical fabric of older town centres. And their popularity means that customers appear happy to travel considerable distances. Refusal to permit this sort of investment can be counter-productive as customers may, if rival centres exist, simply drive to these even if they are some distance away, thus reducing the amount of retail business and associated employment in conventional shopping areas and adding to overall car use.

A further paradox concerns the efficiency with which large stores carry out their operations. This may be seen as an environmental and economic bonus: but large-scale modern stores also have several disadvantages and adverse consequences. They rely on, and have helped increase the use of road transport. They take trade from more traditional forms of retailing and so threaten the viability of conventional high streets. And they can accentuate the tendency for local needs to be met from almost anywhere in the world.

Recommendation

Development control and other decisions which influence retail location should be based on a comprehensive assessment of environmental impact.

THE SELF-SUPPORT ECONOMY

Just as it is important to acknowledge walking and cycling as important modes of transportation despite their absence from many economic measures or sector-based transport policies, so activity within the home deserves proper attention as part of the wider economy. What is sometimes called 'sweat equity' – unpaid work, often a form of DIY, and frequently regarded as a leisure pursuit or a domestic obligation – makes a large contribution to well-being and is a major, if sometimes rather incompetent, force for house maintenance.

This kind of self-support economic activity goes much further. It helps explain the extension of car ownership to social groups whose income is well below that required to meet the full costs of motoring where repair and maintenance is carried out by commercial garages. Growing vegetables and fruit in gardens or allotments, skill in food preparation and storage, and the ability to make or repair clothes, footwear or furniture all make a direct contribution to well-being and can have an important effect on diet, real income and self-confidence.

Planning can play a part in the process of enabling individuals to take control over as much as possible of their own lives, as has been shown by the long tradition of encouragement for smallholdings and allotments which has continued – to good effect – in some inner city community-based and 'city farm' projects.

The main implications for the planning of a growing self-support economy are long term. More home-based activity requires appropriate provision. It favours larger homes, more land for outbuildings and outdoor activities, better standards of sound insulation, and a general reduction in net residential densities. While these are sometimes seen as contrary to sustainability objectives, the alternative of attempting to suppress or limit home-based pursuits has more serious consequences.

Failure to provide for domestic activity means that it spills over into 'public' space (the pavements and streets of many inner urban areas, for example). Inadequate provision speeds the obsolescence of some types of property, while the generous layout and surroundings of, for example, many interwar semi-detached housing estates helps explain their continuing popularity. The failure of many medium- and high-rise housing schemes can be explained, in part, by the mistake of ignoring the economic dimension of domestic life.

Recommendations

New residential development should make positive provision for the full range of home-based activities. This should include space for household growth and changing domestic needs (for example usable loft space and basements, adequately sized gardens, and oversized garages).

Individual empowerment should be encouraged by ensuring that initiatives are not blocked by rival interests or unsympathetic assumptions. In particular, small firms and would-be individual house builders should not be at a disadvantage because of limited land allocations monopolised by a few large developers. Where necessary, special land allocations should be made for self-build housing and for small firms which seek land rather than premises.

HOME-WORKING

Using information technology to enable to people to work at or near their homes has obvious benefits. It can curtail peak commuter flows, reduce the need for office accommodation, and improve the job prospects of a wide range of people who are unable or unwilling to travel to work or who live too far from centres of employment.

Within the European Community, more than 50 per cent of employment now involves some use of information and telematic systems[5] and the opportunities for reducing travel are considerable. There has been some scepticism about how large such savings might be, some forecasters arguing that people often combined journey-to-work trips with other trips and that the reduction would therefore be minimal. But a study in Los Angeles of travel patterns of people before and after they began working at home showed the total number of daily journeys halved; more important, the trips that were made by home-workers were shorter, leading to the total number of miles travelled being reduced to a fifth of the previous level.[6] Apart from the contribution that such a reduction can make in congestion and local pollution, the global effects are not insignificant: cars are now the source of 20 per cent of the UK's greenhouse gas production.

The benefits of home-working for the employer are many, ranging from lower overheads from reduced office accommodation to possibly lower salary bills from moving work to low-wage areas. The worker can benefit too: journey-to-work time is nil; and there can be greater flexibility to cope with domestic needs, such as taking children to school.

But the likelihood of a large proportion of workers switching rapidly to working from home is inhibited by a number of factors, most of which planning authorities can influence.

First, many existing homes impose the same restraints on home teleworking as on the kinds of self-support activities described previously. Usually, some private space is a necessary prerequisite for teleworking, especially if the advantages of flexible working times are to be gained. Privacy may also be a requirement where the information being handled is confidential (on-screen information can be reasonably protected, but teleworking normally includes using the telephone as well as the computer).

Second, most people work not just for money but also enjoy the social contacts that come from sharing an office. This may be less important for people who obtain real satisfaction from their job, but for those involved in routine, often quite boring, work, the stimulus of having other people around may be a necessity. A more feasible teleworking option for many may therefore be the local telecottage, situated within the village or community and perhaps shared by workers from more than one company. Apart from the social benefits of such an arrangement, other facilities can be shared too, such as photocopiers, TV-conferencing, and higher-level (and more expensive) information technology equipment. Confidentiality can be an issue, but in most cases can be overcome by careful design both of the office space itself and of the information technology systems.

The third problem arises from the fact that many parts of the country – including most rural areas – still rely on copper wire telephone systems, whose low capacity inhibits the transmission of large quantities of information. This may be unimportant where the teleworker can have the majority of the information being used permanently down-loaded on to his or her local computer (as, for example, with BT's experiment of devolving directory inquiries to home teleworkers). But where on-line information exchange is important (for example, for a researcher who needs access to data banks or for a design engineer who needs to be up to date with the developments made by colleagues working on the same project), then this lack of a high capacity communications network can be a major inhibition. So the extension of the high capacity fibre optic communications network to replace copper telephone wires is an urgent priority.

The extension of fibre optic cabling to individual homes offers potential advantages beyond teleworking. Perhaps the most important is likely to be access to facilities providing education and entertainment. Tele-banking is already growing, but experiments with tele-shopping show a marked reluctance on the part of consumers to use the service, partly because many people enjoy the shopping experience and partly because of the distrust of choosing goods without seeing them in actuality. It may well be people with special needs – those with disabilities or needing the reassurance of ready access to help and advice – who benefit most from the enhanced capacity of the new technologies to access and convey, interactively, information rapidly in both audio and visual form.

In the medium term, it seems likely that teleworking will lead to the break-up of many traditional work patterns. Not only will more people be able to work at times to suit them, but they may well work for more than one employer or even mix genuine self-employment with a salaried job.

It also seems likely that many workers will continue to need to visit a main office for part of their working time, if only because face-to-face contact is a natural social requirement. This, in turn, will encourage the development of alternative head office working practices, for it is too-obvious a waste of resources to keep specified desk space empty except for occasional visits by a teleworker. This is likely to lead to an extension of so-called 'hot desking' – where work-stations are available for anyone to use, with personal belongings and files and so on usually held in a small trolley that is simply wheeled to the nearest empty desk.

Of course, there are risks in teleworking. The Banking, Insurance and Finance Union (BIFU) has been strongly opposed, citing worries about health and safety, the risks of sexual harassment from managers visiting home workers, and the fact that isolated teleworkers have little power in negotiating terms and conditions of employment. The Manufacturing, Science and Finance union (MSF) has taken the opposite view. 'If your company is re-locating, it's far better if you can't move to be able to work from home than lose your job,' commented MSF's national officer for financial services. MSF has sought to turn the objections on their head by developing its own electronic mailbox service to enable members to seek help and advice instantly.

Recommendations

Environmental plans should investigate the contribution that teleworking can make to achieving sustainable livelihoods and, where appropriate, provide both for local teleworking centres and for new housing developments to be designed for home-working.

The provision of high capacity fibre optic telecommunications networks should be a priority for rural areas as well as urban centres.

There are grounds for optimism in the changes which are now affecting workplace practice. Home-based work and telecommunications which allow commuting trips to be substantially reduced, growing recognition of the contribution of the self-support economy, and increasingly strict environmental controls and business expectations, all favour sustainability objectives. So does the 'greening' of many firms and other organisations.

However, such beneficial trends are against a backdrop of continuing centralisation and the growing physical separation of customers and suppliers. The gap between home and work is getting wider and people are increasingly less able to meet their own needs on their own terms and from the areas in which they live. These paradoxes and contradictions require positive intervention to realise the potential of parts of the overall economy that will otherwise be suppressed by rival interests, to the overall cost of us all.

CONCLUSIONS

Environmental concerns are now accepted as an integral and fundamental part of economic progress. Good practice spread slowly at first but has since accelerated. Recent national legislation and current and prospective legislation from the European Community combine to set higher standards. At the local level, firms working in partnerships with local authorities and voluntary groups are now establishing environmental partnerships.

All these initiatives imply that the future development of the economy is likely to proceed towards the achievement of higher environmental standards. Three key aspects of the pathway towards such raised standards are the 'greening' of business, the introduction of 'green' priorities in economic development and planning policies and actions, and the generation of more sustainable attitudes in relation to the wider issues related to life-styles and ways of earning a living.

Planning the Sustainable City Region

Michael Breheny and Ralph Rookwood

INTRODUCTION

Levels of intervention

Previous chapters have made it clear that, in order to achieve a more sustainable world, radical policies will have to be introduced at a variety of spatial and governmental levels. At inter-governmental level, agreements on environmental protection are required. At the national government level, legislative and fiscal changes, plus general example setting, could make a profound contribution to sustainable development. Finally, at the local government and local agency level – which in the UK covers all bodies from the regional to the very local – there are many positive actions that can be taken, some of which have been described earlier in this report.

These levels of possible intervention are increasingly difficult to achieve as we move from the local to the global. It is therefore encouraging that it has been at the international level that some of the earliest initiatives have been taken – in response to world-wide concern at the dangers posed by global warming – requiring implementation at national and local levels. Uneven though action 'on the ground' has been, it is also encouraging that many initiatives have been taken at a variety of levels in response to localised perceptions and opportunities, without necessarily waiting for direction 'from above'. Progress in practice is dependent on action at all three levels, preferably more or less simultaneously in order to minimise the risk of 'too little, too late'.

Whereas previous chapters have called for action at all three levels, as appropriate, this chapter has a narrower focus: to consider the implications for the shaping or reshaping of our physical environment, for the decisions that are being made daily about developments in both town and country, and for the planning system that exists in Britain to guide those decisions in line with approved objectives. Planning objectives have always included environmental protection and improvement in some form – usually to safeguard or enhance local (mainly urban) living conditions – but until recently these objectives have rarely included much about safeguarding the natural world. Now that the vital importance of the latter has been recognised, it is important to see what changes in planning objectives are necessary for this purpose. These changes necessarily relate mainly to the sub-national level, where policy meets design and where objectives are given their physical form.

This chapter focuses, then, on this sub-national level of intervention. It ranges from the regional to the local and tries to blend them together in an effort to indicate appropriate environmental policies across a multiplicity of circumstances: from central cities to remote rural areas. The whole we call the 'Social City Region'. Although different approaches are appropriate at different spatial scales and in different governmental circumstances, it is essential that they are both devised and implemented in an integrated, complementary fashion.

Policy initiatives that fit into this integrated approach have been put forward in each of the sectoral chapters. This chapter takes a different 'cut' at the problem by putting forward recommendations of two kinds:

1. those that link sectors by referring to appropriate sets of strategic urban and rural policies; and
2. those that relate to the institutional and governmental changes that may be required to deliver policies.

SUSTAINABLE TOWN/SUSTAINABLE COUNTRY POLICIES

It is clear that a major strategic factor determining sustainability is urban form; that is, the shape of settlement patterns in cities, towns and villages. In principle, it is obvious that urban form will affect patterns of private transport, which in turn will affect fuel consumption and emissions. By the same token, the viability and patronage of public transport facilities, and also consumption and emissions, will be affected by urban form. Such form may also affect rates of conversion of land from rural to urban uses and, by extension, the loss of habitats for flora and fauna. Certain urban forms and types of changes to those forms might also involve the loss of green spaces and habitats within urban areas.

It seems obvious, then, that urban form at all scales may be a significant determinant of the prospects for sustainability. It is also obvious, again in principle, that environmentally desirable urban forms may be less desirable in economic and social terms. The implication is that trade-offs have to be made. For example, higher urban densities may lower overall quality of life. Medium to low density housing has long been the preferred choice of many in the UK. Although the European Commission may denigrate the idea of suburban living, it remains the ideal for many people. There may also be a conflict between high urban densities and the desire to 'green the city'.

Urban form and sustainability are thus linked in principle; but is it possible to argue with any degree of certainty that some types of urban form are more sustainable than others? Debate on the issue[1,2] has tended to focus only on large cities. However, this is not sufficient. At each scale in the urban hierarchy, sustainability requires specific initiatives. But for maximum effect, these initiatives need to be co-ordinated. This is why the question of appropriate measures is addressed here in a multiplicity of situations.

THE CONTEXT FOR SUSTAINABLE URBAN DEVELOPMENT

Before pursuing these issues about urban form and sustainability any further, it would be wise to take stock of the major trends in the UK that are currently determining patterns of urban change. It may be that some of these are so powerful that policies that aim to reverse them are doomed to failure. The question may be: how can trends be best manipulated to move towards more sustainable forms of urban development?

The restructuring of industry, the decline of the older industrial cities and the growth of new activities in cleaner and rural environments have been touched on in Chapter 8. Together with the dispersal of population into villages and small towns, these trends are well recorded; but their implications are often resisted by many who wish to sustain the size of cities or protect the countryside from intrusion. However, the trends of the last 30 years have built a disproportionate potential for growth into a large part of the rural lowlands of Britain.

Census data, presented by a typology of districts, show these trends very clearly. The typology adopted by the Office of Population, Censuses and Surveys (OPCS) extends from the largest metropolitan districts to the most remote rural areas at the extremes[3]. The population change figures for each of these types are given in Table 9.1 for the three decades from 1961 to 1991. The table records the persistent drift of people away from the metropolitan areas and, since 1981, from the industrial districts of Wales and Northern England to the smaller towns and rural areas.

Table 9.1 *Population change, 1961–91, for types of area in England and Wales*

	1961–71		1971–81		1981–91	
	000s	**%**	**000s**	**%**	**000s**	**%**
England and Wales	2,629	5.7	262	0.5	−57	0.1
Greater London Boroughs						
Inner	−461	−13.2	−535	−17.7	−147	−5.9
Outer	−81	−1.8	−221	−5.0	−171	−4.2
Metropolitan Districts						
Principal cities	−355	−8.4	−386	−10.0	−258	−7.4
Others	412	5.5	−160	−2.0	−327	−4.2
Non-metropolitan Districts						
Large cities	−41	−1.4	−149	−5.1	−98	−3.6
Smaller cities	38	2.2	−55	−3.2	5	0.3
Industrial Districts						
Wales and Northern Regions	118	1.3	42	1.3	−72	−2.1
Rest of England	342	5.0	158	5.0	59	1.8
New Towns	337	21.8	283	15.1	133	6.1
Resort and Retirement	3461	2.2	156	4.9	174	5.2
Mixed and Accessible Rural						
Outside SE	6272	1.9	307	8.8	156	4.1
Inside SE	9602	2.1	354	6.8	162	2.9
Remote Largely Rural	399	9.7	468	10.3	328	6.4

Source OPCS (1992), 1991 Census

This process of decentralisation of population, and also jobs, is the major postwar geographical trend in the UK, as in many Western countries. Some commentators suggest that this process is so strong that it constitutes 'counter-urbanisation'; that is, not simply a process of extended suburbanisation but a clear rejection of urban living. Some researchers had suggested that this process was being reversed in the 1980s, with a 'return to the city'. However, the 1991 Census preliminary results show that the decentralisation process in the UK is clear and persistent. As Figure 9.1 shows, there is a neat inverse correlation between population growth and population size over the 1981–91 period. The larger the city, the greater the population losses; the more remote the area, the greater the gains.

There is also a social dimension to these losses and gains: this process has had a polarising social effect by leaving behind in the inner cities those with the poorest life chances – the poor, the unemployed, the low skilled, the elderly and minority ethnic groups. The corollary is that areas gaining from decentralisation tend to have become even more solidly middle class, relatively affluent and environmentally defensive. There are progressive exceptions to this pattern, such as the post-war new towns, which have provided a high quality of life to working class in-migrants from the large conurbations.

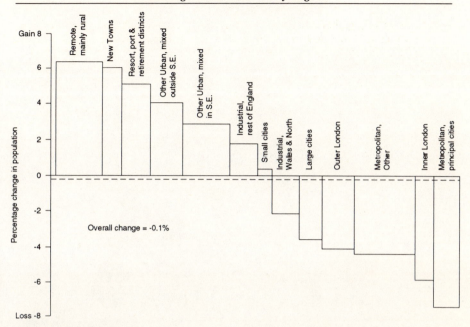

Source OPCS (1992)

Figure 9.1 *The relationship between population growth and population size, 1981–91*

The decentralisation process, then, has important linked economic and social dimensions. In considering the environmental consequences of this process, these must not be forgotten.

The effects of these decentralising changes on the population geography of England and Wales is very marked. Figure 9.2 shows population change by district in England and Wales for the period 1981–91. The areas of fastest growth are concentrated in non-metropolitan Southern and Central England. Thirty years of shifting population has been accompanied by parallel shifts in employment and a strengthening of recipient local economies. Although these areas have been hit severely by the current recession, there is a generally held assumption that they will nevertheless prosper relatively when the economic climate improves.

The result is that the greatest potential for growth lies in the shires of Central and Southern England, in an area extending from Cornwall to Lincolnshire and from Kent to Shropshire. Department of Environment household projections, which take some account of likely migration, suggest that over the twenty years 1991–2011 these same counties will have the highest rates of household growth in the country.

At a finer geographical scale, Breheny, Gent and Lock[4] have also considered this question of the future location of development. They begin by reviewing recent evidence on the proportion of housing development that has taken place as urban infill. Survey evidence suggests that this proportion varies across the country between 30 per cent and 60 per cent of all housing. They suggest that a reasonable assumption in the future is that, on average, up to 50 per cent of future housing development will take place within existing urban areas. This assumes continued containment policies. Possibly, this figure will be an over-estimate if current concerns over 'town cramming' become more widespread.

All these projections must be treated with caution, of course, but there seems little doubt that, for another generation at least, new development will continue to be focused

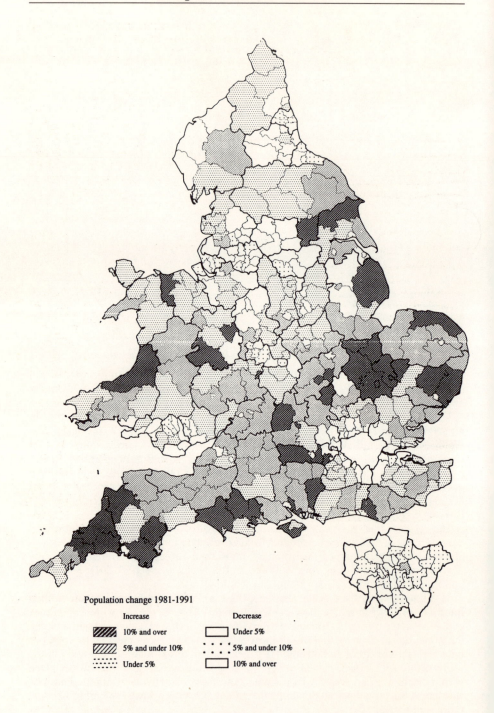

Population change 1981-1991

Increase

▨ 10% and over

▧ 5% and under 10%

⬚ Under 5%

Decrease

☐ Under 5%

⬚ 5% and under 10%

☐ 10% and over

Figure 9.2 *Population growth for districts of England and Wales, 1981–91*

on the lowlands of Southern and Central England, and that within this area much of the pressure will be on greenfield sites in the countryside rather than urban sites.

THE COMPACT CITY PROPOSAL

All this evidence is important to the debate on urban form and sustainability. However, it is particularly important because it casts doubt on a solution to the urban form issue that has gained considerable support: the notion of the 'compact city'. The European Commission, for example, has argued that the high density, mixed use, city is likely to be energy efficient because it reduces travel distances and maximises prospects for public transport provision. In addition, the Commission argues, the compact city provides a superior quality of life for its residents. Suburban development, pejoratively referred to as 'sprawl', creates both high energy consumption and an inferior quality of life.

The Commission's view is a radical one. It suggests that future urban growth should be accommodated within the boundaries of existing urban areas: '...avoid escaping the problems of the city by extending its periphery; solve its problems within existing boundaries'. The compact city solution is also espoused by Friends of the Earth[5] and by other commentators such as Sherlock.[6] This view has been challenged on a number of grounds.[7] Some researchers doubt the superiority of the compact city on energy consumption grounds, arguing that decentralisation of jobs and houses has reduced journey lengths and that congestion in urban areas offsets any gains resulting from shorter journeys. One definite problem with the compact city proposal is that it requires a complete reversal of the most persistent trend in urban development in the last 50 years; that is, decentralisation. As demonstrated above, this 'Canute-like' proposal would simply be impossible to achieve, regardless of whether it is desirable or not.

At the other extreme are proposals for further decentralisation, both physical and institutional. Lower density alternatives to the compact city are proposed, on the very 'quality of life' grounds that the European Commission espouses. The proponents of this approach[8] point to the substantial decentralisation from cities as evidence of the problem of high density urban living. They assume that large tracts of surplus agricultural land are now available for development. They argue that improved telecommunications will facilitate much more localised activities and obviate the need for much of the travel that we see today. It is also argued that decentralised low densities provide environmental gains in terms of the use of ambient sources of energy and home food production. Others suggest that technical breakthroughs, particularly in the form of electric cars, will solve many of the energy consumption and emission problems. Some see an opportunity for decentralised living based on a return to 'rural values'.[9]

THE SOCIAL CITY REGION

The TCPA has strong reservations about all such extreme solutions. They are usually impracticable, unrealistic and undesirable. Even though each may have some merits, as comprehensive solutions they are entirely inappropriate. A detailed critique of these extremes has been argued elsewhere, but it will suffice simply to demonstrate their inadequacies.

The compact city solution is naively based on the idea that urban decentralisation, which has been the dominant urban trend in all Western countries since 1945, can suddenly be stopped and then reversed. Policies of urban containment will no doubt continue to be appropriate, but they must be realistic. This solution also fails to accept that sustainability must balance environmental and other aspirations. There is little point in creating an alienated community for the sake of energy conservation from high densities. The alternative decentralised solution is also based on naive assumptions. If it worked, it would be undermined. Large numbers of people seeking the rural 'good life' would destroy the very idea. Likewise, it is unrealistic to assume that by growing their own vegetables and having fax machines, people would stop travelling. Such a solution might also be socially regressive, condemning the poor to remain in the increasingly undesirable cities as everyone else leaves for the countryside.

Many of the arguments about the role of urban form in increasing sustainability are technical in nature. To some degree the various assertions are empirically testable. However, results are to date rather inconclusive. Nevertheless, sufficient evidence and experience is available to suggest that certain policy stances on urban form can be adopted. One line of argument says that in the absence of clear evidence about the relationship between urban form and energy consumption, and in the absence of any clear view on the prospects for new technologies, a robust policy stance should be adopted in the short term. This is the approach supported by the TCPA: to move towards greater sustainability while ensuring that no harm is done; a version of the 'precautionary principle'. In these circumstances, any attempt to prescribe some simple, single over-riding policy (such as the high density compact city) in order to reduce the impact of urban areas on natural ecosystems is unrealistic and incapable of successful implementation. What must be addressed is the whole inter-dependent regional complex – here christened the Social City Region, adapting the terminology used by Ebenezer Howard. What must be developed, in pursuit of future sustainability, is a whole set of distinctive policies attuned to the varying conditions and environmental potential of the different parts of the region but complementary and mutually reinforcing.

This message is therefore necessarily more complex than the 'compact city' prescription for the way forward – necessarily because the modern industrial world is much too diverse for simplistic rules. However, we recognise that some short formulation is necessary to encapsulate the main essentials of our alternative approach. We therefore propose that the basic principle to be followed in developing planning policies for future development in accordance with sustainability principles should be expressed as follows.

Recommendation

In planning for new development and in reshaping or adapting existing development in order to achieve long-term sustainability and a healthy relationship with the natural environment, the basic unit for the development of appropriate environmental standards shall be the whole of the Social City Region, varying the standards (for example for densities, urban form or transport systems) to suit differing conditions, while ensuring that policies are complementary and that the sum total for the region as a whole contributes to the realisation of the approved sustainability objectives.

To meet these varying conditions, we propose that a variety of approaches be considered to suit particular settlement types within the overall Social City Region. These proposed sets of ideas as to what might be appropriate in a multiplicity of circumstances we have called the 'MultipliCity' approach to sustainability.

It would be possible to produce a very lengthy classification of these settlement types in order to put forward proposals for each. However, in the interests of manageability, we suggest a six-fold typology, all components of the Social City Region itself. This is listed in Table 9.2, with typical areas given to indicate what we have in mind in each case.

Table 9.2 *Classification of the components of the Social City Region*

Area Type	Example
Social City Region	Greater Manchester, Strathclyde
1. City – centres	Glasgow, London
2. City – inner area	Handsworth, Birmingham; St. Ann's, Nottingham
3. City – suburbs	Sutton, London; Jesmond, Newcastle
4. Small towns and new communities	Henley, Clitheroe
5. Mixed urban-rural	Oxfordshire, North Yorkshire
6. Remote rural areas	West Scotland, Northumberland

This typology in types 1 to 6, from large inner city to remote rural areas is, in effect, a simplification of the OPCS classification of Urban Areas discussed earlier.

The following sections look in more detail at some of the principal changes needed in order to achieve future sustainability, first taking the region – the Social City Region – as a whole and then examining each of the six settlement types separately.

CHANGES NEEDED FOR FUTURE SUSTAINABILITY

A number of powerful forces have combined to disperse urban development widely throughout extensive regions, the various parts of which are heavily inter-dependent and strongly inter-acting. These forces include the specialisation and large-scale concentration of modern production, the reliance for distribution on fewer and larger warehouses and large long-distance lorries, the development of convenient long-distance commuter rail services, the increased speed and availability of information technology and communication systems, the failure of the property market and the planning system to maintain sufficient affordable housing close to workplaces, and the decline in the environmental quality of large cities for both living and working.

This wide dispersal of urban development means that strategies for controlling future physical development, whether in town or country and whether for sustainability objectives or not, must be capable of adapting to a wide range of local conditions and must provide not only for improved design of new development but also for the reshaping of existing urban areas. The short time available for successfully avoiding environmental catastrophe means that the latter are of particular importance, since this is where the majority of people will be living during the few decades in which the widespread conversion to sustainability standards must be achieved.

In the sections that follow we set out briefly what we consider to be the principal changes in development strategies that will be needed in the various parts of the city region, in order to achieve the reduced environmental impact which is essential if cities and their dependent areas are to stop inflicting further damage on the natural environment at a rate and scale that cannot be accommodated. In effect, this means broadening the objective of the existing physical planning system – which has been to control 'development' (as statutorily defined) so as to achieve certain aims *within* our built environment – to include the relationship *between* this built environment and the world of natural ecosystems. These strategies for urban and rural development still concern the ways in which, firstly, we design and construct our built environment and, secondly, we manage and use our physical infrastructure; but the criteria for making policy choices must now include the objectives for natural resources, energy, pollution and waste, and their implications for buildings, production and transport as set out in earlier chapters.

Some measures are, of course, common to all parts of the city region, such as:

- reductions in pollution and waste
- greater efficiency in using energy and scarce materials
- more environmentally friendly transport systems
- minimising the separation of homes from jobs and services.

Other measures differ widely according to circumstances, for example:

- densities reduced in some areas but increased in others
- activities decentralised from some locations but more tightly clustered in others
- the need to replace buildings by greenery in some areas but to do the reverse in others.

Nevertheless, in spite of these differences in what will be most appropriate in particular local circumstances, there are certain objectives which must guide all future development if an acceptable rate and scale of progress – taking the region as a whole – are to be achieved. The main objectives are given in Box 9.1.

BOX 9.1 The Social City Region: Changes needed for future sustainability

NATURAL RESOURCES

1. Increased biological diversity, including positive measures for encouraging wildlife.
2. Big increase in biomass (trees and other green plants) in both town and country.
3. Replacement instead of depletion of groundwater reserves and good quality topsoil.
4. Much greater use and production of renewable materials in place of scarce finite ones.

LAND USE AND TRANSPORT

5. Shorter journeys to work and for daily needs.
6. Much higher proportion of trips by public transport.
7. More balanced public transport loadings to minimise fuel consumption.
8. Greater local self-sufficiency in non-speciality foods, goods and services.
9. More concentrated development served principally by public transport.

ENERGY

10. Greatly reduced consumption of fossil fuels.
11. Increased production from renewable sources; eg sun, wind, tides and waves.
12. Reduced wastage by better insulation, more use of CHP, local power generation.
13. Form and layout of buildings better designed for energy efficiency.

POLLUTION AND WASTE

14. Reduced emission of pollutants, especially from industry, power stations and transport.
15. Comprehensive measures to improve the quality of air, water and soil.
16. Reduction in total volume of waste stream.
17. Greater use of 'closed cycle' processes.
18. Much greater recovery of waste materials through recycling.

CHECKLIST FOR MONITORING PROGRESS

1. Pollution reduced by:
   a) establishing the environmental capacity of the region for emission of pollutants;
   b) refusing permission for any development that would result in the total volume of emissions exceeding the regional capacity;
   c) setting up inducements and penalties to cut existing emissions.

2. Natural resources conserved by:
   a) encouraging rehabilitation rather than redevelopment;
   b) stimulating regional production of renewables to replace finite non-renewables;
   c) adopting conservation measures to save topsoil.

3. Total volume of waste stream reduced by measures such as:
   a) reducing business rates for firms using 'closed cycle' processes;
   b) introducing graduated charges for waste collection.

4. Increased recycling of most waste materials including:
   a) recovery of scarce inorganic materials for reuse;
   b) composting of organic wastes.

5. Reduced energy consumption and increased percentage from renewables by:
   a) programme for raising energy efficiency of all buildings to at least minimum sustainability standards;
   b) increased use of solar gain;
   c) greater use of combined heat and power systems;
   d) development of wind farms and wave power.

6. Major increases in biomass, both urban and rural, by:
   a) more community forests and other rural tree planting;
   b) protection of existing urban open space and creation of new open space in areas of deficiency;
   c) additional urban tree planting and other green vegetation;
   d) gardens on flat rooftops;
   e) more green areas in new development projects.

7. Regional water supplies augmented and consumption reduced by:
   a) tree planting to maximise rainwater retention in watersheds;
   b) metering consumers with graduated charges favouring low consumption;
   c) applying 'closed cycle' methods to water use;
   d) separating 'grey' water for filtering and return to groundwater reserves;
   e) reducing urban run-off by use of more permeable paving, providing natural channels and lagoons in place of closed drains.

8. Urban decentralisation and dispersal reduced by:
   a) greening and decongesting inner cities;
   b) making inner city housing more attractive by eliminating excessive densities, designing for 'defensible space';
   c) increasing average densities in city suburbs and small towns;
   d) using more concentrated forms for new development.

9. Commuting distances reduced by:
   a) more local production to meet local needs
   b) local employment to match local skills;
   c) more telecommunication-based home-working, especially in rural areas;
   d) more mixed development;
   e) more housing in major employment centres;
   f) more complementary development in adjoining small towns to reduce reliance on distant large cities;
   g) building balanced new communities.

10. Public transport made more attractive and economic by:
    a) concentrating more mixed-use development at public transport nodes;
    b) co-ordinating land use and public transport to achieve more balanced commuter flows;
    c) creating more dedicated public transport routes;
    d) improving frequency and reliability of services;
    e) raising densities to complement improved public transport.

11. Road traffic reduced by:
    a) locating new development so as to reduce travel demand;
    b) using opportunities to reshape urban areas to reduce private motorised trips;
    c) refusing permission for new car-based out-of-town retailing and business parks;
    d) pricing road use on congested routes;
    e) reducing car parking provision and increasing charges where public transport available;
    f) more pedestrian-priority areas.

Figure 9.3 *The social city region*

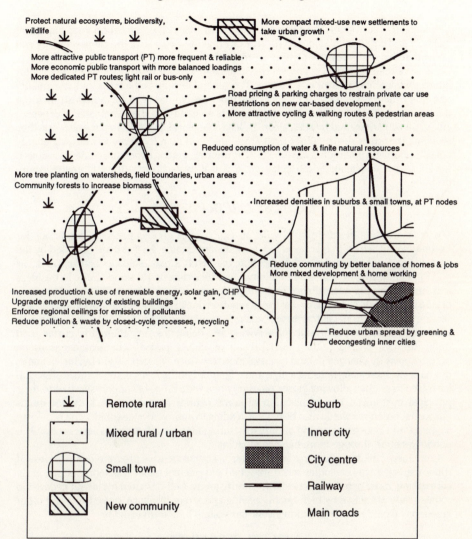

Protect natural ecosystems, biodiversity, wildlife

More compact mixed-use new settlements to take urban growth

More attractive public transport (PT) more frequent & reliable
More economic public transport with more balanced loadings
More dedicated PT routes; light rail or bus-only

Road pricing & parking charges to restrain private car use
Restrictions on new car-based development
More attractive cycling & walking routes & pedestrian areas

Reduced consumption of water & finite natural resources

More tree planting on watersheds, field boundaries, urban areas
Community forests to increase biomass

Increased densities in suburbs & small towns, at PT nodes

Reduce commuting by better balance of homes & jobs
More mixed development & home working

Increased production & use of renewable energy, solar gain, CHP
Upgrade energy efficiency of existing buildings
Enforce regional ceilings for emission of pollutants
Reduce pollution & waste by closed-cycle processes, recycling

Reduce urban spread by greening & decongesting inner cities

Remote rural	Suburb
Mixed rural / urban	Inner city
Small town	City centre
New community	Railway
	Main roads

161

CITY CENTRES

Although often surrounded by declining inner areas, many city centres remain as important business and entertainment hearts to large city regions. Because of the intense activity and traffic that this generates, city centres are major foci for energy consumption and pollution. Because of their dominance, city centres also have a major bearing on the prospects for future sustainability of their city regions. The general decline in the environmental quality and ease of access in cities – both cores and inner areas – has been a major 'push' factor in the profound process of decentralisation that is so central to the sustainability debate. If cities can be revived and be seen again as desirable places in which to live and work, thus reducing the wider dispersal of urban areas, they will go a long way to reducing energy consumption and pollution. Conversely, if the improved environmental standards required for long-term sustainability are achieved, this will in itself make the city centres more desirable.

LAND USE AND TRANSPORT

The concentration of different activities in city centres creates the ideal conditions for maximum reliance on public transport, walking and cycling. All these are impeded by the present scale of road traffic and congestion; the result is excessive fuel consumption, air pollution damaging to health and buildings, wasteful delays and unreliability in business and other trips, poor accessibility, and a degraded street environment. The present pattern of land uses results in a high level of trip generation due to the squeezing out of housing and service industries from central areas, causing heavy reliance on long-distance journeys to work and additional road traffic for servicing and deliveries. Any attempt to curtail road traffic through pricing (either road pricing or higher parking charges) needs to be accompanied by changes in land use designed to reduce trip generation by, for example, dramatically increasing housing within and adjoining central areas or much more provision for mixed uses, thus allowing closer proximity of a wide range of support services to their principal customers. Decentralisation of some central area activities to major multi-purpose sub-centres would also be helpful, leading to improved accessibility and providing scope for the necessary central area restructuring and contributing to more economical public transport through more balanced loading.

Combined with these land-use adjustments, a comprehensive programme for improved traffic management – including more attractive and efficient public transport, reductions in car parking, more extensive pedestrian-priority areas, well-designed cycle and pedestrian routes made attractive by high-quality paving and street furniture, more trees and other greenery – would reduce pollution levels and sustain long-term viability.

NATURAL RESOURCES

These are significant both in terms of the value of natural features within the city and of the demands made by city development on resources imported from elsewhere. Parks, riversides and other water features, trees, 'green architecture' and wildlife contribute greatly to the attraction and health of cities, as both history and property values show. The greening of the city, especially the city centre, is one of the major lessons that the past has to teach us about how to enhance the value of cities as places in which to live and work. Further greening has the environmental merits of carbon dioxide absorption and the maintenance of flora and fauna and so on; it also has the merit of making city cores more attractive to residents and hence assisting the reversal of the process of out-migration.

City centres are by their nature major consumers of investment capital and natural resources and must make their contribution to the conservation of scarce world resources by reducing their demands wherever possible. Redevelopment should be refused except in those cases where a positive net contribution to sustainability objectives can be achieved by, for example, lower consumption of energy and non-renewable materials.

ENERGY

City centres are large-scale intensive users of energy within buildings, particularly in offices and shops. They must therefore play a major role in implementing effective energy conservation policies in existing buildings, encouraged and assisted by a comprehensive programme of incentives and penalties, technical advice and public exhortation. Integrated environmental planning and building regulations should require all new buildings to be substantially more energy efficient. Rydin[10] explains the relationship between commercial logic and conservation measures in the property industry. Such an understanding is needed if planning policies are to be effective in persuading developers to achieve net reductions in energy consumption. New forms of building – shape, orientation, cladding and glazing – will be needed to maximise solar gain and the use of renewable energy. CHP systems must be used in business and residential developments wherever possible.

WASTE

Commercial activities in urban cores produce large quantities of waste, much more of which must be recycled. Companies must be persuaded through appropriate regulations and differential charging to reduce the volume of waste and to assist recycling through separating waste products before collection. Given the large scale, local authorities must be responsible for collection and recycling jointly with any regional agencies.

Box 9.2 City centres: changes needed for future sustainability

CHECKLIST FOR MONITORING PROGRESS

1. More attractive for living as well as working.
2. Less dependence on long journeys to work.
3. Increased amount of affordable housing relative to total employment.
4. Selective decentralisation of employment.
5. Improved quality of housing through, for example, reduction of excessive densities and redesigning for 'defensible space'.
6. Greener, with more natural features, especially trees and water.
7. Augmenting local open spaces to meet shortages.
8. Exclusion of non-essential road vehicles.
9. Improved access by high-quality public transport.
10. Reduced car parking with priority for essential users.
11. Progressive reduction in road congestion and traffic delays.
12. Greater self-sufficiency of local areas for daily servicing.
13. Increasing the provision of more continuous and attractive cycling and pedestrian routes.
14. Increasing pedestrian-only and pedestrian-priority areas.
15. Better energy-efficiency standards in all buildings; greater use of solar gain.
16. Reduced consumption of fossil fuels; more use of CHP.
17. Reduction of total waste stream and greater percentage recycled.

Figure 9.4 *City centres*

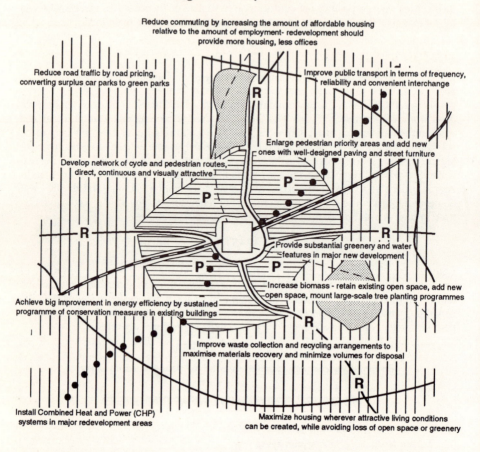

Reduce commuting by increasing the amount of affordable housing relative to the amount of employment- redevelopment should provide more housing, less offices

Reduce road traffic by road pricing, converting surplus car parks to green parks

Improve public transport in terms of frequency, reliability and convenient interchange

Enlarge pedestrian priority areas and add new ones with well-designed paving and street furniture

Develop network of cycle and pedestrian routes, direct, continuous and visually attractive

Provide substantial greenery and water features in major new development

Increase biomass - retain existing open space, add new open space, mount large-scale tree planting programmes

Achieve big improvement in energy efficiency by sustained programme of conservation measures in existing buildings

Improve waste collection and recycling arrangements to maximise materials recovery and minimize volumes for disposal

Install Combined Heat and Power (CHP) systems in major redevelopment areas

Maximize housing wherever attractive living conditions can be created, while avoiding loss of open space or greenery

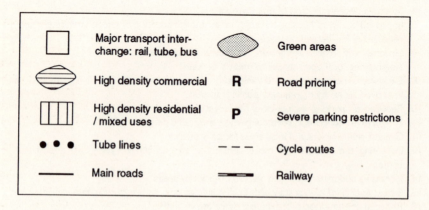

☐	Major transport interchange: rail, tube, bus	(green)	Green areas
(hatched)	High density commercial	**R**	Road pricing
⊞	High density residential / mixed uses	**P**	Severe parking restrictions
● ● ●	Tube lines	– – –	Cycle routes
—	Main roads	▭	Railway

THE INNER CITY

In many respects, inner city areas may pose the greatest complexities for the application of sustainability criteria. In terms of proximity to central area employment, high housing densities, mixture of housing and other land uses, lower car ownership ratios and greater use of public transport, they would appear even in their present form to exhibit more fully than other areas the characteristics necessary for future sustainability. Yet of all the six area types discussed here, inner cities have over recent decades proved to be the least popular locations for living and working.

The lesson is clear: their compactness, higher densities and proximity to work and public transport will have to be combined with other qualities – or possibly give way at least partially to other qualities – if these areas are to be made sufficiently attractive to reduce the pressures for urban dispersal.

These are the areas where getting the balance right will be critical in creating a desirable living environment, giving precedence to measures such as 'greening' – with more open space and more trees and more provision for natural flora and fauna – traffic calming and the exclusion of through traffic, and the creation of safe areas for children's play and walking. The over-riding aim in many of these areas will have to be the steady elimination of those factors which have been driving people out and, in the process, destroying the community spirit and self-help networks which are also important components of a sustainable home environment. In some areas, this may well mean that housing densities must drop or the mixture of uses be reduced to eliminate incompatibilities, contrary to the sustainability policies appropriate elsewhere.

LAND USE AND TRANSPORT

Because of their existing compactness and complexity, alterations to the inner city structure will need especially careful design to suit local circumstances. Typically, the emphasis is likely to be on correcting the deficiency in local community facilities, reducing overcrowding, and improving the design of housing areas to provide more attractive surroundings and more 'defensible space'; the net effect will probably be some overall reduction in housing densities, even though some individual sites may be suitable for an increase. Some regrouping of business uses may be necessary to eliminate nuisance and to provide the more up-to-date operating conditions which are essential if the mixed-use character of these areas is to be maintained.

One objective of any such regrouping will be improved accessibility; but new traffic management schemes must be designed to reduce the blight of excessive road traffic. Through traffic will have to be rerouted and traffic calming measures widely used to create larger areas with safer, quieter streets and less polluted air. Networks of safe and attractive routes for walking and cycling then become easier to develop, adding to accessibility and further reducing the need for motorised trips. These restraints on road traffic must be accompanied by major improvements in public transport – in frequency, reliability and ease of transfer – with more use of electric vehicles, both buses and trams, to further reduce noise and pollution.

Where existing buildings are too old and decayed for rehabilitation to be practicable or desirable, urban renewal schemes must be used to introduce better environmental practices, replacing old polluting factories and energy-inefficient housing and providing improved routes for public transport. Proposals for 'urban villages' – developed on large derelict sites – offer the prospect of dramatic rejuvenation of parts of inner city areas. Such 'implants' are intended to provide all the characteristics – jobs, housing, recreation, local identity, quality of life – of viable communities in previously depressed, and often dying, areas. However, where sites have been derelict long enough to become wildlife habitats, this rare asset of nature near the heart of the city may best serve sustainability objectives by being retained to offset any local open space deficiency.

NATURAL RESOURCES

Because of the typical lack of open space and greenery throughout large parts of old inner city areas, every redevelopment scheme needs to make some provision for trees and other vegetation to add visual delight and to help increase the total biomass in the city. The use of permeable paving materials around new planting will help maintain it as well as reducing excessive rainwater run-off. In addition, more use could be made of open rainwater channels leading to streams and ponds in open spaces as part of the growing network of natural features that is needed for 'greening the city'. The reduction in road traffic will provide space for many more tree-lined streets, especially in areas that have re-acquired a sense of local identity and community.

ENERGY CONSERVATION

Since these are the areas where age and obsolescence often combine to require either complete redevelopment or major rehabilitation works, there will be scope both for reducing total demand for energy by requiring all such schemes to incorporate the best standards for heat-conserving insulation, and for increasing the share of renewable energy by maximum use of passive solar gain and combined heat and power.

Box 9.3 The inner city: changes required for future sustainability

CHECKLIST FOR MONITORING PROGRESS

1. Residential areas becoming more attractive through being less congested, greener, cleaner, quieter and safer.
2. Residential areas increasingly freed from through traffic, protected by traffic calming for local traffic.
3. Reduction in excessively high densities and additional local open space in areas of worst deficiency.
4. Improvements in design of mixed use areas to reduce nuisance and improve access and facilities for small businesses.
5. Increased variety in housing types, tenures and prices, attracting a wider range of income levels.
6. Better provision of community and leisure facilities, available to both local residents and employees.
7. Developing policies revised to provide for compactness and maximum accessibility to jobs and leisure opportunities while also creating attractive living and working conditions.
8. Improved frequency and reliability of public transport, both bus and light rail.
9. Expanding network of attractive routes for cycling and walking.
10. Active programme for major expansion of trees and other vegetation; protection and enhancement of natural features.
11. Increasing percentage of buildings adapted to reduce energy consumption, reduce heat loss and make more use of solar gain.
12. Development of CHP as part of redevelopment schemes; reducing dependence on external sources of power.
13. Reduction of total waste stream from housing and businesses.
14. Collection, separation and disposal of waste, arranged to maximise percentage of waste materials recovered and recycled.

Figure 9.5 *The inner city*

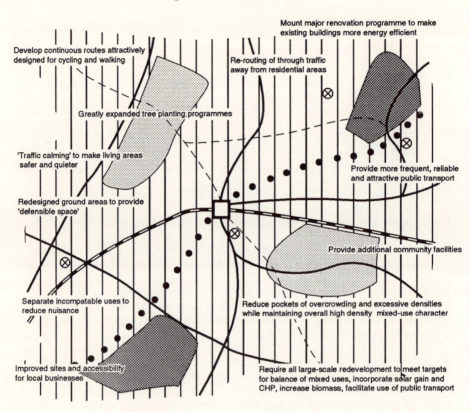

Mount major renovation programme to make existing buildings more energy efficient

Develop continuous routes attractively designed for cycling and walking

Re-routing of through traffic away from residential areas

Greatly expanded tree planting programmes

'Traffic calming' to make living areas safer and quieter

Provide more frequent, reliable and attractive public transport

Redesigned ground areas to provide 'defensible space'

Provide additional community facilities

Separate incompatable uses to reduce nuisance

Reduce pockets of overcrowding and excessive densities while maintaining overall high density mixed-use character

Improved sites and accessibility for local businesses

Require all large-scale redevelopment to meet targets for balance of mixed uses, incorporate solar gain and CHP, increase biomass, facilitate use of public transport

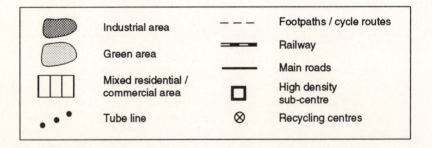

Industrial area		Footpaths / cycle routes	
Green area		Railway	
Mixed residential / commercial area		Main roads	
Tube line		High density sub-centre	
		Recycling centres	

SUBURBS

Suburbs constitute one of the greatest challenges. They contain a high proportion of the population and the existing housing stock, and will continue to do so throughout the period in which the change to more sustainable forms of urban development must be accomplished. In their present form, however, they are very wasteful of energy and generate a high proportion of trips by private motor vehicle. The love of nature and the individual private home are combined par excellence in the suburb, but the lack of variety in density and land use reduces accessibility to employment and services, increasing the reliance on motorised trips and making energy conservation more difficult. The application of sustainability criteria will thus require changes in the spatial arrangements of the suburb. The introduction of these various changes, involving a gradual adaption of life-styles to new environmental and economic constraints, needs to be done with the maximum involvement of the residents if it is not to be seen as an unreasonable interference with cherished existing values.

LAND-USE AND TRANSPORT

One possible approach to creating more sustainable cities – and one that affects the suburbs directly – is that of 'decentralised concentration'. This approach promotes sub-centres in cities and larger towns to take some of the pressure from the traditional single core. This reduces congestion and facilitates the development of additional public transport systems. These centres would be people-intensive nodes – workplaces, retailing and leisure facilities – developed around rail and bus systems. Suburb-to-suburb public transport systems should be developed to cater for many trips which now take this form but which currently can only be completed conveniently by car. In the short term, such systems might be based on buses (although deregulation has made this more difficult). In the long run, rail, light rail and tram systems might contribute. There may be opportunities to increase residential densities in some areas, but care must be taken not to lower environmental standards through town cramming. Opportunities should be taken to create a greater mixing of activities. This might facilitate shorter, local trips to work and to services. Edge-of-town retail and business parks should be resisted; opportunities might be found to locate these in the enhanced suburban centres.

NATURAL RESOURCES

As well as variations in architecture, services and other facets, differences in vegetation in gardens, parks and other natural areas (biomass) can all enter the calculations of sustainability. The quantity and quality of water is increasingly becoming an issue in many areas as a result of environmentally damaging processes which must now be changed. The careful husbandry of water will become essential. Soakaways must be provided for surface water run-off, even if temporarily stored in lagoons which double as nature areas. This will require land to be set aside for the purpose. The use of permeable materials will prevent the sealing of the ground and should be part of good practice, as should the reuse of grey water. The treatment of sewerage by reed beds and other sewerage 'farms' is feasible using green belt space.

Green matter is essential for a healthy environment. A proactive management of all biomass resources, and a concern for increasing carbon dioxide absorption, will place additional importance on open spaces and their management. Areas will need to be set aside for planting to counteract the effects of building: twenty new trees for each house is suggested. Existing 'green assets', including rough ground serving as natural wildlife habitats, must not be sacrificed nor excessive infill permitted in the search for increased densities or more varied and concentrated development. The greater diversity in suburban form apparent since the Second World War needs extending. Traditional allotments should be retained for food growing purposes, as well as for their contribution in disposing of green waste and adding to total biomass. They could be used for local fish-farming where water is available, as well as bee-keeping and intensive food production of an organic nature.

ENERGY CONSERVATION

Detailed planning policies should contribute to making new build substantially more energy efficient. New forms of building with outer conservatory-like skins will seek to maximise the use of renewable energy. Opportunities should be taken wherever possible to develop CHP systems.

WASTE

Reducing the total volume of the waste stream is a prime requirement through changes in packaging habits and greatly-enlarged recycling. At the neighbourhood level, sufficient land area needs to be allocated for recycling collection centres. Careful siting will be necessary in predominantly residential suburbia for materials which generate noise in handling. Composting stations might be located at allotments to deal with that fraction of green waste which cannot be dealt with at individual homes. At a district authority level, (population of, say, 100,000) a materials recovery and processing facility will be needed for all recyclable waste, including industrial waste, where this is the appropriate scale. For some materials – such as tyres – only one or two facilities nationwide may be required. Residual waste can be incinerated for district heating.

Box 9.4 Suburbs: changes needed for future sustainability

CHECKLIST FOR MONITORING PROGRESS

1. More intensive development along public transport corridors.
2. More mixed-use zones for combined living and working.
3. Higher density mixed-use development at neighbourhood centres and public transport nodes.
4. Using redevelopment opportunities to achieve a greater variety of housing types and residential densities, with higher densities in suitable locations, especially where easily accessible to public transport and other services.
5. Growing network of safe and convenient routes for walking and cycling.
6. Reduced impact of motor vehicles on local neighbourhoods through progressive exclusion of through traffic and more extensive use of traffic-calming measures.
7. Enhancement of open spaces, improving ecological function in terms of biodiversity, wildlife habitats, urban forests and increasing total biomass to act as pollution 'sinks'.
8. Developing green corridors linking open spaces and any remaining areas of natural vegetation.
9. Greater retention of rainwater run-off, development of streams and ponds for conservation and landscape purposes.
10. Reducing water consumption, reuse of filtered grey water and increased return of used water to the ground.
11. Greater recycling of waste, reducing volume and landfill needs.
12. Increased involvement of local residents and community groups in schemes for waste recovery and other conservation measures.
13. Reduction in total energy consumption, with increasing percentage of buildings brought up to sustainability standards for conserving heat and power, and increased use of CHP and solar gain.
14. Increased share of energy obtained from renewable sources.

Figure 9.6 *Suburbs*

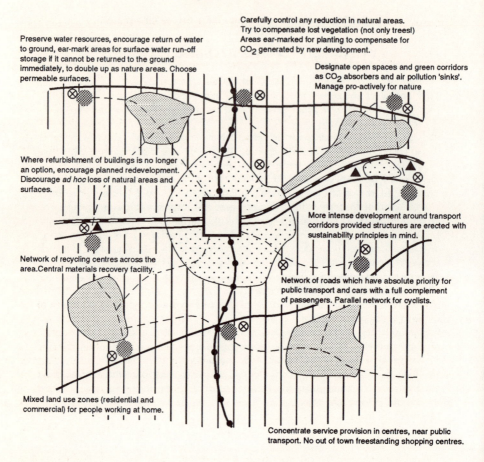

Preserve water resources, encourage return of water to ground, ear-mark areas for surface water run-off storage if it cannot be returned to the ground immediately, to double up as nature areas. Choose permeable surfaces.

Carefully control any reduction in natural areas. Try to compensate lost vegetation (not only trees!) Areas ear-marked for planting to compensate for CO_2 generated by new development.

Designate open spaces and green corridors as CO_2 absorbers and air pollution 'sinks'. Manage pro-actively for nature

Where refurbishment of buildings is no longer an option, encourage planned redevelopment. Discourage *ad hoc* loss of natural areas and surfaces.

More intense development around transport corridors provided structures are erected with sustainability principles in mind.

Network of recycling centres across the area.Central materials recovery facility.

Network of roads which have absolute priority for public transport and cars with a full complement of passengers. Parallel network for cyclists.

Mixed land use zones (residential and commercial) for people working at home.

Concentrate service provision in centres, near public transport. No out of town freestanding shopping centres.

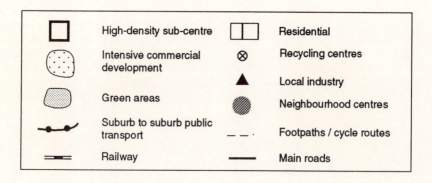

□	High-density sub-centre	⊞	Residential
⬭	Intensive commercial development	⊗	Recycling centres
⬭	Green areas	▲	Local industry
•–•–•	Suburb to suburb public transport	●	Neighbourhood centres
▭	Railway	– · – ·	Footpaths / cycle routes
		——	Main roads

SMALL TOWNS AND NEW COMMUNITIES

The small town is one of our most successful types of community. It acts as a service centre for other towns and villages and has many of the characteristics of sustainability. At this level, however, local circumstances are likely to vary considerably. Many small towns, particularly in accessible, lowland areas, have grown rapidly in recent years. They have been seen as almost the ideal living environment: providing a semi-rural, economically buoyant, small-scale living environment, but with sufficient services to provide a high degree of self-containment. In the coming years, these towns will remain under pressure unless decentralisation from the large cities slows down considerably. Many of these towns have historic centres and other historic areas where the introduction of energy-saving measures and other changes to achieve sustainability objectives would be unacceptable unless carried out sensitively. There is no doubt, however, that many sustainability measures – such as pedestrianisation, taming the motor car, reduction of car parking, and rehabilitation instead of redevelopment in order to conserve scarce materials – would greatly assist the conservation of historic features.

LANDUSE AND TRANSPORT

As a result of their rapid growth, many small towns now have severe traffic problems. In sensitive, congested centres road pricing or severe traffic restraint measures may be appropriate, particularly in historic towns. Care must be taken, however, to ensure that the result is not simply a shift of traffic to other less restrictive towns nearby. Again, public transport has to be promoted. In some cases, an overall increase in the size of the town will facilitate improved public transport. With a single accessible node, the centre becomes particularly important, and in the case of historic towns particularly sensitive: it must carry the burden of those activities that are people intensive. Thus, the centres will have to carry those business and retailing activities that should be resisted on the edge of town. If towns are close together, then linking public transport may be important. It may be appropriate to take opportunities to achieve a greater mixing of uses. There may be circumstances in which infilling, and hence higher densities, might be appropriate in such towns. Densities should be increased near to public transport facilities, while activities, such as distribution, should be located on the edge of town near to major roads.

These positive changes will have to be complemented by strong restraints on any further edge-of-town retailing and offices together with measures such as road pricing and higher parking charges to reduce the volume of road traffic. New large-scale traffic generators should be permitted only where well served by public transport. Where nearby towns are complementary in terms of their job and leisure opportunities, accessibility by public transport should be improved so that groups of towns become more self-reliant and less dependent on more distant, bigger cities.

The building of new communities would, of course, provide the best opportunity for achieving forms of urban development that fully meet sustainability standards. Particular attention will need to be paid to:

- overall layout;
- pattern of land uses and transport;
- design of buildings;
- energy and transport systems;
- minimum generation of pollution and waste; and
- maximum provision for trees, water, wildlife and a high level of biomass.

New settlements could provide the models, demonstrating for all to see and experience what the full application of sustainability principles is like in practice; they could provide the vision towards which the gradual restructuring of existing urban areas could be directed.

NATURAL RESOURCES

The more balanced and more self-servicing urban areas which sustainability requires are already to be seen to some extent in Ebenezer Howard's Garden Cities and the later New Towns. For example, Redditch used the study of microclimate to aid environmental conditions and built separate drainage systems to create strings of lakes. In Milton Keynes, the system of open spaces planned into the structure of the town provides space for planting millions of trees, attractive routes for cycling and walking, open-air recreation close at hand, and gives ample scope for increased biomass and the further working out of ecological principles.

In older towns, there is room at the edges for developing all these ideas, together with new ones such as using the incineration of residual (non-recyclable) waste in local CHP systems for supplying greenhouses with energy for intensive horticultural production – a better alternative to paying farmers to simply set aside land. Policies for developing smallholding areas on the outskirts would encourage greater self-sufficiency in supplies of basic foods and more local employment. Local supplies of organic fertiliser could be obtained by mixing green waste with treated sewage sludge, reducing the need for expensive imports of artificial fertilisers.

ENERGY CONSUMPTION AND WASTE

Measures to reduce both of these will be needed here as much as elsewhere, and will be similar to those described for various other parts of the Social City Region. Where the overall density is high enough, there may be scope for greater self-sufficiency by combining power generation from renewables and CHP schemes with intensive area-wide heat and power conservation schemes.

Box 9.5 Small towns and new communities: changes needed for future sustainability

CHECKLIST FOR MONITORING PROGRESS

1. Reduced rate of growth in road vehicle mileage.
2. Increased percentage of trips by public transport.
3. Growth of non-motorised movement, cycling and walking; increased mileage of safe attractive routes for cycling.
4. Increased density of activities near public transport nodes.
5. Ecology centre actively promoting sustainability concepts and goals.
6. Urban audit published regularly, measuring air and water pollution, energy efficiency and recycling.
7. Business network, developing ways of promoting local use of local produce and improving the attractiveness of local markets.
8. Reductions in energy consumption in existing buildings.
9. Reduced per capita consumption of fossil fuels and increased percentage obtained from renewable sources and district CHP schemes.
10. Growing contribution to integrated sub-regional waste system in terms of reducing total waste stream, closed-cycle processes and recycling.
11. Creative management of water for conservation and landscape purposes.
12. Increases in tree planting and other plant life, and total biomass.
13. Enhancement of nature throughout all parts of the urban area.
14. Redevelopment normally refused permission when rehabilitation would require less use of scarce natural resources.
15. Conserving historic areas while improving energy efficiency.
16. Increasing involvement of community groups and schools in making a direct contribution to sustainability targets.

Figure 9.7 *Small towns and new communities*

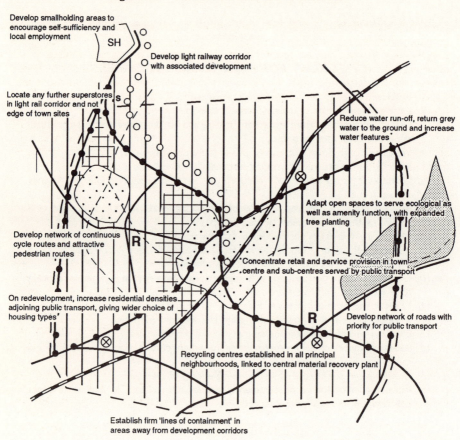

Develop smallholding areas to encourage self-sufficiency and local employment

SH

Develop light railway corridor with associated development

Locate any further superstores in light rail corridor and not edge of town sites

Reduce water run-off, return grey water to the ground and increase water features

Adapt open spaces to serve ecological as well as amenity function, with expanded tree planting

Develop network of continuous cycle routes and attractive pedestrian routes

Concentrate retail and service provision in town centre and sub-centres served by public transport

On redevelopment, increase residential densities adjoining public transport, giving wider choice of housing types

Develop network of roads with priority for public transport

Recycling centres established in all principal neighbourhoods, linked to central material recovery plant

Establish firm 'lines of containment' in areas away from development corridors

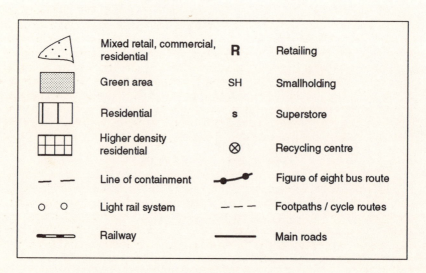

	Mixed retail, commercial, residential	R	Retailing
	Green area	SH	Smallholding
	Residential	s	Superstore
	Higher density residential	⊗	Recycling centre
— —	Line of containment	•—•—•	Figure of eight bus route
o o	Light rail system	– – –	Footpaths / cycle routes
	Railway	——	Main roads

MIXED URBAN-RURAL AREAS

These areas will bear the brunt of continued economic restructuring and potential growth, particularly in South and Central England. The high rate of growth (see Table 9.1) is likely to continue as people leave the bigger urban centres seeking home environments which are less congested, less polluted, more spacious and with easier access to the countryside. This rapid growth may eventually slow down if travel costs rise steeply in the drive to cut pollution levels, and if large cities are successful in creating more attractive living conditions. However, current trends cannot be reversed quickly and substantial further growth seems inevitable, creating intense pressure on the environment but also opening useful opportunities to guide development in sustainable ways. Current set-aside policies for taking land out of agricultural production will also strongly affect these areas.

LAND USE AND TRANSPORT

Many of these areas have reasonably complete road and rail networks but have experienced major changes in accessibility with the rapid growth of private road traffic, decline in bus services and the improvement of long-distance commuter rail services at the expense of local lines. Because settlements are small with limited facilities and agricultural employment is low, many areas have increasingly changed from being mixed-use, mixed-income and relatively self-sufficient for jobs and daily needs to being dependent on more distant, large towns and cities for jobs, shopping and services, and even for affordable housing as commuters have moved in and pushed house prices out of the reach of local people. The result is more and longer trips for more purposes and greater dependency on the private motor car. Low densities and long utility runs per household add to energy inefficiencies.

New development in recent decades has exaggerated all these characteristics which are incompatible with long-term sustainability. The continued pressure for growth does provide considerable scope for correcting some of the worst deficiencies but the application of sustainability principles in these areas will require strong policies combining land use and transport objectives, applicable to all localities within an overall regional strategy.

New development should normally be to higher average densities, but much more varied to meet a wider range of household types and incomes and closely related to fixed lines of rapid public transport. There should be provision for areas or pockets of low density where there are opportunities for combining home and workplace (including smallholdings) and for more individual self-sufficiency in terms of energy supply, composting waste and on-site sewage treatment. All new development, apart from minor infilling, should be designed to achieve, first, an improved balance of homes and workplaces (to reduce long-distance work trips) and, second, an improved balance of commuter flows (to make full use of public transport capacity, giving more economical public transport and less fuel consumption).

NATURAL RESOURCES

New and existing settlements should be interspersed with community woodlands, good agricultural land protected from further urban encroachment and small holdings or market gardens for small-scale production linked to local markets, with intensive and innovative food producing areas on the best soils. As with the new community forests, the use of trees as the dominant feature in mixed areas can work wonders in assimilating development into the landscape.

These areas must continue to accommodate gravel extraction and other mineral workings in locations not requiring excessive trip lengths. Their role in the environmentally safe disposal of non-recyclable wastes will be an important part of any regional strategy for future waste disposal avoiding pollution of ground or water supplies. Quantity as well as quality of water is becoming an increasing problem, requiring both lower consumption, reduction of rainwater runoff, re-use of grey water, and redesign of drainage and sewage systems to separate out non-sewage bearing flows and using them for recharging groundwater reserves.

NEW SETTLEMENTS

Many of these objectives will be more readily achieved through the building of balanced new settlements rather than the single-use unbalanced extensions to existing settlements which have been typical of speculative development in recent decades. Given that only a fraction of future housing demand can be met within existing urban areas, there is a strong case for regional and sub-regional strategies to include the building of new settlements designed on advanced 'sustainable development' principles as an alternative to both 'town cramming' and further peripheral sprawl.

ENERGY

As elsewhere, big savings are possible through more compact new development and better designed buildings and by using all opportunities for passive solar gain and incorporating CHP systems in most projects.

Box 9.6 Mixed urban – rural areas: changes needed for future sustainability

CHECKLIST FOR MONITORING PROGRESS

1. Increased number of service sub-centres supported by higher densities and linking public transport services.
2. Better balance of homes and workplaces throughout the sub-region to achieve more even public transport loadings.
3. Improved capacity of local producers to serve local markets for daily goods and services.
4. Increased local job opportunities and social choice.
5. Increasing percentage of trips by public transport.
6. Greater diversity of new development: some achieving energy efficiency through better design; some having greater self-containment for energy and food supplies.
7. Substantial share of new development in new settlements designed to match sustainable development standards fully.
8. Integrated sub-regional waste systems to reduce waste streams; minimise landfill and maximise recycling of hard materials; compost organic waste; provide fuel for CHP plants; and improve the separation of toxic materials to prevent ground and water pollution.
9. Major increases in community forests, tree planting, and total biomass.
10. Reduction in water consumption and increasing ground-water reserves.
11. More use of passive solar gain and CHP systems.
12. Increasing percentage of existing buildings meeting full energy-efficiency standards.
13. Active landscape programmes for raising biological diversity, protecting natural features and greening urban areas.

Figure 9.8 *Mixed urban – rural areas*

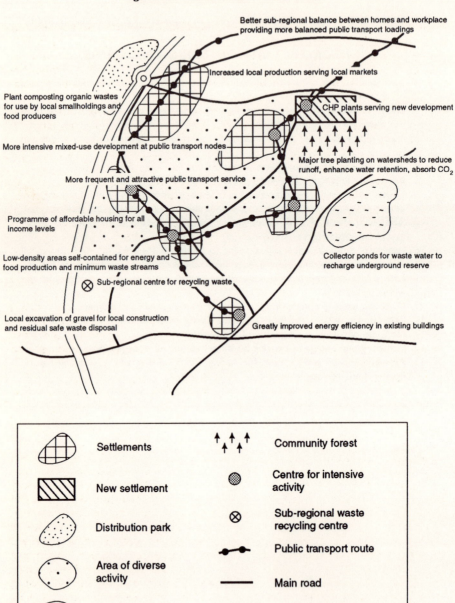

Better sub-regional balance between homes and workplace providing more balanced public transport loadings

Increased local production serving local markets

Plant composting organic wastes for use by local smallholdings and food producers

CHP plants serving new development

More intensive mixed-use development at public transport nodes

Major tree planting on watersheds to reduce runoff, enhance water retention, absorb CO_2

More frequent and attractive public transport service

Programme of affordable housing for all income levels

Low-density areas self-contained for energy and food production and minimum waste streams

Collector ponds for waste water to recharge underground reserve

⊗ Sub-regional centre for recycling waste

Local excavation of gravel for local construction and residual safe waste disposal

Greatly improved energy efficiency in existing buildings

Settlements		Community forest	
New settlement		Centre for intensive activity	
Distribution park		Sub-regional waste recycling centre	
Area of diverse activity		Public transport route	
Balancing lake		Main road	
		Dual carriageway	

REMOTE RURAL AREAS

These areas contribute least to the total environmental damage caused by modern industrialised society, by reason of their small and scattered total populations and their predominantly non-urban and non-industrial life-styles. However, they are likely to have an increasingly important role to play in achieving sustainability targets for the region as a whole: for a greatly enlarged supply of renewable energy; for greater regional self-sufficiency in food and timber; for major increases in forest cover; for augmenting regional water supplies; and for their valuable leisure resources of natural beauty and peaceful havens well away from the rush and pressures of areas more dominated by urban demands and values. The demands for all these are bound to grow, partly as a continuation of established trends and partly as the inevitable result of the search for greater sustainability for the region as a whole.

It is likely that remoter rural areas will continue to receive in-migration – a well-established trend that general regional policies in pursuit of greater sustainability are unlikely to stop. Densities, however, are likely to remain low. There is no reason to think that any general drive for more concentrated forms of urban development would have much impact here. Other objectives will have much greater relevance, including greater reliance on local sources of energy, food and natural materials; home- and community-based employment; and better provision for energy and water conservation and for recycling of recoverable wastes. Happily, the search for greater regional sustainability will necessarily slow down or reverse the centralisation of production and employment which has until now left these remoter areas with vulnerable economies, substandard services and associated social problems. However, new institutional arrangements may be needed to promote sustainable development practices, in particular to achieve integration in land management, settlement planning, transport operations and resource development.

LAND USE AND TRANSPORT

The economic circumstances of such areas vary considerably. Some have received jobs and people as a result of decentralisation, sometimes making up for the decline in traditional employment and therefore remaining economically and socially viable. Others have suffered from job losses, increasingly inadequate public transport and obsolete public services and community facilities. With their emphasis on greater self-sufficiency in the local economy, enhanced local production to reduce unnecessary road transport, and improved public transport services, sustainability policies should provide greatly improved prospects for the future of these hitherto disadvantaged areas. However, economic viability will be partly dependent on a balanced package of measures, sensitively adapted to local conditions, including, for example: improved jobs and services in locations well served by public transport; transport improvements aimed primarily at improving sub-regional accessibility rather than long-distance commuting; wider application of the 'tele-cottage' principle to facilitate home-working or small new enterprises in more (and, indeed, in less) remote areas and for combining smallholdings with tele-linked businesses; and development of local distribution networks aimed at efficient servicing of local markets.

NATURAL RESOURCES

The UK has one of the largest potentials for wind energy in the whole of Europe and the opportunities for exploiting this are located largely in the more remote rural uplands, especially in the West. Ways will have to be found of designing and developing windfarms in these areas without causing unacceptable damage to their natural beauty. The other major sources of renewable energy (wave and tidal power) are less concentrated in remote rural areas, so it will be a function of the energy strategy for the region as a whole to determine how much wind power in remoter areas needs to be developed relative to these other sources and other locations in order to meet energy sustainability targets.

Changing agricultural policies and measures to deal with 'surplus' farmland are already creating opportunities for more varied activities, including tourism and leisure activities, and for more forestry and forestry-based products. Some of these areas are, after all, the 'rainforests' of Britain, amply provided with water and favourable conditions for plant growth and biological diversity – valuable assets in achieving a balanced and sustainable development for the region as a whole. Special audits to identify the potential for renewable resources of all kinds will be necessary.

ENERGY CONSUMPTION

If these areas are to become principal suppliers of wind- and water-generated electricity to the rest of the city region, expanded research programmes and careful detailed planning and design will be necessary to minimise any adverse effects on the local environment. To meet local demand, small-scale local power stations will help to reduce distribution losses; CHP schemes will be viable in some settlements; and – as elsewhere – making all buildings more energy efficient will be a major contributor to the important goal of reducing overall consumption.

Box 9.7 Remote rural areas: changes needed for future sustainability

CHECKLIST FOR MONITORING PROGRESS

1. Expansion of total biomass through increasing forests, tree planting along field boundaries and roadside verges, and protection of areas of natural vegetation.
2. Increasing biological diversity, including avoidance of monocultures and protection of wildlife habitats.
3. Growth of groundwater reserves, protection of watersheds.
4. Reduced pollution of streams and ground-water.
5. Increased composting of organic wastes and reduced use of artificial fertilisers.
6. Increasing production of energy from renewable sources: wind, wave, tide, geothermal.
7. Reduced consumption of fossil fuels.
8. Progressive upgrading of all buildings to meet new sustainability standards for energy efficiency.
9. Improved public transport in terms of frequency and convenience, improved accessibility, more attractive travelling conditions.
10. Reduction in long-distance commuting.
11. Growing self-sufficiency of the local economy in terms of the capacity of the sub-region to provide a greater variety of job opportunities and to supply daily goods and services from local sources.
12. Better telecommunications to aid homeworking.
13. Publication of regular audits on waste, pollution, energy and water.
14. Regularly updated plans for integrating land management, settlements, transport, and resource development.

Figure 9.9   *Remote rural areas*

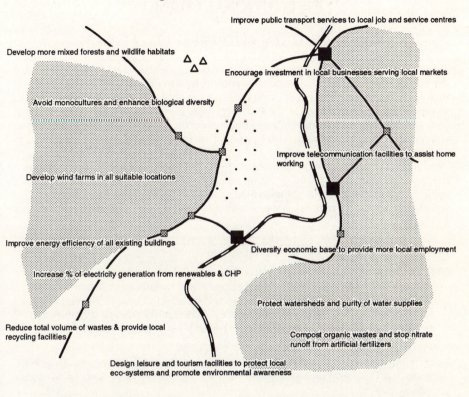

Improve public transport services to local job and service centres

Develop more mixed forests and wildlife habitats

Encourage investment in local businesses serving local markets

Avoid monocultures and enhance biological diversity

Improve telecommunication facilities to assist home working

Develop wind farms in all suitable locations

Improve energy efficiency of all existing buildings

Diversify economic base to provide more local employment

Increase % of electricity generation from renewables & CHP

Protect watersheds and purity of water supplies

Reduce total volume of wastes & provide local recycling facilities

Compost organic wastes and stop nitrate runoff from artificial fertilizers

Design leisure and tourism facilities to protect local eco-systems and promote environmental awareness

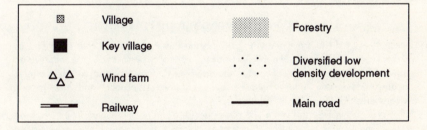

▨	Village	▨▨▨	Forestry
■	Key village	· · · · · ·	Diversified low density development
△△ △	Wind farm		
⊐⊏	Railway	——	Main road

SUSTAINABLE TOWN, SUSTAINABLE COUNTRY – INSTITUTIONAL CHANGE

DELIVERING SUSTAINABLE URBAN DEVELOPMENT

The previous sections have proposed a detailed policy agenda for achieving sustainable development at local levels. The question now is how to deliver such initiatives at the regional and local level? In considering the arrangements to do this, a basic principle to be adopted is that plans at all levels should be more closely co-ordinated. The TCPA is convinced that policy initiatives should fully reflect the desires and aspirations of local communities. Thus, consistent with the aim of effective implementation (as argued in Chapter 1), we strongly support the European Commission's notion of 'subsidiarity' – which requires that decisions are made at the lowest effective level. However, it is also the case that each layer of policy making must be consistent with that above it. This applies most obviously in the planning field, where local plans should be consistent with structure plans, which in turn must be consistent with regional objectives and national guidance.

Recommendation

Policy making must encompass the twin principles of subsidiarity and plan consistency, avoiding excessive centralisation and maximising the involvement of those whose daily living environment will be affected by new development, while ensuring that there is consistency between the details of proposed development and the broader policies at regional and national levels.

If new policy vehicles are introduced to deal with sustainable development, as we have suggested in Chapter 1 and will pursue below, then these must also follow these principles.

BOX 9.8 Community involvement in Leicester

Leicester – styled the 'Environment City' – has set up eight specialist working groups with representatives from the public, private and voluntary sectors to guide and develop action around the built environment; the social environment; food and agriculture; economy and work; energy; waste and pollution; transport; and the natural environment.

The groups involve more than 120 senior decision and policy makers from the three sectors. The groups aim, within the framework of a twenty-year plan, to build on Leicester's significant achievements in moving towards greater sustainability and to achieve realistic and practical solutions to such problems as car dependency. The involvement of all sectors of the community – including business – is seen as crucial if genuine changes in the environmental field are to be accomplished.

Although the concern here is with the local scale, there are, of course, constraints imposed on local action by national governments. Thus certain desirable initiatives at the local level require changes in central government regulations and practices. A good example of this is the case of appeal decisions where local authorities have refused permission on environmental grounds. To date, the Department of the Environment has not been very sympathetic to such arguments. However, if central government is serious about achieving sustainability objectives, it must encourage local authorities to use their planning and other environmental control functions for this purpose.

Recommendation

Central government advice and appeal decisions must actively promote and support local planning authorities in their attempts to achieve environmental improvements and sustainability objectives through their local plans and development control decisions.

In the absence of elected regional governments, and pending the reorganisation of some elements of local government, it is essential that the fullest possible use is made of existing arrangements to implement environmental policy. The present and developing system of regional guidance can make a greater contribution to environmental policy. Although developed within the land-use planning field, this is the only vehicle available at present for the discussion and adoption of any regional-level policies. Because it is an informal system, albeit one that is currently being promoted strongly by central government, it has a largely advisory role, setting a context for structure plan policies. Environmental statements are now very much to the fore in regional advice being prepared by regional conferences. However, these tend to take the form of generalised statements. Regional guidance could usefully go further in considering the consequences of regional-scale settlement patterns and transport systems and in proposing changes that will improve sustainability. Debates and policy formulations at this scale need not be too constrained by the land-use origins of the system. A number of regional conferences are finding the system to be a suitable vehicle for addressing non-land-use issues.

Recommendation

Regional guidance should give more detailed advice on environmentally sustainable development patterns within regions.

Although in the short term such improvements to the treatment of environmental issues in regional guidance is highly desirable, we believe this should be viewed as an interim arrangement only. The experience to date strongly indicates that the present arrangements for dealing with major development and environmental issues of regional or national significance – in terms of both policy formation and implementation – are inadequate and will only be effectively handled by setting up a regional level of government capable of preparing and operating long-term strategies. The arguments and proposals for doing so are detailed in the TCPA report *Strategic Planning for Regional Development*.[11] These arguments apply especially strongly to policies for sustainable development and their prospects of being effectively implemented would be greatly strengthened if these strategic bodies existed at the regional level to guide and support the local action which is needed to make national policies work in practice.

Recommendation

A regional level of government should be established to prepare strategies for future development, with special reference to the need for effective implementation of national policies for environmental protection and future sustainability.

At the local level, the new system of unitary authorities – assuming regional government

– should provide an effective means of implementing environmental policy. At both elected regional and unitary authority levels, however, a new integrated approach to such policy is crucial. It is therefore suggested that it be a statutory requirement that regional and unitary authorities produce integrated environmental plans, as suggested in Chapter 1. An informal system, even if backed by central government – as, for example, with regional guidance – would be far less effective.

Recommendation

Legislation and regulations should be amended to require regional and local authorities to prepare Integrated Environment Plans (IEPs), which state environmental objectives, policies, targets and responsibilities.

In Chapter 1 it was suggested that integrated environmental planning must recognise three crucial characteristics of environmental processes: their trans-media nature, through air, land and sea; their trans-sectoral nature, as they cut across traditional policy boundaries; and their trans-boundary nature, as they cut across political frontiers. These characteristics imply an integration of analysis and policy formulation that will be novel to most agencies. But they also imply organisational arrangements that may have to be novel too. Despite efforts at 'corporate planning' in the 1970s, whereby all local government services were to be co-ordinated within a planning approach, local authority activities remain largely compartmentalised within departments. However, environmental concerns cannot be the sole preserve of a single department. It is essential that all local environmental initiatives, at regional and local levels, are co-ordinated.

Recommendation

Organisational arrangements must be devised in regional and local agencies to enable genuinely integrated environmental policies to be formulated and implemented.

Integrated Environmental Plans would probably be best co-ordinated from a chief executive's department. Contributions to the plan would come from individual departments, but within a clear co-ordinated framework. The environmental agenda to be addressed by regional and local integrated environmental plans would be determined in each case, as the discussion of settlement types earlier in this chapter has demonstrated. However, some indication can be given here of issues that might be addressed:

- new urban form and energy consumption (residential, workplace, retail and leisure locations, varieties of urban densities etc);
- existing urban form and energy consumption;
- promotion of public transport patronage;
- promotion of CHP;
- trade-offs between environmental and other criteria;
- waste disposal arrangements;
- telecommunications;
- habitat protection and creation;
- urban greening;
- recycling schemes;
- building controls;
- urban densities.

BOX 9.9 An integrated approach – the London Borough of Sutton

Starting from a short, robust policy statement in 1986, Sutton Council has gradually set out to change its attitudes and work practices to make them more environmentally relevant. Accepting that not everything can be done at once, steady progress has, nevertheless, been maintained. Where an issue has been tackled, such as recycling, it has not been seen in isolation but as part of wider issues, in this case including waste avoidance, waste collection, waste disposal and the finding of markets for recovered materials. For example, the Council uses its purchasing powers to generate a higher demand for recycled products.

Faced with limited resources, Sutton Council has achieved its results by redistributing resources and by setting up special funds, such as an energy conservation fund. Monitoring of implementation and a gradual change of attitudes and aptitudes by staff has played an important role.

Cumulatively, the effect of Sutton's work in the fields of the preservation and enhancement of nature, environmental education and recycling have all started to contribute to a more sustainable future. Of particular importance are the efforts to involve the community. The overriding principle in Sutton's work is to concentrate on the manageable, to be imaginative, and to maintain continuity. Crucially, it is accepted that, whatever the circumstances, everybody can make a contribution here and now.

The distinction between the appropriate agendas for regional and local integrated enviromental plans will depend on circumstances. However, clearly the regional level would need to establish the objectives and targets for the region as a whole and provide facilities or support beyond the resources of individual local authorities (for waste disposal and recycling, for instance). Local authorities would devise the programmes of action which would be appropriate to their local circumstances, while also contributing their share of the overall regional effort. In the absence of regional strategies, some local authorities have already taken major initiatives in promoting environmental awareness in their areas, setting up local conservation programmes and schemes for waste recovery and recycling – such as Leicester City Council's 'Environment City' scheme (see Box 9.8) and the London Borough of Sutton's council-wide programme for involving all council departments and community groups (see Box 9.9). Such initiatives need to become standard practice throughout the country – with such active government support as is necessary in terms of power and resources.

Recommendation

All local councils should take the lead in creating an awareness and understanding of environmental issues, in developing council-wide programmes for at least a number of priority issues such as energy conservation and waste recycling, and in involving local residents – with positive support, as necessary, from central government.

Effective planning for sustainable development will rely heavily on good information, both about the current state of the environment and about the various key factors which have been identified as requiring change if environmental sustainability is to be achieved. One essential source of data will be local environmental audits which will be required to measure the amount and rate of change in conditions such as the level of pollutants in air, water and soil, the degree of biodiversity, and the reserves of essential resources including water and topsoil. Equally important will be an organised programme of regular monitoring to measure progress in changing those key environment-influencing factors which are the subject of sustainability policies and for which specific targets have been set in the IEP, for example energy conservation, transport efficiency, development of renewables and proportions of waste materials recycled.

Recommendation

Local environmental audits should be carried out and published regularly by the appropriate regional and local authorities in order to establish to what extent sustainability policies are having the intended effect.

Monitoring of key environment-influencing factors and the regular publication of results should be required as an integral part of every Integrated Environment Plan in order to assess the extent and rate of progress in achieving the sustainability targets set in the plan.

Monitoring is not an end in itself, however. It has to be the basis of further action: either to take action to ensure that missed targets are achieved in future or as the basis for the amendment of policy.

RESOURCES

If more sustainable policies are to be developed for our towns and our countryside, it will be essential to have earmarked financial resources available both to fund specific projects and to assist in paying compensation where appropriate. One potential source of such resources is for government to impose a tax on the increase in land value that arises from the granting of permission for development and to use the proceeds for environmental purposes. As suggested in Chapter 2, it seems entirely appropriate to use 'betterment' in this way, as it is physical development itself that causes so many environmental problems.

Vast amounts of money change hands when land is developed. A retailer may pay as much as £10 million for 2 hectares of farmland that has planning permission for a superstore. This enhanced value reflects the profit anticipated by the retailer, but it is considered by many people to belong to the community whose collective actions brought services and population near enough to the site to justify its development. The potential value of the land is only realised with the grant of planning permission. In the past 45 years three attempts to collect this betterment have been made, each to be abandoned by following governments mainly for political reasons. However, the different schemes were repudiated before there had been sufficient research to assess their full effects and to identify the causes of apparent land shortages.

At the other end of the economic scale, land values fall when land is abandoned, as, for example, in areas of industrial decline. Grants are given to reclaim such land. Industrial rehabilitation is desirable but it seems illogical to grant in aid the recovery of lost land values in derelict land while refusing to collect the enhanced value from developing land.

The 'polluter pays' principle has become a catchphrase of the sustainability debate. The aim is to make the instigator of environmental problems pay for the remedial action required to correct these problems. There is a debate, however, as to how the polluter should pay. One possibility is that the polluter should be directly responsible for the cost of remedial action. Another possibility is that the public sector should carry out remedial action, funded by taxation on the polluter.

Where the polluter is the developer of land, one obvious way of taxation is through a betterment levy, charged as a proportion of the increase in land value arising from the granting of planning permission. An alternative would be the levying of an 'impact fee'. This idea is currently being promoted as an alternative to the current system of negotiable planning gain agreements. The planning gain or impact fee arrangement has to date been intended to provide for public infrastructure provision, rather than for remedial environmental objectives. However, in principle, it could also be used for the latter purposes. In making a choice between the use of impact fees or betterment to fund environmental rehabilitation, our preference is for betterment. It is a 'real' value tested by the price at which the land changes hands. It is thus likely to be scaled according to the scale of the potential environmental impact caused by development.

However raised, the funds should not be treated as general taxation but as a fund to meet the costs of remedial environmental work and to compensate communities adversely affected by economic restructuring. Because restructuring is national in its repercussions, and because related shifts in land value are both regional and national, the fund will need to operate nationally and regionally. Nationally it would be able to support communities in transition and suffering the more acute forms of growth or decline. Regionally, support would be available for the development of public transport, energy efficiency in buildings and renewable resources.

Recommendation

Effective implementation requires the establishment of a Sustainable Land Development Fund, to be sourced from a betterment tax on the increase in land value that arises from the granting of planning permission. The fund should be used for environmental improvements and community compensation.

Two obvious problems arise from this suggestion. One is the question of the means by which monies from this fund are distributed; the other is the likely loss of Fund income – and hence loss of environmental protection – in times of recession. Some means can be devised to resolve both problems. Both would involve equalisation; one geographical and the other temporal. In the first case, it should be possible to devise a formula to switch funds from areas of high fund income to areas of severe environmental problems. In the second case, monies can be held back in high-yielding years to compensate for low income in years of economic recession.

The authors wish to acknowledge the help of Ray Green in the preparation of this chapter. Figures 9.1 and 9.3 to 9.9 were drawn by Heather Browning and Judith Fox.

10

Making it Happen
Ralph Rookwood

INTRODUCTION

In the course of one or two generations we have come to recognise that we live on a small finite planet in which all living things are part of complex inter-related ecosystems that are being disrupted at an increasing rate; what is more, these ecosystems may be fatally damaged by processes which act against nature instead of in harmony with it.

Many of these damaging processes are urban, or urban generated, and their conversion to environmentally acceptable standards raises some major 'town planning' issues. Even the agricultural and forestry practices which cause most environmental concern are largely aimed at supplying urban consumers.

There is no clear dividing line between the natural and the built environment when considering the processes that need to be reformed in order to achieve long-term sustainability. There is, however a division between those development processes which determine the shape and quality of our physical environment – whether in town or country locations – and those that do not. Our concern is with the former, and with the kind of planning necessary to create a sustainable physical framework for our increasingly urbanised society.

Throughout this report, therefore, the recommendations have been concerned with those development decisions which legislators and investors, developers and builders, and the relevant professional designers (architects, engineers and town planners) can influence and which they could help to become more 'environment friendly'. These are the decisions which the planning and building legislation and regulations help to shape and which will have to change if the objective of long-term viability is to be achieved.

The general evidence in Chapter 1, as in all reports since *The Limits to Growth* in 1972, is that the risks of failing to change our development habits is too great to be acceptable and that the increase in these risks is still outstripping our actions to reduce them. More radical action is needed. Such action must be more widespread, involve many more people, and be sustained at a high level for a long time just to reach the crucial turning point where risks start diminishing instead of worsening. The precautionary principle – 'taking action now where there are good grounds for judging either that action taken promptly...may avoid more costly damage later or that irreversible effects may follow if action is delayed[1] provides a key indicator for action.

The major changes that this will require in political and economic organisation are only beginning to be recognised. Of course, some welcome changes are already under way, both in politics and in industry, and the need for change is now more widely acknowledged than ever. But too many of the changes that are already taking place are relatively superficial and the rate of change is far too slow to achieve even the minimum targets for securing a viable long-term future. We still face the risk that a rather casual acceptance of 'thinking green', coupled with the adoption of comparatively minor measures introduced at a very leisurely pace, will be regarded as sufficient.

The government White Paper *This Common Inheritance* (1990) was a welcome first step but its message was weakened by its lack of clear priorities and the incongruity of mixing global doom with cathedral repairs and litter collection. Some of the physical planning proposals were welcome in themselves; but the serious environmentalist could justifiably view their total practical effect as the equivalent of rearranging the plant tubs on the decks of the *Titanic*. Although the Environmental Protection Act is already making some impact and promises some worthwhile achievements, a real sense of urgency is still lacking, as is any evidence of a comprehensive programme of action which seriously confronts the unprecedented rate of deterioration in the natural environment. 'Too little too late' is still a serious danger.

The next section therefore concentrates on a limited number of fundamental, but essential, changes in the political and economic framework for making decisions about the built environment. We regard these as the necessary prerequisites which society must adopt if our earlier detailed recommendations for change are to be implemented in the practical worlds of investment decisions, policy frameworks, planning strategies and financial evaluations.

Many of these, however, are necessarily more about tomorrow than today. What is equally important is to multiply rapidly the actions already successfully being taken within the existing framework. Some of the pioneers have been mentioned in previous chapters: they include enterprising local councils, far-sighted businesses, public spirited community groups, and the occasional central government department taking more than a legislative or regulatory role (see also Box 10.1). We therefore suggest in the later section entitled *'Preparing early action programmes'*, that all the principal bodies or interest groups that influence the reshaping of our physical environment should, without delay, prepare programmes of action within the existing planning framework to accelerate progress on environmental issues while the more fundamental changes needed for ultimate success are being worked out.

This chapter concludes with two further sections. The first proposes the construction of a number of demonstration projects to provide practical evidence of what can be done. The second, in the form of an epilogue, provides a feet-on-the-ground vision of what a sustainable community could be like in the fairly near future if best current practice plus the recommendations from this book were adopted.

TEN GENERAL 'RULES OF CONDUCT' FOR SUSTAINABLE DEVELOPMENT

RULE 1: FUNDAMENTAL CHANGES IN ATTITUDES

The most common concluding statement of many analyses and reports on this subject is a warning that a major change in attitudes is absolutely essential if environmental catastrophe is to be averted. Considering the importance attached to this, surprisingly little has been said about it. For example, whose attitudes are we discussing? Attitudes about what? What must be done to change attitudes?

We have therefore thought it right to start with these questions, presenting our initial attempt at some practical answers.

It is clear, of course, that the crucial objective is a change in *behaviour*, in particular a change from activities and processes that abuse the natural world to alternatives that respect its limitations. Our growing awareness of inhabiting 'only one earth' since the Stockholm Conference of 1972 has not yet been matched, twenty years later, by changes in our behaviour either as producers or consumers, on the scale and at the rate that is needed.

Since this general failure to respond is not due to any lack of specific and well-substantiated advice as to many of the actions required, the emphasis on the fundamental importance of a change in attitudes seems entirely justified.

BOX 10.1 A sustainable market town

In 1990, Eagle Star announced plans for a new market town at Micheldever Station in mid-Hampshire designed to satisfy the Brundtland definition of sustainable development, meeting the needs of the present without compromising the ability of future generations to meet their own needs. Specifically, the planners have addressed such issues as reducing road congestion and the need to travel; saving energy; minimising waste and pollution; enhancing the landscape; water conservation; ecology; quality in design and construction; and future management procedures.

A balanced and largely self-contained community is envisaged, comprising 5000 new homes of mixed sizes, types and tenure with jobs, shops, schools, open space, and health, sports and community facilities provided to meet the daily needs of local people. Travel will be minimised by ensuring that no home is more than half a mile from the town centre and school and no more than a mile from job opportunities. Attractive and direct cycleways and footpaths will help persuade people to leave their cars at home for local journeys, with bus services providing links to external rail, bus and coach services. Micheldever main-line railway station is in the centre of the proposed town. Development will be located so that cars can use spare capacity on local main roads without creating congestion; the internal road network would be designed to disperse traffic through the town.

A design code is being developed aimed at minimising energy consumption, especially in individual homes. The code will specify high insulation standards; low energy consumption appliances; and solar power and other renewable energy sources will be considered as supplementary power sources where practical. The planners are also investigating providing a district heating scheme, possibly using a combined heat and power system; one option under consideration is to fuel this with locally sourced straw as a bio-fuel.

The possibility is being considered of designing homes in a way that encourages waste sorting for separate collection in order to maximise recycling. In addition, commercial, retail and light industrial users of property in the town will be required to pursue a good practice recycling and waste minimisation code that will be enforced through covenants.

Centuries of intensive agricultural practice have diminished biodiversity in and around the Micheldever site. The plan for the new town envisages retaining the vast majority of trees and hedgerows of ecological value. But the planners also intend to develop new habitats for plants and wildlife as part of the master plan. Initiatives include the establishment of new native woodland, chalk grassland and aquatic features. These would be interlinked to form a network of green corridors throughout the market town and linking into the adjacent countryside. Crucially, a maintenance plan for new and retained habitats will be devised as part of the comprehensive management plan for the whole town.

This future management plan is designed to ensure that Micheldever station market town can be sustained for future generations. It would be based on a Town Trust which would enable residents to participate in the design of the community during the construction period. Public participation has already begun, with regular 'Focus Group' meetings held throughout Hampshire. Focus Group members represent the interests of more than 4300 Hampshire people who would like to live in the new market town and who hold 'Shire Certificates'. (These entitle the holder to be among the first to view or reserve a home in Micheldever.) Focus Groups are making a significant contribution to the planning process, with the proposals for sustainable development being a good example of that participation.

So far as urban development is concerned, the recommendations in the previous chapters constitute a further attempt to highlight the necessary changes in the way that we design, construct and use our physical framework for living. However, without a change in attitudes, it would be foolish to assume that these recommendations will be any more effective than the many that have preceded them.

But whose attitudes are we referring to? Although the answer should ideally be, to some extent, *everyone,* any concerted programme must be directed mainly at identified key groups of decision makers and opinion formers in industry and business, in central and local government, in the professions, in education and the media, and in the environmental pressure groups. The activation of enlightened individuals will, as always, be crucially important: a passionate personal advocate is worth more than any number of learned reports. But the advocate needs ammunition and a receptive climate of opinion.

BOX 10.2 The road to survival

'Until a realisation of the relationship between man and his environment has become part of our education and a principal basis of its orientation, a long-range improvement of land use is improbable. We must understand this relationship, sense it so deeply that it colours our feeling about children, country, laws, survival, foreign relations, and nearly every other thought and emotion we have...

'If we ourselves do not govern our destiny, firmly and courageously, no-one is going to do it for us. To regain ecological freedom for our civilization will be a heavy task. It will frequently require arduous and uncomfortable measures. It will cost considerable sums of money. Democratic governments are not likely to set forth on such a step and rocky path unless the people lead the way.'

Source William Sloane Associates (1948) *Road to Survival*

We must also recognise that attitude and behaviour are symbiotic and mutually reinforcing. Mere exhortation is not enough. Regulations, prices – anything that changes the relative costs and advantages of acting in certain ways – not only force a change in behaviour but also lead to important changes in attitude.

So what must be done to change attitudes? We *propose* a concerted programme in which the following would be key elements.

- *Environmental census and projections.* The government's decision to publish relevant statistics annually in an accessible form is a potentially valuable first step provided that:
  1. The basic data are actually being collected. Government cuts in recent years (such as the abolition of the Soil Survey) are incompatible with a commitment to provide an adequate range of meaningful data.
  2. Data are published by an independent body free from the influence of vested interests, whether political or industrial.
  3. Data are produced on a standard set of environmental indices so that trends and rates of change can be calculated.
  4. Current data are accompanied by projections showing the probable future if present trends continue.
- *Monitoring targets.* Having established a set of sustainability indices and targets (see Rule 3 below) to be publishing annually, monitoring should check:
  1. the extent to which targets are being achieved;

2. the factors either contributing to or impeding progress.

Central government, local government, and business enterprises above a certain size should all take part, perhaps competing for awards marking outstanding achievement.

- *An integrated education and publicity programme.* An organised programme for the production of educational materials at all levels, from primary schools to universities, should be commissioned (possibly by both the Economic and Social Research Council and the Science Research Council), coupled with the parallel production of television programmes and video tapes selling at subsidised prices to encourage widespread distribution and supported by government funding. Also included should be a Householder's Do-It-Yourself Manual. Local Environmental Information and Advice Centres should be established in all major towns to stimulate local interest and action.

  What must not be overlooked is that no such programme for creating a better-informed public can succeed without more open government and greater freedom of access to official information.

- *Publicising and rewarding major achievements.* Because the scale of the problems will discourage many people and the rate of progress will, at least initially, be disappointingly slow, it will be important to give high-profile recognition to schemes which have proved to be successful. Examples have been given elsewhere in this report of some successes in local government (see Chapter 2) and industry (see Chapter 7). Even so, there are good reasons for feeling pessimistic about our ability to change society enough and in time, with debilitating effects on our determination to take corrective action. The best antidote will be full awareness of successes already being achieved. National, regional and local awards made annually, with lively publicity in all the media, and with displays in the Environmental Information Centres will all help to create the groundswell of public opinion needed to develop programmes of action widespread enough to match the scale of the problems.

The other 'Rules of Conduct' outlined below will also make their contribution to changing attitudes through greater awareness and understanding, by requiring or inducing changes in behaviour which will in turn influence attitudes.

RULE 2: FACILITATING INNOVATION AND REPLICATING BEST PRACTICE

Disseminating current best practice and providing readily accessible technical information about actions that are both environmentally beneficial and profitable will not only be part of the 'changing attitudes' process but will also make a valuable contribution to the learning curve of implementors. While making current best practice the norm would lead to an enormous improvement on the present situation, a massive rethink in many fields will be required before the current environmental deterioration is reversed. Speeding up the rates of both innovation and replication will need to be a specific objective of both public policy and industrial strategy. Penalties for causing environmental damage, combined with positive incentives for developing new processes and more benign practices, are going to be needed as part of an intensive campaign over the next decade or two.

We *propose* that the relevant government departments – particularly the Departments of Trade and Industry, Environment and Transport but with positive support from the Treasury and the proposed new Environment Agency – should be directed to prepare Environmental Support Programmes involving the following:

- financial incentives to encourage energy saving, pollution abatement, waste reduction and recycling, including special allowances for environmental capital investment;

- tax penalties for environmentally damaging practices;
- financial support for pilot projects;
- funding for research, especially on ways of facilitating innovation and on counteracting factors which inhibit the spread of best practice.

RULE 3: ESTABLISHING SUSTAINABILITY INDICES AND SETTING TARGETS

Measuring and publicising regularly the extent to which quantifiable targets are being achieved will be an essential part of creating the managerial, political and public awareness on which adequate progress (in terms of both scale and rate) will depend. The question of what is adequate is not yet wholly defined but will undoubtedly mean first limiting the growth of and then reducing the major environmental risks to the global environment (for example, CO_2 emissions, losses of topsoil and forest cover, unrecycled wastes, river and sea pollution). For this purpose, more work will need to be done to establish indices for measuring improvements in sustainability and then adopting specific targets – at national, regional and local levels – to which action programmes and monitoring can be geared.

To some extent these targets are already being set through international negotiation and through the European Community, especially for those factors such as air and water pollution which are most prominent in crossing national boundaries. Some of these have implications for the built environment, at least indirectly, but it will be clear from the recommendations in earlier chapters that there are a number of more specific factors for which targets have yet to be set.

As part of the general process of 'think globally, act locally', it would be useful to consider how these relate to some general indices for measuring improvements in sustainability. For this, we have followed the lead given in the recently published guide to sustainable development *Defending the Future*,[1] adapting its proposals to the particular focus of this report. Our approach has been to select those indices which relate most directly to the major threats to the global environment and which are capable of regular measurement. Taken as a group, these should enable any country to assess whether the sum total of all the measures being taken by all the agencies involved is sufficient to make a positive contribution to global environmental health. Our proposed general indices are given under five headings corresponding to the basic goals of sustainable development set out in Chapter 1. This list is not intended to be comprehensive; the selection includes the most significant indicators of progress, concentrating on those directly or indirectly influenced by changes in the way we handle physical development, building standards and urban design.

The use of energy and materials ('conservation of resources') goal

- Reductions in per capita consumption of specified scarce resources, particularly materials used in all forms of construction.
- Reduction in the proportion of non-renewable energy usage in the primary production of building materials and in the construction and maintenance of buildings.
- Increasing investment, and related tax incentives, in technologies:
  1. which replace non-renewable forms of energy by renewables.
  2. which improve energy efficiency or reduce waste and pollution.
- Increasing the proportion of passenger miles travelled by public transport.
- Decreasing the length of average daily journeys (for work, shopping and leisure).

Ecological processes and environmental worth ('enhancing environmental quality' goal)

- Reductions in the total volumes of waste requiring disposal.
- Increasing the proportion of waste being recycled into usable products.
- Improving the balance between the rate of usage and the rate of replacement of key renewable resources.
- Reductions in the production of major air and water pollutants.
- Increases in area of diversified mature forest.
- Increases in areas of biological diversity protected and available for future use.
- Increasing price differentials so as to discourage environmentally damaging consumption and encourage more environmentally benign consumption.

Balance between the built and natural environments ('balanced development' goal)

- Reductions in the rate of expansion of urbanised areas.
- Increases in the proportion of green open space and the number of trees in urban areas.
- Increases in the number and extent of areas covered by Nature Conservation Orders protecting vegetation in areas of wildlife interest or importance.

Society and culture ('social equity' goal)

- Reduction in the number of people suffering a degraded quality of daily living environment.
- Reducing the differential in resource consumption between the profligate rich and the needy poor to offset the unavoidable increase in consumption resulting from improving the living standards of the most deprived, while reducing the average consumption of the population as a whole.
- Greater equality in the incidence of the costs and benefits of resource conservation and pollution control.
- Long-term costs and benefits (those borne by future generations) are given greater weight relative to short-term costs and benefits in the calculation of development profitability.

Policy, economics and institutions ('personal and political participation' goal)

- Reduction in the number of decisions affecting the local environment taken without the active involvement of those whose living conditions are affected.
- Increasing the number of local initiatives to achieve sustainability objectives by local government, local businesses and community groups.

Regular reports containing the relevant statistics for each of these general indices for measuring progress will be important for informing everyone concerned about the success or otherwise of the policies and programmes adopted in pursuit of more sustainable forms of development. However this *post hoc* account of achievements up to the present is not in itself a management tool for organising the work ahead. For that purpose, sets of specific targets for the periods ahead will be needed.

RULE 4: MAXIMISING SCOPE FOR INITIATIVES AT ALL LEVELS

The urgency of moving quickly in the changeover to sustainability requires increased action at all levels. The following issues all need to be actively explored and promoted:

- community involvement,
- decentralisation,
- positive incentives,
- removal of institutional and fiscal barriers,
- the creation of policy and administrative frameworks conducive to the achievement of sustainability objectives.

In order to get things moving at both global and local levels there must be some institutional reorganisation, with the centralised nation-state ceding powers upwards to international organisations and downwards to regional and local bodies.

In particular, much greater freedom and positive encouragement for local initiatives is an urgent necessity in Britain, where increasing over-centralisation of government, industry and finance is inhibiting action. In Chapter 2 we have referred to the initiatives already being taken by the more progressive local authorities even within the constraints currently imposed on them. The potential for a major expansion of worthwhile action at this level is clearly there, provided that central government follows up its statements of general principle with more positive encouragement.

We endorse the words of the Prince of Wales when he said in London (March 1991):

> *We can all too easily get caught up in global negotiations whilst forgetting that people need to be free to pursue sustainable development for themselves. The reconciliation of environmental protection with economic advance essentially comes down to a mass of local problems. These all add up to global issues, but the solutions are local. Providing the right conditions for solutions at the local level is the challenge for governments.*

In pursuit of this objective, we *propose* the following:

- central government to give a specific remit to local government to adopt as standard practice sustainability principles into all operations, particularly with regard to reducing energy consumption, waste disposal and recycling, pollution control, and greening of the local environment;
- central government to exempt local government expenditure for these purposes from its calculations of spending limits;
- local government to encourage a strong community involvement at all stages of developing policies and practices in environmental matters;
- local authorities to encourage the setting-up of partnership schemes for sustainability with community groups, schools, interested industrialists and businesses, and statutory undertakers;
- local authorities to stimulate continuing local debate about these issues, through community centres, youth organisations and schools;
- major national industries and businesses, including the privatised utilities, to be encouraged to co-operate with local government in these changes and to promote decentralised initiatives within their own organisations;
- as part of any proposals for the reorganisation of local government, the provision of suitable machinery to ensure that major developments having regional environmental impacts are located and designed so as to comply fully with sustainable development criteria.

RULE 5: REDEFINING 'GROWTH' IN TERMS OF 'QUALITY OF LIFE'

There are serious doubts that economic growth (at least as currently measured) is compatible with sustainability. However, it is also possible to argue that growth is essential for making the very changes on which sustainability depends. Like other black and white arguments which obscure reality, the concept of growth needs breaking down and examining in order to establish what kinds of growth are beneficial and improve the quality of life and what kinds of growth are positively harmful, either to personal lives or to the environment. Growth in road accidents or in the number of sick requiring medical care are not signs of a better society, yet the money spent on both contributes to the Gross Domestic Product (GDP).

We know that GDP is a seriously flawed and misleading measure because it counts 'bads' as well as 'goods', yet this is the measure that is always used to tell us whether or not we are 'progressing'. As a result, environmentally necessary changes such as stronger pollution controls are sometimes resisted on the grounds that they would impede the growth of GDP. We need to follow the lead already taken by a growing number of economists – such as The Other Economic Summit – in recent years and by some international organisations in establishing a set of measures which indicate improvements in the quality of life and which could replace GDP as our measure of progress. We would then be in a much more informed position to judge whether 'growth in good living' is compatible with long-term viability and a sustainable global ecology.

These would not, of course, measure the production of those things needed to assist our conversion to more sustainable forms of development. But then neither does GDP. It is likely that, in addition to a composite 'quality of life' index, we will need a further composite index which tells us whether we are expanding our total national output of goods and services produced in conformity with sustainability principles and/or which improve our capacity to live and work in a sustainable way.

The defining of these composite indices to replace GDP is beyond the scope of this report, but we have no doubt of its fundamental importance in resolving the apparent conflict between economic growth and sustainable development.

We therefore *propose* that, as part of its programme for adopting better environmental practices, the government should commission a review of current work on these issues to identify any further research that may be necessary and to produce an alternative to GDP as a measure of national progress.

Ideally, of course, such an alternative should be agreed internationally, since comparative national performance in terms of GDP is well established as a measure of how well or badly government policies are thought to be working. Any work along these lines should therefore have strong international links and might well be best organised under the joint auspices of the United Nations Environment Programme and the United Nations Development Programme, or by an independent body such as the International Institute for Environment and Development.

RULE 6: REDEFINING 'COSTS' AND 'PROFITABILITY'

The basis for adequately reflecting externalities (including long-term ones) in costs before assessing comparative profitability will require further thought, leading to changes in accounting practices and taxation criteria. Pearce[3] has made a start and the 'polluter pays' principle is being accepted as a legitimate idea, if not yet much practised. But sustainability will require recognition of other damaging practices not resulting in direct pollution. For example, the use of timber from non-sustainable logging operations which poses as much of a threat to our future as the more obvious discharge of non-assimilable effluents.

Taxable allowances and other financial incentives and penalties will need to be mobilised as part of the general campaign to discourage waste and encourage recycling, to discriminate in favour of closed-cycle processes, and to penalise the use of non-renewable resources wherever renewables are potential alternatives. A useful start has been made by the government (see *This Common Inheritance*, Annex A) on research into appropriate economic instruments, but a more vigorous pursuit on a wider front is necessary if the opposition of vested interests and conventional wisdom is to be overcome.

It is encouraging that some businesses have already found that the adoption of waste-reduction measures can add to profitability, and that pollution-control processes can produce marketable products, and that some local authorities have found ways of reducing waste-collection and disposal costs through organised recycling programmes. The fact that progress is already being made without special financial incentives is a good reason for moving quickly in the use of fiscal measures designed to increase the profitability of environmentally benign processes and thus to help accelerate progress to a level more commensurate with the need.

We therefore *propose*:

1. That immediate steps be taken for setting up schedules of charges for a selected list of the major pollutants and the major non-renewable resources as a basis for levying at the earliest possible date:
   – penalties for polluters
   – penalties for use of non-renewable resources to create a financial advantage from using renewable alternatives.
2. That the relevant research councils should be provided with extra funds for commissioning studies on:
   – the adjustment of accounting norms regarding the time-scales for depreciation and for much longer-term returns on investments (especially on physical infrastructure)
   – financial incentives and pilot projects for conversion of industrial processes to those compatible with long-term sustainability.

In one way or another, these are all to do with redefining profits, which is likely to be even more influential than redefining growth in adapting balance sheets to support the kind of investment decisions compatible with sustainability criteria.

RULE 7: LONGER-TERM PLANNING AND BUILDING HORIZONS

Ideas about what time-scales are realistic will have to change drastically from the short-termism which has become increasingly common in recent years. Forward planning for between 30 and 150 years is being seriously urged, at least for certain purposes such as depreciation, frequency of capital replacement, and the return on certain investments. Equally, the balance of advantage between redevelopment and the refurbishment of existing buildings is bound to be affected, as are design and construction standards, if ideas about the normal life-span of buildings are to be appreciably extended.

The implications for consumption of scarce materials need to be more influential in such decisions, as well as the implications for total energy consumption. The proposals under Rule 6 for redefining profits would, of course, have an important effect here. But we also need to be clearer about the potential contribution of both building design (see Chapter 6) and town design (see Chapter 9) so that we are not only being pushed by finance but also led by design standards aimed at long-term sustainability.

Much progress has already been made, particularly on the energy efficiency of buildings, but much less is known about the implications of a radically extended life-cycle for buildings. The implications of adopting a much longer time-scale for town design and for the physical planning process generally have hardly begun to be explored.

We therefore *propose* that studies should be carried out by both the planning and the building design professions, together with the building industry and the relevant research institutions, aimed at producing conclusions and recommendations within two years as to the design implications of adopting long-term objectives for buildings and urban areas compatible with sustainable development criteria.

RULE 8: CONTINUITY OF POLICY AND FRAMEWORKS FOR DECISION MAKING

The points made above about longer financial horizons and long-life design criteria have their equivalents in the fields of politics and administration. Our need to develop a fundamental shift in perspective about time-scales and our treatment of the environment will be frustrated without substantial continuities in policy which transcend electoral cycles and political differences. What is needed are some consistent 'rules of the environmental game' which can gradually be absorbed as a daily living code affecting all decisions which are environmentally significant, whatever the (inevitable) variations within the rules as to how the game is currently being played.

The adrenalin of political confrontation will have to give way to some measure of consensus, at least about the more critical environmental imperatives. Government budgetary horizons, Treasury rules, even electoral systems, may all need to change to facilitate longer-term planning ahead, as well as more consistency of approach. Short-term *ad hoc* decision making is simply not compatible with sustainability, and the political/administrative implications of this need to be worked out.

Happily, public opinion surveys indicate that some greater measure of common ground among the major political parties would be welcomed. However, the difficulties standing in the way of such a fundamental change in the conduct of public affairs are formidable. The inertia of conventional wisdom and ingrained conventions and procedures in administration, and the traditions of political life, all constitute a hurdle that will be extremely difficult to surmount. Except in response to an extreme and immediate threat – such as that posed by a major war – changes normally only come slowly. Week by week, it is becoming more certain that the environmental crisis which faces us is just as extreme as a major military attack: but the immediacy is yet to be felt by many. How then to achieve the radical change in public administration that is required?

It seems likely that, in Britain, a frontal attack on the administrative and political barriers to a sustained environmental strategy would be defeated by the vested interests committed to maintaining the status quo. It is true that government spokespeople have stated that the government's general commitment to 'green' principles is intended to penetrate all departments and be taken into account in all policies. However, there is no evidence so far of a willingness to contemplate fundamental changes of the kind discussed here. We believe that much stronger pressure will have to be exerted. Where could such pressure come from?

It seems to us that it will need the combined forces of the following:

- international pressures of the kind now demanding agreement on measures to combat global warming;
- internal popular and political pressure generated by the application of the 'rules of conduct' outlined above, which should lead to a better informed public that is more aware of both the needs and the possibilities.

However, such pressures will no doubt have to be accompanied by some more rigorous and formal investigation into the detailed changes that would have to be made to permit the adoption of the long-term policies, implementation programmes and budgets that are crucial to success.

We therefore *propose* that there should be a Royal Commission on Procedures for Implementing Long-term Environmental Strategies, drawing on the best available knowledge about both the theory and practice of budgeting and decision making, and the relationships between central and local government, directed to study and make recommendations about what changes would best facilitate greater long-term continuity in the implementation of environmental policies to achieve sustainable development.

RULE 9: ENVIRONMENTAL STANDARDS, CAPACITY LIMITS, AND IMPACT ASSESSMENTS

Experience has already shown that, while voluntary standards are useful, progress is speeded up when governments impose standards to which private businesses and public authorities can respond without suffering competitive disadvantage or being stalled by institutional inertia. The profound effect on motor vehicle design worldwide in response to the California state legislation on exhaust emissions is a striking example in the environment field.

The making of progress towards quantified targets, referred to earlier, will be partly dependent on the setting of progressively more stringent standards of environmental performance, covering a wider range of factors than hitherto. Such standards must be national, operated by an independent body with sufficient powers and resources to enable prompt investigation of any breaches of environmental standards and able to secure early remedial action. We believe that the effectiveness of such a body will depend on it operating with a strongly decentralised regional structure, since the regions are the areas within which major environmental impacts can best be assessed; regional administration is also close enough to local government to establish effective working relationships with local environmental control staff.

If, however, more stringent standards of environmental performance simply result in each individual source producing less pollution while the number of polluting sources is growing, the result may still be a damaging growth in the total volume of pollutants. A clear example is air pollution from motor vehicles, where the growth in the number of vehicles is adding more pollution than is being saved through cleaner exhausts. A current proposal for a huge sludge-burning plant along the Thames estuary illustrates the same point: local environmental health officials are confident that the plant can be designed to perform much more cleanly than the most stringent standards would require but the throughput will be so great that the total load of pollutants affecting the sub-region would be seriously increased.

It is clear, therefore, that, in addition to reducing pollution from existing sources through the setting of more stringent standards, there must also be controls to ensure that the total load of pollutants is, first, prevented from growing and then progressively reduced. We need to establish the concept of environmental capacity limits which must not be exceeded. This is, of course, the concept behind the international agreements to stabilise CO_2 emissions from the major industrialised nations by 2000. In practice, this means that there will need to be regional emission limits to ensure that new development within a region does not create a net increase in the total load of pollutants. This would mean, for example, that the sludge-burning plant mentioned above would only be permitted if the developers could provide for a reduction in pollutants elsewhere in the region sufficient to offset the output from their own operations.

The combination of stricter emission standards for individual existing plants plus the 'no net increase' rule for new ones would gradually result in reducing the stress on the natural environment, and might even do so rapidly enough to deflect the present negative trends before they reach the critical point of no return. Anything less seems doomed to failure.

Although control of pollution may be the most urgent single issue for immediate action, long-term viability also requires action to deal with the other major environmental impacts. These include the problems posed by waste collection and disposal, waste reduction and closed-cycle processes, and the substitution of non-renewables by renewables (bearing in mind that this will also make an important contribution to easing pollution problems). Appropriate environmental standards will also be required for each of these.

BOX 10.3 High-level environmental assessments

'At present...EIA procedures are required only for individual projects. We are however in the process of putting forward proposals for a new Directive which will require assessments to be included at a higher tier in the decision-making process, that is, during policy making, plan and programme planning. This *strategic environmental assessment*, as we are calling it, will aim to ensure that new developments are sustainable within the ecological and global context.

'The need to integrate environmental considerations into policy, plan and programme formulation has long been recognised by the Commission. Decision makers within the member states have also begun to realise that it is more appropriate to prevent environmental impacts at pre-project stage, prevention being better than cure. We believe that higher-level environmental assessment raises the importance of environmental considerations to that of other aspects of development, such as financial and technological concerns. This would encourage decision makers to take into account environmental goals along with social and economic aims.

'For example, using an alternative mode of transport could not be considered in an EIA of a new road link, since this would no longer be a realistic alternative as the decision has already been made to build a road. Likewise, the use of an alternative energy source could not be considered during a nuclear power generation plan inquiry. However, the environmental implications of different modes of transport or energy sources can be considered at policy or plan level during a strategic environmental assessment.'

Source Laurens J Brinkhorst, Director-General for Environment, Nuclear Safety and Civil Protection, Commission of the European Communities (speaking at the Annual Conference of the TCPA, November 1990)

An important issue in relation to this, and one that is particularly relevant to the built environment, is the question of environmental impact assessments. It is clear that these must be more widely applied in Britain as part of a more comprehensive programme of environmental measures. Developments within the European Community will, in any case, require this to be done. The proposal by Brinkhorst (see Box 10.3) for 'higher-level' environmental assessments at the pre-project policy and plan-making stages indicates the scope of action that is probably required.

The question remains as to where the responsibility is to be placed for ensuring that the whole range of targets related to long-term sustainable development objectives is being achieved. For this purpose, we *propose* that there should be a single national body, with its independence and terms of reference established by statute, responsible for preparing and revising as necessary – and in accordance with the government's overall environmental policies – a coherent set of national objectives for waste and recycling, pollution and non-renewable resource substitution. These objectives would incorporate: environmental performance standards; environmental capacity limits; and requirements for environmental impact assessments. This organisation would also be responsible for reporting annually on how these objectives were being met. Whether the new Environmental Protection Agency proposed by the government will have a sufficiently wide remit to be able to undertake this role remains to be seen.

We also *propose* that the practical job of actually achieving these objectives through the enforcement of standards and through the approval processes for new development should be organised and co-ordinated at the regional level, with appropriate arrangements for involving both the environmental health staff of local authorities and the development control staff of the reformed environmental planning process described in Chapter 9.

RULE 10: DIVERSIONARY FINANCE FOR LONG-TERM SURVIVAL

Our national defence budget, in the military sense, is very big in absolute terms and also accounts for an unusually large proportion of the total national budget. Although sometimes criticised, it is nevertheless generally accepted as necessary for national security. The realisation is now growing that the adverse world environmental trends pose just as big a threat to our national security and it is legitimate to argue that the financing of environmental defence will have to be given the same kind of status as our traditional defence budget in terms of having a high priority claim on our financial resources.

However, even the military budget has to be justified in relation to other competing claims and the financing of necessary environmental measures will be no exception. Where is the money to come from, remembering that there is widespread agreement that the critical 'make or break' period is that up to the year 2010, with the next ten years vital for establishing a major acceleration in the rate at which environmental protection measures are made effective?

We believe that an important principle to be used in identifying potential environmental funding is what we have called the 'diversionary principle'. By this we mean the deliberate diversion of money from activities or processes which are environmentally damaging to ones which are environmentally or ecologically essential for our long-term security. A good example is the diversion of money from road building (with its consequent encouragement of increased air pollution) to public transport infrastructure. Other examples might include more resources for rail and fewer for air travel, more for better insulation and energy-saving equipment with fewer for power stations, more for waste reduction and fewer for waste disposal, and more for electric power generation from renewable sources and fewer for nuclear. And since we are talking about national survival, it is only right that the government should reassess whether our future would be better protected with one less Trident submarine and the money spent instead on shielding the natural world from further damage. The potential savings from even these few examples are enormous and would support a big expansion in essential environmental safeguards.

In view of the severity of the environmental risks ahead, some diversion of funds away from some familiar but essentially trivial expenditures would quickly answer the question 'Can we afford these changes?' One has only to look at the huge sums spent annually on luxuries and non-essentials to be quite clear that there is no truth in the view that resources on the required scale are not available. Changing priorities may well be painful (as well as being dependent on changing attitudes, as discussed earlier), but there is no absolute shortage of finance to prevent action on the scale required.

There is one further point concerning affordability which is of great significance. As Parry has pointed out,[4] 'examples abound of doing better with less'. The industrial leaders that are investing in more energy-efficient, less waste-producing processes are finding valuable savings and potentially increased profits as a result of adopting more ecologically sound methods. For example, the London Borough of Sutton has been spending somewhat more per tonne on its waste recycling and waste reduction programmes than on conventional collection and landfill disposal but the gap is closing and it expects soon to be matching conventional costs and then under cutting them as landfill costs rise. To be frightened by statements anticipating major price increases as a consequence of adopting environmentally benign processes cannot be justified by the accumulating experience so far. The initial investment required for making changes must be found, and in some industries the sums are very large. But the prospect of future savings, and of future profits, is proving sufficient in an increasing number of cases to justify the added initial expenditure.

We *propose* that studies be put in hand at an early date by the Department of the Environment to identify those areas in which the diversionary financing principle could be applied, where public expenditure on environmentally damaging activities could be switched to activities which conform to its general environmental objectives. The Department should then make proposals for changing investment priorities accordingly.

We also *propose* that a special Environmental Conversion Assistance Fund be established for the purpose of making grants or loans to small businesses who do not have the capital resources needed to convert their operations so as to be more energy efficient, produce less waste, recycle more or use closed-cycle methods.

DEMONSTRATION PROJECTS

SUSTAINABLE NEW COMMUNITIES

To achieve maximum impact on the public imagination and understanding, a complete new settlement designed on wholly sustainable lines and displaying the very best of current practice could be of great value. We believe that the most dramatic demonstration of the possibilities would be achieved by building at least one, and preferably several, new communities embodying the best of known technologies and design; such developments could also provide an opportunity for extending these and trying out new ideas and technologies without the constraints that will inevitably limit what can be done by adapting existing towns.

The long history in this country of planning and building new communities to serve a variety of purposes has been the subject both of praise and of controversy about objectives, about design, and about the quality of life so provided. But public attention has tended to concentrate on some particular issue currently in dispute, such as 'New Town blues' or 'prairie planning'; this has often obscured the scale of the overall achievement. Yet 2 million people in Great Britain now live in one or other of the 28 New Towns built in the 47 years since the approval by Parliament of the New Towns Act in 1946. In spite of some disappointments and mistakes – inevitable while learning how best to proceed – there is now good evidence of the social and financial success of the New Towns. The scale of their contribution to postwar needs for a large increase in good quality housing and modern premises for business activities to provide an improved living and working environment is a matter of simple fact.

Also a matter of simple fact is the huge unmet need which still exists for additional housing (between 2 and 3 million according to published official figures) which current building programmes, even without the current recession, cannot possibly meet. The closing down of the New Towns programme, the severe cuts in council house building which have never been matched by an equivalent increase in private construction or housing association activity, have together resulted in a large gap between demand and supply.

Once the current slump in the construction industry and the economy generally is corrected, there will therefore have to be another spurt in building activity of all kinds, within which new communities could once again play an important role. This will be a unique opportunity to ensure that the necessary environmental standards (for energy saving, conserving scarce resources, limiting pollution and providing more efficient transport) are applied from the beginning to the whole of a community. This is the context in which we are proposing that there should be at least one new community, and preferably several in different regions, commissioned as a demonstration project. No amount of writing and talking can be as effective in changing attitudes and improving standards generally as a practical example in which theory is tested and opportunities provided for experiment and for generating new ideas.

We therefore *propose* that, as an important contribution to the achievement of the government's 'green' policies, land should be acquired under the New Towns Act for the construction of several new communities in areas of housing shortage in order to demonstrate and to further the practical application of the sustainable development principles described in this report.

It should be noted that some valuable work has already been carried out and published on the location, design and financing of new communities, as part of the TCPA/Rowntree Foundation New Communities Competition held in 1990–1.

SUSTAINABLE URBAN RENEWAL

In addition to creating new communities, it is important that there should be urban renewal projects to demonstrate the application of sustainable development principles to existing urban areas. For many decades ahead, most people will still be living within existing built-up areas and adequate progress cannot be made towards vital environmental objectives unless these areas also become less wasteful of energy, less polluting of air and water, more 'nature friendly', more effective in recycling materials, and much more environmentally efficient in their transport systems. It is not enough to ensure that every major new development is built to meet high environmental standards. It is also crucial that the steady but fragmented replacement and refurbishment of existing buildings is also carried out to high environmental standards.

We therefore *propose* that all major urban authorities should be encouraged to designate selected urban renewal schemes in which there would be the maximum use of techniques for improving environmental performance short of total rebuilding, with appropriate government assistance in the form of grants and tax exemptions to assist the owners and developers involved. The standards achieved would generally be less than in completely new communities. However, the total contribution to national targets would be greater, provided that all urban renewal was carried out to the best practicable standards. The purpose of the demonstration projects would be to lead the way, providing the evidence necessary for inducing more widespread adoption.

PREPARING EARLY ACTION PROGRAMMES

It is not surprising that earlier chapters have contained so many recommendations for action on such a wide variety of fronts. Our growing understanding of the need to stop abusing the natural world clearly calls for fundamental rethinking at all levels about the future development of our increasingly industrialised and urbanised societies and about our current operating practices. Action programmes are therefore bound to be multi-faceted: the steps already taken – from Stockholm in 1972 to Rio de Janeiro in 1992 – demonstrate the many difficulties in trying to make sure that all our sectoral policies (energy, transport, building, urban form and so on) are compatible with each other and are all pulling in the same direction.

Conditions are ripe for confusion and delay, yet time is not on our side. All the analyses of trends, rates of change and critical thresholds, while not agreeing on all details, have one important message: early action is essential to reverse the most damaging trends if we are to be reasonably sure of not passing the point of no return, the point beyond which environmental catastrophe becomes inevitable.

In these circumstances, we *propose* that everyone who has any responsibility for, or influence on, the design or management of our physical environment should draw up without delay an Early Action Programme aimed at reversing the trends that now threaten the ecological health of the planet. Taking the action programmes as a whole, certain basic principles should apply:

1. Action should start without delay. Our knowledge is incomplete and is likely to remain so. But there are enough areas where scientific and technical knowledge is sufficient to indicate actions to minimise known dangers and where delay awaiting absolute certainty carries a much bigger risk. Some actions should be selected because they have the potential to produce early results in response to urgent problems; others because the time-scale is such that, although the target is more distant, action must start soon to avoid passing the point of no return.
2. Everyone needs to be involved; problems and solutions are so interconnected, and time-scales now so short, that complementary action on all fronts seems essential for success. In all organisations (whether government or business) where major spending and investment decisions are made, this means the adoption of a basic corporate philosophy which gives 'environmental health' equal status with conventional measures such as efficiency or profitability.
3. Additional resources will be required. Initially at least, extra costs will be incurred to make possible the necessary changes; this investment, however, will be made for conventional reasons – to avoid danger, to secure future savings, and to create a better future. It should be possible to attract the necessary popular and political support to provide the necessary funds to protect the world's natural ecosystems (which constitute our own life-support system). After all, considerable resources are currently devoted to purposes that are much less esential.

It would be helpful if these Early Action Programmes specifically addressed the five goals of sustainable development set out in Chapter 1. For this purpose the goals may be restated as:

GOAL 1: CONSERVATION OF RESOURCES

– Maintenance of a continuing supply of resources for future generations
– Efficient use of non-renewable energy and mineral resources and recycling
– Development of renewable alternatives
– Protection of biological diversity.

GOAL 2: BUILT DEVELOPMENT IN HARMONY WITH THE NATURAL ENVIRONMENT

– Minimising the consumption of energy and scarce natural resources
– Maintaining the productivity of land
– Buildings designed for long life, adaptability, and low resource consumption
– Form and location of human settlements to minimise adverse impacts on nature
– More energy-efficient and less polluting transport systems.

GOAL 3: PROTECTION OF ENVIRONMENTAL QUALITY

- Avoidance or reform of processes that pollute or degrade air, water and soil
- Restoration of areas degraded or grossly polluted
- Protecting and enhancing the regenerative capacity of the land
- Elimination of processes that endanger human health
- Safeguarding the integrity and continuity of natural ecosystems.

GOAL 4: SOCIAL EQUITY AS BETWEEN INDIVIDUALS, SOCIETIES AND GENERATIONS

- Devising patterns of trade, aid and investment that diminish inequalities
- Reducing extremes of wealth and poverty which inhibit environmental care
- Restraining the rich and powerful from unsustainable resource exploitation
- Encouraging forms of economic development that reduce social inequality.

GOAL 5: CHANGING VALUES AND ATTITUDES THROUGH PARTICIPATION IN ENVIRONMENTAL DECISIONS

- Developing greater sharing of responsibility among all levels of decision making, from local to international
- Encouraging and empowering local initiatives to achieve sustainability goals
- Promoting more widespread knowledge about environmental problems and the actions needed to counteract them.

In preparing the Integrated Environmental Plans proposed in Chapter 9, county and district authorities will need to take into account the Action Programmes prepared by other bodies. It is important that the various programmes reinforce each other and contribute to common objectives. But, because early action is necessary, it is vital that neither should be delayed pending preparation of the other. Closer co-ordination between IEPs and Action Programmes will have to evolve in the light of experience and as ways are gradually found – through careful monitoring of results – of creating the most effective relationship between plans and implementation.

There have been similar pleas for early action before and it is worrying that these have largely gone unheeded. Vested interests have no doubt contributed to this, but it would seem that sheer inertia has been even more important. Most of us, both individually and collectively, have not been sufficiently motivated to make the necessary changes. So there remains a fundamental need to identify and use 'levers of change' powerful enough, and pervasive enough, to induce a decisive break-away from long-established means of doing things. With this in mind, we *propose* that every early action programme should contain measures to bring the following motivating factors into play:

- *Awareness* both of problems and solutions. While it is true that awareness of environmental issues has been gradually growing, it needs to become more widespread and more specific in terms of what is doing the most damage, what is the time-scale for taking corrective action, and what the effects of various changes would be. We cannot always have a London or Los Angeles smog to dramatise the dangers, but it should be possible to demonstrate 'if present trends continue' scenarios vividly enough to stimulate demands for early action.
- *Current costs*: In industrialised money economies, differentials in prices are clearly prime motivators, hence the 'polluter pays' proposals and the necessity to

anticipate changes in charging regimes to encourage fuel economy, to favour renewable sources of energy and raw materials, to reduce travel distances, and the other essential measures recommended elsewhere in this report. Since we are all conditioned to minimise current costs, adjusting cost differentials to serve environmental ends should be a prime motivating factor built into every action programme. Of course, such shifts should be applied incrementally to ease the consequential changes, with compensating provisions where necessary to ensure that the impact on individual living standards is not inequitable.

- *Future savings/profits*: Investment today to secure future savings or to generate future profits is common practice for both individual households and business firms. However, such investment depends on sufficient funds being available after current needs are met. To be effective in achieving sustainability objectives, many of the proposals in this report will necessarily affect most households and businesses, many of whom will not have the additional funds required. So necessary financial help – whether in the form of loans, grants, tax concessions or other financial inducements – will need to be built into the action programmes.

Epilogue

A Vision of a Sustainable Community: The Moderley Example

Ralph Rookwood

A story of an imaginary town where the political will was found to apply sustainability principles to the design and operation of buildings, utilities, parks and transport. The town becomes famous as a demonstration of how to change attitudes and create a much more enjoyable living environment while safeguarding the future.

Having become genuinely worried about global warming, acid rain and toxic wastes and convinced that big rises in fuel costs were soon coming, Joan Garnett had experienced several shifts in mood.

First, a feeling of being a helpless victim of major forces beyond her ability to influence, much less control. Second, a growing irritation that officials and national and local politicians were more talk than action. Third, a growing suspicion that such action as was being taken was trivial and ineffective. Fourth, frustration that, although she was reading more and more often about good examples of successful waste recycling, energy saving and similar schemes, nothing much was happening in her own town. Finally, a growing conviction that only if everyone who claimed to be concerned, including herself, became actively involved in taking action wherever possible was any progress going to be made.

That was ten years ago and it was hard now for any newcomer to believe that ten years earlier things had been so different. Joan Garnett was now chairperson of Moderley Council's Sustainable Development Committee. The council was run by a coalition of environmentally minded people from the three main political parties who, not always without difficulty, were willing to moderate their philosophical differences in order to implement a programme of environmental protection under the popular slogans 'Think global, act local' and 'Protect the future, benefit now'. The results were now clear to see.

It had taken a while to gather any momentum. It was only when the international agreements to speed up the reduction in emissions of CO_2, SO_2 and NOx, coupled with 'polluter pays' penalties for exceeding the new and more stringent standards, had resulted in big increases in the costs of heating, electricity and travel that people generally began to start wanting to turn awareness into local action. Even then, the normal bureaucratic delays almost certainly would have stifled local initiatives if the old central government controls over local spending and local programmes had remained in force.

Happily, although the major objectives of those pressing for constitutional reform and the strengthening of local democracy had only been partially achieved, the government had agreed that expenditure by local authorities designed to reduce pollution and waste disposal problems should be excluded from local government spending limits. This boost to local initiatives, coupled with the stricter standards set by the newly formed national Environmental Protection Agency, gave councils such as Moderley the opportunity they needed.

The local priorities were clear. *Environmentally* they were:

- to reduce air pollution (motor vehicle exhausts; excessive emissions from such sources as industry, power stations and hospitals; methane from waste tips);
- to reduce ground-water pollution from industry, waste tips and agriculture;

- to reduce environmental damage from road traffic;
- to increase the recovery of usable materials for recycling;
- to protect and strengthen 'nature' within the urban scene;
- to create a lively community awareness and involvement in improving the local environment while also contributing to international programmes to protect the planet.

Financially the priorities were:

- to stop the growth in waste disposal costs (council budget);
- to reduce heating and electricity costs (council, business and household budgets);
- to reduce transport costs and improve the viability of public transport (council and household budgets);
- to strengthen the local economy by increasing the use of local suppliers, thereby reducing transport demand and supporting local employment.

The council's Environmental Audit had identified the major sources of pollution, the major avoidable wastes and the most promising opportunities for conserving energy. Wherever possible, when professional or scientific skills were not essential, the audit had involved local citizens, community groups and schoolchildren as part of the deliberate policy of encouraging active public participation. The initial scepticism was fairly quickly overcome when the council produced its first programme, committing itself to investments designed to produce early benefits and cash savings, together with a less endangered future.

It helped that the council could quote the example of other authorities who were already successfully implementing similar programmes in other parts of the country. The idea of matching – and perhaps bettering – existing 'best practice' proved an appealing one. The council was therefore well placed to respond to the Environmental Protection Agency's new scheme, launched jointly with the Local Authority Associations, for annual awards to those councils achieving the best progress in meeting or exceeding the new environmental standards.

Perhaps the most encouraging result of the council's initiatives was the change in public psychology away from the fatalistic view that 'global warming and all that' was somebody else's responsibility and beyond local influence, to a stimulating belief that people were not helpless and that making an effort locally was going to make a difference.

Joan Garnett and her colleagues were well aware that such a change of attitude was a fragile thing, especially in the early days. They knew that to save energy and reduce waste on a really significant scale would take ten or twenty years. They also knew that there had to be tangible results, visible improvements, in year one and every year thereafter, combined with a deeper shift in outlook and expectations. There needed to be an understanding that it was possible, as well as necessary, to set some long-term targets and to achieve them by steady, measurable, progress. Like rebuilding the cathedral spire, seeing progress each year measured against a known long-term target was an important part of building public support and confidence.

They were now seven years into their long-term programme, long enough to see substantial improvements already achieved and to have confidence that progress in many cases could be faster than earlier cautious estimates. Local enthusiasm, local pride and local ingenuity were proving more fruitful than the best-informed opinions had earlier thought possible.

MAKING A START

It had not been too difficult, in the first flush of enthusiasm, to get the council to agree in principle to the priorities, both environmental and financial, mentioned earlier. What was more difficult, once the process had begun of elaborating these into a detailed programme of specific measures, was to establish and maintain some clear picture of the overall strategy to use in resolving conflicts and measuring progress. This was true for council officials, for committees, for business firms, for voluntary groups and for the general public. All would need to contribute in some way in making necessary changes, but all had particular interests to defend, and often disagreed strongly about the best tactics and the priorities for action.

A regular flow of information, equally available to all, was needed if some broad consensus about the facts and the possibilities was to be developed. If this was to be a real effort by the whole community, any division between 'them' and 'us' had to be avoided from the outset. Hence the decision to set up an Environmental Resource and Information Centre (ERIC) in a prominent position in the town centre. ERIC had quickly become a much-used part of the local scene. The centre consisted of:

- a data bank and library;
- a permanent exhibition linking global and local issues;
- an ecology advice unit;
- a current programmes and projects display;
- a progress review display in which a number of key indices showed progress already achieved against targets.

There had been all sorts of doubts and heart-searching, and fierce argument, about the wisdom of setting up such a prominent progress review, for fear of providing political opponents with ammunition to discredit the whole programme. However, Joan Garnett and her closest colleagues were convinced that an adequate rate of progress would never be achieved without the spur of widespread public awareness, either of shortfalls calling for increased effort or of successes creating the confidence essential for continuing the programme. Their arguments finally won the day and the progress review became one of the most influential instruments for maintaining public understanding, as well as official cohesion. A crucial element in this was the use of three sets of targets:

1. *International* – for greenhouse gases, acid rain, deforestation, desertification and coastal pollution;
2. *National/regional* – for air pollution, river pollution, toxic waste disposal, energy consumption;
3. *Moderley* – for air pollution, waste disposal, recycling, public transport, road traffic impacts, energy consumption, local economy, water management, and natural ecology.

The purpose of the triple set of targets was, of course, to develop a stronger sense of the concept 'Think globally, act locally' and to set local achievements against the wider objectives to which the local programmes were designed to contribute.

YEAR 7 PROGRESS REVIEW

Standing inside ERIC, as Joan Garnett often did on her way to council meetings, she was particularly interested in the new electronic display boards summarising the latest environmental information – always a matter of keen local concern.

Air pollution figures were good, but the leakage from the municipal waste dump, which had been closed since the 1970s, was becoming an increasing concern. The pollution effect on the ground water was being monitored and proposals about how to deal with it was the subject of a very complicated report to the council. If only previous generations had taken a bit more care!

She liked the panel which calculated the ecological benefits of recycling for each ward of the city. It did seem that there was room for considerable improvement, in some areas more than others, although people seemed to be taking much more notice now that they were able to receive feedback on their own behaviour and its environmental implications.

This feedback process had been of particular importance for the 'Equity: Everybody Benefits' part of the total sustainability programme. When the programme was launched, people had tended to think of it as a package of changes solely to protect and improve the physical environment. The idea that there also had to be a social dimension took longer to be recognised, as well as being politically more touchy, tending to attract the label of being a left-wing idea whereas the programme as a whole had been carefully shaped to be essentially apolitical. However, as more and more minority and special-needs groups became involved in debating the detailed implications of the various changes – with their effects on living costs and affordability as well as accessibility, for example – the need for some fair distribution of both costs and benefits became better recognised.

In practical terms, it was not such a big step from ensuring that transport changes should not disadvantage the physically handicapped to ensuring that energy-saving improvements were also available to the financially handicapped. After all, the target of a major reduction in energy consumption was certainly unattainable so long as the poor continued to be a big proportion of the most energy wasteful households, as the Environmental Audit had clearly shown.

Another display panel at the centre was entitled 'Nature in the City' and gave the results of the fifth biennial species survey. It was staggering to see how the diversity of species had increased over time and how pleasant the town had become – the visible results of some very hard work implementing a far-reaching long-term strategy. She recalled earlier demands for more 'soft' areas, water areas, and a much more careful use of all land to maximise its natural potential. Verges now flowered, the tree population had tripled, grass cutting in open spaces was much reduced and the many natural meadows were proof of the success of the policy. A much-admired new feature was the twenty large ponds which had been created as part of the drainage alterations aimed at retaining a large part of surface water run-off; these now provided superb wild life refuges within the city, although the growing heron population was becoming a problem.

Perhaps the most successful use of open space was the transformation of former allotments to community 'farm parks' with the theme of 'food in the city'. Two allotment sites had recently been turned into active urban farms, practising fish farming, bee keeping and poultry farming. The experiment had been made possible by an EC subsidy which now encouraged growing food in the immediate vicinity of potential customers.

She was reminded by this particular display that she was supposed to bring home a bag of ladybird larvae as the annual invasion of greenfly had just started: this was one of the initiatives started at the Ecology Advice Unit some five years ago to deal with the results of the authority's policy of banning pesticides in the locality.

Next to the 'Nature in the City' display and the 'Pollution Control' display was the section on 'Waste Disposal and Recycling', where the cross-links among all three were very much in evidence. The incineration of sludge had been outlawed in the mid-1990s to cut toxic emissions. The alternative of processing sludge to produce marketable fertiliser was not possible unless household sewage was kept separate from contaminated industrial effluents. Following successful trials, the separated foul sewers were now in place and the new digester/fertiliser plant would be operating from next year. It was fortunate that early reed-bed experiments had been carried out.

What was causing even more widespread interest, however, was the use of biological composting toilets in one complete area of the New Town which had made development possible without any main sewerage system. The savings had been huge, including not just the cost of the sewers themselves but also the cost of the major extension to the sewage treatment works that would otherwise have been necessary. The composting toilets produced a small volume of dry safe compost suitable for use on the local allotments or gardens or for sale to the Moderley Council to fertilise the extensive parks system. The liquid produced by the composting process, also safe and odourless, joined the 'grey' water from baths and basins for use in watering gardens or to soak away in simple below-surface drainage pits.

Since the composting toilets used much less water than conventional flush toilets (about one-sixth as much), the regional water company benefited both environmentally and financially. Overall demand was less, so extraction rates from rivers and underground aquifers were reduced; in addition, the proportion of water supplied to customers which was returned to the ground was appreciably increased. The net effect was to make a valuable contribution to the vital objective of preventing any further lowering of the water table. With other towns now following suit, the financial benefit – through reducing the need for capital investment in reservoir and treatment works capacity – was considerable.

Complementary action had been taken to deal with surface water run-off by channelling it through kerb-side runnels into small streams feeding the large recreation lake. Industrial effluents were treated on site by individual companies either singly or jointly, with an emphasis on recovery of all reusable materials, resulting in comparatively small volumes of waste transported by road tanker to one of three destinations: the sub-regional toxic waste disposal unit where high charges were a strong incentive to keep volumes small; or the town's sewage plant, which still operated on a reduced scale for final treatment of some liquid wastes; or to the sub-regional landfill sites where safe non-recyclable solid wastes were used for landscape restoration in gravel works and quarries.

The proposals for houses with toilets not connected to mains drainage had caused enormous controversy when first proposed. The newspapers had played up public fears about health risks and the local water company had objected to this radical departure from traditional methods. Gradually, as scientific tests on trial installations confirmed the absence of health risks, both public and expert opinion moved in favour of the new approach, finally acknowledging the two major benefits: this domestic closed-cycle system dramatically reduced the volume of organic wastes (since kitchen wastes were also consumed in the composting units) and eliminated the need for any sewage collection and treatment; and the major saving in infrastructure costs reduced the cost of the new houses. In the end, furious opposition gave way to enthusiastic support and the scheme was now one of the town's environmental lessons of most interest to visitors, many from places still struggling to expand the capacity of conventional sewage treatment systems and cope with the difficulties and expense of raising effluent quality to match the stringent EC standards which had been found necessary to reverse the deterioration of rivers and coastal waters.

Visitors were also impressed by the recycling display which summarised the results already achieved by the reorganised Resource Recovery Service: volumes and value of reusable materials (nearly 60 per cent recovery for both glass and paper) and council savings through greatly reduced landfill costs. Joan Garnett remembered seeing, as she left the house that morning, the Resource Saver vehicle with its separate compartments for presorted glass, metal, paper and compostable organic material; what was most notable was the small size of the little trailer attached to the vehicle which collected any household waste which couldn't be recycled. Since the latest price rise to £5 per pound charged by direct debit for the non-recoverable waste which was weighed at the kerbside, everyone made strenuous efforts to reduce the waste their household generated. This was just as well, since the last landfill available within 200 miles had reduced Moderley's allocation to 300 tonnes for the next year.

She also remembered walking past the new recycling centre, which now dealt with over 80 per cent of all waste in Moderley. Most of it was put to good use and had generated many jobs in the process. It was rewarding to see the adjacent industrial complex where, among other 'green' products, the latest type of photo-voltaic energy-saving devices were manufactured for sale throughout the EC. This particular enterprise had started as a joint venture among a group of authorities looking for radical ways of cutting their energy consumption. They had to underwrite five years of production; now it was a roaring success.

There was no time for her to visit the 'Energy Saving' and 'Transport' sections but there was evidence of the major advances in both in the main car park outside, where all the vehicles were linked up to a solar fuel station. These had sprouted up all over the city since the Borough Environmental Engineer had spent a fortnight rallying his solar-mobile in the Swiss alps. The effectiveness of the solar fuel stations was such that a one-hour refuelling lasted for 100 miles of travel. The council, together with the other major employers in the town, now had an all-electric vehicle fleet. The big debate currently was whether or not Moderley should shift to the new hydrogen-cell vehicles, which had taken such a long time to develop.

Leaving ERIC and walking along the bustling city road, Joan Garnett could not help reflecting on the big changes that had taken place here. Every time she breathed deeply in the fresh air she realised how beneficial the reallocation of road space in favour of public transport, cycles and pedestrians had been. Initially, the sceptics had poured scorn on the proposals and had mocked the change of name from Highways Committee to Transport Efficiency Committee. However, the Sustainable Development Committee had refused to accept the inevitability, or even the practicality, of the Department of Transport trend projections showing huge increases in road vehicle ownership and trip mileages; there was no possibility of expanding road capacity at anything like that rate. Such expansion could only mean increasing congestion and more frequent delays, with all the additional costs and inconvenience this would entail – an unacceptable prospect in itself, quite apart from undermining air pollution targets by preventing any reduction in total vehicle emissions. An exhibition 'If Present Trends Continue' had driven the point home and it only needed the first doubling of fuel costs to make a radical new approach to traffic in Moderley not just acceptable but actively demanded.

Now that the system had settled down after the initial teething troubles, people looked back at the clogged roads and poor public transport of the past with disbelief. How could they have put up with it for so long? It had taken people some time to give up their ingrained private car habits, but the new, regular, and reliable bus schedules giving a fast and frequent service to all the main destinations had proved to be a more convenient, and cheaper, alternative for many trips. The result was an actual reduction in private car mileage, permitting the extensive pedestrianisation of the city centre and sub-centres, with the attractive refurbishment which had made many streets and squares the lively social centres which were now one of the city's most notable new features.

Road pricing and increased parking charges had helped to provide some of the capital investment required, augmented considerably by the legislation which provided for the decentralisation of all road tax revenues, with all commercial vehicle taxes going to the new regional authorities and private vehicle taxes going to the local authorities. Another decisive step was taken when the City Council was able to emulate the Californian example by an LEnB (local environmental bye-law) which completely barred any vehicle that did not fall within the zero-emission category. Joan Garnett had been surprised to hear of the dramatic reductions in respiratory diseases when she last met her old friend the senior registrar at the local hospital. Of course, this change had also been helped on its way by the EC carbon tax which had been so strenuously resisted in the early 1990s.

IMPACT ON THE PHYSICAL FORM OF THE CITY

Visitors were often surprised that Moderley's well-known radical programme demanding that all new development, and all major investment, must contribute to future sustainability had not had a bigger effect on the city's physical appearance. The pedestrianised centres, much admired as they were, were after all only a tiny part of the total urban scene. The linear parkways, heavily planted with trees and extensively linked with pedestrian and cycle routes that were gradually becoming continuous, were becoming a more prominent feature of all neighbourhoods, both old and new. But, after all, most of the town had been built in pre-sustainability days and the 'Conserving Scarce Resources' part of the programme stressed the importance of keeping existing buildings and retro-fitting for energy saving rather than rebuilding, except where redevelopment could show major environmental gains.

Moreover, much of the energy-saving investment, such as the city's restructured drainage system, was hidden away. Wall and roof insulation, double and triple glazing, low-consumption light bulbs, internal heat pumps for recycling heat from waste water, and similar measures which were such an important part of the campaign for reducing energy consumption ('Live better with less'), had little effect on external appearances. Even the increasing use of Sterling CHP (combined heat and power) engines was not very obvious.

What did show, of course, was the widespread use of solar panels and the increasing number of wind generators mounted on the roofs of the higher office buildings, these now attracting no more attention than television aerials. More conspicuous was the major wind energy park with its large cluster of windpower generators on high ground on the outskirts. However, this was an isolated feature akin to the cooling towers of the old coal-fired power station: its chimneys were now fitted with sulphur scrubbers and it was only competitive with alternative sources because of the resulting sales of gypsum to local builders, together with the sale of 'waste heat' to the nearby district heating scheme.

Where new buildings had been constructed, Joan Garnett was struck by the beauty – initially strange although now becoming familiar – of the design features intended to maximise solar gain and natural ventilation as part of the 'closed cycle' building design philosophy. The visual effect proved to be particularly attractive in cases of infill or replacement housing with their sun-trap conservatories resembling their Edwardian predecessors, very popular for providing a superb in-house atmosphere.

MODERLEY NEW TOWN

The one area where the effect of the sustainability programme was most evident was in the complete new neighbourhood of Moderley New Town which formed the major extension of the town on one side. Nobody called it a suburb because it was so unsuburban in character. This was partly the result of more compact layouts and building forms, with a greater use of wide-front terraced houses (reducing heat loss while permitting efficient noise insulation and better-proportioned gardens). But it was also the result of much greater variations in layout and density, with some areas having plot sizes big enough to permit a variety of life-styles that were more self-contained in terms of food production, small workshops, personal energy supply and waste disposal.

Even with this greater variety in urban form, gross densities overall were higher than in the old conventional suburbs, an important factor in meeting one of the principal design criteria: ensuring that a high proportion of all dwellings should be within easy walking distance of a sizeable shopping and local service centre, primary school and local recreation facilities. This had sharply reduced the necessity to use the private car for daily journeys.

But it was the mixed-use character of the new area that was an even bigger reason for it being so unsuburban in feel. And it was the local employment thus provided that was another important factor in reducing private car mileages. The huge rise in fuel costs had made this highly desirable and the decentralisation of many routine office jobs through the widespread use of improved telecommunications had made it a practical alternative to the old long-distance commuting-to-work practices. A valuable added bonus was how much easier it was for men and women to fit together work and family commitments.

Laying on high capacity fibre optic cable links as standard fitting to all houses had greatly reduced unit costs and the rapid growth of tele-cottage and tele-village operations had greatly improved the efficiency of home and local working. Added to this were the sizeable number of small workshops which had been encouraged by mixed-use planning policies for the area, some in private houses or gardens, others in localised purpose-built groups. All these workshops had been required to be non-polluting, with minimal noise and traffic generation.

Joan Garnett smiled when she remembered the heated discussions about work going on in residential areas and the difficulties of convincing her colleagues that mixed land use actually had some overall benefits. All that changed the day the council altered its structure and offered its services through 50 one-stop service points. Now half of the council's 2000 employees worked either at home or at one of the many decentralised workstations. Many of the city's other major employers had also taken advantage of these new possibilities, so achieving major cost savings in reduced car fleets, parking costs and public transport travel subsidies.

The contribution of Moderley New Town to the council's main sustainability objectives was, of course, a question that was continually being asked. The council knew that most environmental gains had to be achieved within the older areas of the town. But it was a matter of national, as well as local, concern to find out just how much more could be achieved in areas purpose-built with these objectives in mind. The results from the first years were already better than expected, especially in terms of air quality, reduced traffic impacts, energy and water conservation and accessibility to daily services. But the biggest benefit had been in terms of the general quality of life and neighbourhood spirit.

The latest report on the lessons from New Town and their implications for the town as a whole was on the agenda of the council meeting to which Joan Garnett was now going. The main purpose of this special meeting was to discuss the next ten-year Environmental Programme. Other items on the agenda included:

- a complete break with centralised energy provision;
- regional co-ordination to reduce environmental impacts;
- the implications of sustainable development criteria on settlement patterns (a recurring item since the early 1990s).

Her mind, however, was mainly preoccupied with the lecture she had agreed to give following the council meeting. Her presentation was to an evening session of an international conference where her brief was to sum up the guiding philosophy which had shaped what was described on the conference programme as the 'Moderley Experiment in Urban Sustainability'. She had the rough outline in her briefcase, hoping that inspiration would enable her to convey to the audience the strength of local feeling that something of real significance for the future, and of real benefit to the quality of life here and now, had already been achieved through the involvement of the whole community. The following extracts from her notes give the essence of her main points.

The Moderley Philosophy

This is a community that emphasises self-reliance, maintaining a diversity of skills, meeting a diversity of needs, and aiming for long-term viability. Investing to serve future needs as well as current ones. Focusing on prevention rather than treatment. Aiming for increasing satisfaction rather than increasing consumption.

With personal satisfactions coming more from personal involvement and creative achievement than from passive consumption of more material goods, the central question 'what will it cost?' is increasingly replaced by a new central question 'what kind of life do we want to create for ourselves?'

More self-reliant in terms of supplying a bigger proportion of its essential needs, becoming progressively less dependent on outside sources for heat and power, water supply and waste disposal, basic foods and fertilisers, employment and recreation. Strengthening the local economy by substituting local products for imports where possible and expanding the productive capacity of local communities.

Sometimes Moderley on its own, sometimes jointly with neighbouring towns. Not regressing to some more primitive self-sufficiency, but becoming better able to shape its own quality of life, making better use of local resources both human and natural, less at risk from adverse external trends.

Being more consciously responsible for its own future, there is a greater willingness to recognise the future's vulnerability to adverse world trends, to take steps that serve global needs as well as local needs, to safeguard the future while serving the present. Pressing local industries to adopt closed-cycle processes is easier when the whole community is doing the same: doing more with less, using less energy and natural resources, producing less waste, taking pride in good husbandry.

The 'fundamental change of attitudes' universally called for as a prerequisite for effectively safeguarding the planet's future has become more common in families, schools and community groups, in local industry and business, and in local government. The growing recognition of an external threat to survival, and the involvement of the whole community in resisting it, had created that deeply valued fellow-feeling that is commonly experienced only in wartime conditions. The cynics who claimed that personal selfishness would always prevail have been proved wrong.

So much for the philosophy. But how does it feel, living here? Not just the fresh clean air, the evidence of nature everywhere with trees and shrubs, avenues and clumps and small woods; an abundance of water features of all kinds, formal fountains contrasting with the canals and streams and wildlife ponds. Something much more intrinsic than 'Britain in Bloom' prettiness and tidiness.

The lively town and neighbourhood centres, with smoothly efficient public transport, general ease of movement and access, a feeling of services operating reliably without dominating or interfering with the complex interplay of human activities. The stimulation of vibrant social activity. Work and leisure mixed. The pleasures of 'life in the round'.

Something in the general mood, more relaxed, less strain and hassle. An awareness of being jointly in control, not helpless victims of external forces. A feeling of community involvement, of pride in surroundings, visible enjoyment, proprietorial feeling like the house-proud owner of a much loved house.

MAKING IT HAPPEN

True to form, however, after this attempt to put across to the audience the essence of the basic philosophy and its results, Joan Garnett concluded by highlighting the practical difficulties and how they were tackled in overcoming opposition and getting the necessary agreement to proceed.

If this strikes you as being a 'cosy consensus' which is too utopian to be true, let me correct any false impressions by assuring you that there *is* no cosy consensus, there never has been at any time while we've been hammering out our policies and the programmes for putting them into effect, and I don't think there ever will be. What we *do* have is a strong majority view which is a fairly durable one precisely because we had to fight hard to create it; a majority view which has become more confident in spite of some mistakes and some defeats, as we have step by step produced successful results – successful, that is, in terms of living in Moderley, but also by being so clearly in step with the evolution of thinking both nationally and internationally.

There's nothing quite so encouraging as the conviction that you're in the lead, that you're setting the pace, that you were far-sighted enough and courageous enough to see what had to be done, and to get on and do it while others were still dithering. But it wasn't easy, so I want to conclude by recalling some of the struggles we had in getting to our present position, and some of the hard lessons we learned along the way.

There were times when the partisan reactions to proposed changes were so fierce that we thought that current self-interest would win out over long-term dangers. There were even more times when people said 'too idealistic' or 'too expensive' or 'politically impossible'. And there were times when we failed to convince our opponents, at least on the first round. But we gradually learned that, although tactics naturally had to vary to suit particular situations, there were some basic essentials that were likely to prevail if we persisted long enough.

First of all, we had to be convinced ourselves that each specific proposal was really necessary in order to make progress towards some agreed target; also that the alternatives, if any, involved higher costs and fewer benefits.

Secondly, we had to go on repeating the reasons why the target itself, and maintaining the momentum, was important.

Thirdly, we had to be careful to maintain our 'holistic' approach, which usually meant that there was a 'package' of changes which only worked properly as a group, so that each individual proposal could be justified both in its own right and as an integral part of the overall package: what we called 'avoiding one-legged proposals'.

Fourthly, we had to combine 'sticks' and 'carrots': penalties had to offer potential benefits; changes involving extra costs had to be accompanied by the prospect of extra profits once the changes were complete; community benefit had to be seen to outweigh, and if necessary compensate for, individual losses.

Fifthly, while maintaining the momentum necessary to get results on time, we had to be sensitive to transition problems and flexible enough with the practicalities of implementation programmes (including financial and technical help and advice where needed) to ease the changeover. Our Implementation Advisory Service was much appreciated for its approachability, and for the way it was able to use its powerful central position and status to mould and adapt broad programmes to individual circumstances.

So my final message to you based on our experience here in Moderley is twofold. Don't underestimate the amount of opposition you are likely to encounter, but do try to distinguish between the two kinds: that due to lack of information and understanding, and that due to real conflicts of interest. You need to deal sympathetically but vigorously with both, and the more success you have with the first, the better your chances of resolving or overcoming the second. Hence the importance we attached to ERIC and the reason I've described its operations to you in some detail.

Sometimes it is only the weight of public opinion, the general mood that you have managed to develop, that will prevail when a particular partisan interest is unavoidably threatened. But more often than you might think, the partisan conflict can be dealt with by a more realistic view of long-term prospects offsetting the current problem, together with positive help in handling transition problems. We all know by now of the many examples where extra costs in the short term have been converted into long-term profits.

So, finally, don't be put off by those who say that however practical the actual proposals in your sustainability programme, it won't be possible to achieve popular or political acceptance. If the case is good enough, and the need is urgent enough, persistence will win out in the end; attitudes *will* change. What we have to fight against most is the real danger of 'too little, too late' when the environmental dangers ahead could well mean disaster if action is delayed.

When opposition mounts, and difficulties multiply, just remember that our best safeguard is '*the precautionary principle,*' and persevere.

The author wishes to acknowledge Helmut Lusser for his help in the preparation of this chapter.

References

CHAPTER 1

1. Prentice, T (1990) *The Times*, 17 May
2. World Commission on Environment and Development (1987) *Our Common Future*, Oxford University Press, p49
3. Howard, E (1889) *Tomorrow: A Peaceful Path to Real Reform*, revised edition (1965) entitled *Garden Cities of Tomorrow*, Faber and Faber, London; Purdom, C B (1949) *The Building of Satellite Towns*, J M Dent and Sons, London; Hardy, D (1991) *From Garden Cities to New Towns and From New Towns to Green Politics*, E and F N Spon
4. HMSO (1990) *This Common Inheritance*, London
5. Commission of the European Communities (1992) *Towards Sustainability*: a *European Community Programme of Policy and Action in Relation to the Environment and Sustainable Development*, Brussels, 27 March
6. World Commission (1987), op cit, p47
7. HMSO (1990), op cit, p10
8. Luper–Foy, S (1992); 'Justice and natural resources', *Environmental Values*, vol 1, no 1, spring, p61
9. Daly, H E and Cobb, J B (1990) *For the Common Good*, The Green Print; Redclift, M (1987) *Sustainable Development: Exploring the Contradictions*, Routledge, London
10. Gorz, A (1980) *Ecology as Politics*, South End Press, Boston, p5
11. Pearce, D, Markandya, A and Barbier, E (1989) *Blueprint for a Green Economy*, Earthscan, London, p170
12. World Commission (1987), op cit, p49
13. Sandbach, F (1984) 'Environmental Futures', in Masey, D and Allen, J. (eds), *Geography Matters!*, Cambridge and The Open University, p184
14. Netherlands National Institute of Public Health and Environmental Protection (RIVM) (1989), *Concern for Tomorrow*. (A National Environmental Survey 1985–2010), National Institute of Public Health and Environmental Protection, Netherlands
15. Carson, R (1962) *The Silent Spring*, Houghton Mifflin, and Pelican, London
16. Giddens, A (1985) *The Nation-state and Violence*, Polity Press, Cambridge
17. HMSO (1990), op cit, p11
18. Ibid, p11
19. Department of the Environment (1991), *Improving Environmental Quality*, HMSO, London
20. Blowers, A (1992) 'Limited Concerns, Intentions Too Modest', *Town and Country Planning*, vol 61, no 1, January, pp3-4
21. Department of the Environment (1991) *Policy Appraisal and the Environment* HMSO, London
22. HMSO (1991) *This Common Inheritance: The First Year Report*; (1992) *This Common Inheritance: The Second Year Report*; London
    Department of the Environment (1992) *The UK Environment*, Government Statistical Service HMSO, London
23. Clough, A H 'Say Not the Struggle Naught Availeth' see for example *Choice of Verse*, Faber, London

CHAPTER 2

1. Elkin T, McLaren D, Hillman M (1991) *Reviving the City*, Friends of the Earth, London
2. Hardy, D (1979) *Alternative Communities in Nineteenth Century England*, Longman, Harlow; and (1991) *From Garden Cities to New Towns*, E & F Spon, London

3. Nicholson, M (1987) *The New Environmental Age*, Cambridge University Press and (1991) *Environmental Policies for Cities in the 1990s*, OECD Paris
4. Cullingworth, J B (1975) *Environmental Planning Vol 1: Reconstruction and Land Use Planning 1939–1947*, HMSO, London
5. Wood, C (1976) *Town Planning and Pollution Control*, Manchester University Press
6. Blowers A (1984) *Something in the Air: corporate power and the environment*, Harper and Row, New York
7. Wood C (1989) *Planning Pollution Prevention – a comparison of siting controls over air pollution in Great Britain and the USA*, Heinemann Newnes, London
8. Buchanan, C (1963) *Traffic in Towns* report for the Ministry of Transport, HMSO, London
9. Hillman, M and Cleary, J (1992) 'A prominent role for walking and cycling in future transport policy' in *A New Transport Policy for Britain* (eds J Roberts et al), Lawrence & Wishart, London
10. DoE (1990) *This Common Inheritance*, HMSO, London
11. Commission of the European Communities (1990) *Green Paper on the Urban Environment*, CEC, Luxembourg
12. DoE (1992) *PPG 12: Development Plans and Regional Planning Guidance*, HMSO, London
13. Raemaekers, J (ed) (1992) *Local Authority Green Plans: a Practical Guide (Working Paper No 39)*, Heriot Watt University
14. *Planning*, no 897, 30 November 1990
15. Jones, G and Stewart, J (1983) *The Case for Local Government*, George Allen and Unwin, London
16. Hurdle, D, and Adams, M (1991) *Global Warming – how the London Boroughs and the Government can respond to London*, London Boroughs Association
17. Association of County Councils (1991), *Towards a Sustainable Transport Policy* and *County Councils and the Environment*, ACC, London
18. OECD (1991) *Environmental Policies for Cities in the 1990s*, OECD, Paris
19. Pearce, D, Markandya, A and Barbier, E (1989) *Blueprint for a Green Economy*, Earthscan, London
20. Webber, M M (1964) 'The Urban Place and the Non–place Urban Realm' in *Explorations in Urban Structure*, University of Pennsylvania Press
21. Elkin et al (1991), op cit
22. Sherlock, H (1991) *Cities are Good for You*, Paladin, London

CHAPTER 3

1. Crosby, A W (1986) *Ecological Imperialism – The Biological Expansion of Europe 900–1900*, Cambridge University Press
2. Bunyard, P, Goldsmith, E, Hildyard, N and McCully, P (1990) *5000 Days to Save the Planet*, Hamlyn, London
3. Meadows, D H and D L, and Randers, J and Behrens, W (1972) *The Limits to Growth*, Pan, London
4. Meadows, D H and D L, and Randers, J (1992) *Beyond the Limits*, Earthscan, London
5. McKibben, W (1990) *The End of Nature*, Viking, London
6. Wiener, M J (1985) *English Culture and the Decline of the Industrial Spirit, 1850–1980*, Penguin, Harmondsworth
7. Pearce, D, Markandya, A and Barbier, E (1989) *Blueprint for a Green Economy*, Earthscan, London
8. Environmental Ethics Working Party (1989) *Values, Conflict and the Environment*, St Cross College, Oxford
9. DoE (1990) *This Common Inheritance*, HMSO, London
10. Schumacher, E F (1974) *Small is Beautiful*, Sphere Books, London
11. DoE (1991) *Policy Appraisal and the Environment*, HMSO, London
12. Royal Town Planning Institute (1986) *The Challenge of Change, RTPI, London*
13. Harrison, F (1983) *The Power in the Land*, Shepheard Walwyn, London
14. Green, R, and Holliday, J (1991) *Country Planning, A Time for Action*, TCPA, London
15. Green, B (1991) *An Environmentalist's View of Policy Needs* published in 'Agricultural Policy and the Environment', Centre for Agricultural Studies, University of Reading

16. Holliday, J C (1986) *Land at the Centre – Choices in a Fast Changing World*, Shepheard Walwyn, London
17. Pitt, J (1991) *Community Forest Cities of Tomorrow*, published in 'Town and Country Planning', TCPA, June
18. Ibid
19. Creative Development Seminars in Rural and Urban Regeneration (1990) *Helping Villages Help Themselves*, 10 Littlegate Street, Oxford
20. Green and Holliday (1991), op cit
21. Green (1991), op cit
22. Wells, H G (1902) *Anticipations*, Chapman and Hall, London
23. Williams, R (1973) *The Country and the City*, Chatto & Windus, London
24. Countryside Commission (1991) *Caring for the Countryside*, Countryside Commission, Cheltenham

CHAPTER 4

1. Schumacher, D (1985) *Energy: Crisis or Opportunity. An Introduction to Energy Studies*, Macmillan, London
2. UN World Commission on Environment and Development (1987) *Our Common Future*, Oxford University Press
3. Patterson, W C (1990) 'The Energy Alternative', Channel 4 TV, London
4. Parliamentary Alternative Energy Group Bulletin, Apr 1991
5. EC (1990) *Green Paper on the Urban Environment*, CEC, Luxembourg
6. CHPA (1991) *Co–Gen*, Bulletin of the Combined Heat and Power Association, Mar
7. British Annual Energy Review 1990, British Energy Association
8. DoE (1990) *This Common Inheritance*, HMSO, London
9. Parliamentary Alternative Energy Group *Bulletin* (August 1991)
10. Friends of the Earth Briefing Sheet *Removing the Windbrakes* (Mar 1991), London
11. Energy Technology Support Unit
12. FoE (1991) op cit
13. CHPA (1991) op cit
14. DoE (1990) op cit
15. Cairncross, F (1991) *Costing the Earth*, Economist Books, London
16. TCPA (1986) *Whose Responsibility?*, TCPA, London
17. House of Commons Energy Committee (1991) *Third Report, Volume 1*, HMSO, London
18. Goldemberg, J, Johansson, T, Reddy, A, and Williams R (1987) *Energy for a Sustainable World*, World Resources Institute
19. Labour Party (1990) *An Earthly Chance*, Labour Party Publications, London
20. DoE (1990), op cit

CHAPTER 5

1. De Swaan, A (1988) *In Care of the State*, Polity Press, Cambridge
2. House of Commons Environment Committee (1986) *Radioactive Waste*, First report, Session 1985–9; House of Lords Select Committee on European Communities (1989) *Nitrate in Water*, Session 1988–9; House of Commons Energy Committee (1989) *Energy Policy Implications of the greenhouse Effect*, Session 1988–9, Sixth Report; House of Commons Environment Committee (1990) *Contaminated Land*, Session 1989–90, First Report, HMSO, London
3. Holdgate, M W (1979) *A Perspective of Environmental Pollution*, Cambridge University Press
4. Bertell, R (1985) *No Immediate Danger*, Women's Press, London
5. Environmental Data Services, Report 209, Jun 1992
6. DoE (1992), *Waste Disposal Planning under an Environment Agency*, HMSO, London
7. Blowers, A (1992) 'Limited Concerns, Intentions Too Modest', *Town and Country Planning*, vol 61, no 1, Jan
8. Smith, D and Blowers, A (1992) 'Here today, there tomorrow: the politics of hazardous waste transport and disposal', *Waste Location: Spatial Aspects of Waste Management, Hazards and Disposal*, Routledge, London

9. Asante–Duah, D K, Saccomanno, F F and Shortreed, J H (1992) 'The hazardous waste trade; can it be controlled?', *Environmental Science and Technology*, vol 26, no 9, Sep
10. DoE (1991), *Policy Appraisal and the Environment*, HMSO, London
11. Chisholm, M and Kivell, P (1987) *Inner City Waste Land*, Institute of Economic Affairs, Hobart Paper 108
12. Blowers, A (1984) *Something in the Air: Corporate Power and the Environment*, Harper & Row, London
13. Hawkins, K (1984), *Environment and Enforcement*, Oxford University Press
14. 'Britain's Buried Poison', *The Observer*, 4 Feb 1990

CHAPTER 6

1. DoE (1992) *Environment in Trust: Global atmosphere and air quality*, HMSO, London
2. DoE (1991) *Housing and Construction Statistics 1980–1990*, HMSO London
3. Connaughton, J N (1990) 'Real low energy buildings', *The Energy Challenge*, RIBA South West, Plymouth
4. Baird, G (1992) Private communication, Victoria University of Wellington, New Zealand
5. Olivier, D (1992) *Energy Efficiency and Renewables: recent experience on mainland Europe*, Energy Advisory Associates, Hereford
6. Connaughton (1990) op cit
7. Leach, G et al (1979) *A low energy strategy for the United Kingdom*, International Institute of Environment and Development, London
8. Brister, A (1991) 'The future for insulation', *Building Services*, Oct 1991, pp43–4
9. Howard, N (1991) 'Energy in balance', *Building Services* May 1991, pp36–8
10. BRECSU (1985), reported in *Energy in buildings*, Sept 1085
11. Vale, B and R (1991) 'The Woodhouse medical centre', *Towards a green architecture*, RIBA, London
12. Lowe, R, Chapman, J, and Everett, B (1985) *The Pennyland Project*, Energy Research Group, Open University, Milton Keynes
13. Olivier (1992) op cit
14. Bordass, W (1990) 'Appropriate methods and technologies for new build and refurbishment: offices', *The Architect and Global Responsibility*, RIBA, London
15. Vale (1991) op cit, 'The NMB Bank'
16. Olivier (1992) op cit, p17
17. Vale, R (1978) *Insulation versus generation*, Open University, Milton Keynes
18. Muthesius, H (1979) (original 1904) *The English House*, Crosby, Lockwood, Staples
19. O'Connor, L (1992) 'Recovering rainwater', *CIBSE Journal*, Feb
20. Cooper, J (1992) 'Creating the greener field site with development', *Green Buildings*, Design Construction Services, Nottingham

CHAPTER 7

1. Breach, I (1989) 'Can you give up your car?' *The Guardian*, 13 Oct
2. DoE (1991) *This Common Inheritance*, HMSO, London
3. Barrett, M (1991) Research paper for Worldwide Fund for Nature, London
4. Goldemberg, J, Johansson, T, Reddy, A and Williams, R (1987) *Energy for a Sustainable World*, World Resources Institute
5. Adams, J (1990) 'Car Ownership, Forecasting: Pull the Ladder Up or Climb Back Down', *Traffic Engineering and Control*, Mar
6. HMSO (1988) *National Travel Survey 1985/86*, London
7. Transport and Environment Studies (1990) *Can Land Use Changes Lessen Car Dependence?*, TEST
8. May, Prof T (1989) *Getting about in Towns: Solutions*, paper given at the TCPA Annual Conference
9. Civic Trust, County Surveyors Society and DpT (1990) *Lorries in the Community*, London

10. National Economic Development Council (1991) *Freight Lines to Europe*, NEDC
11. TCPA (1990) *Community Railway Policy*, evidence of the TCPA to Sub-committee B of the House of Lords Select Committee on the European Communities 1990 (4478/90 Com (89) 564)
12. Bidwell, R and Ernecq, J M (1990) *1992 and the Environment. Implications and Actions*, paper prepared for the IEEP '1992 and the Environmental Seminar'
13. TEST (1991) *The Wrong Side of the Tracks;* Transport 2000 (1991) *Freight and the Environment*, conference
14. Transnet (1990) *Energy, Transport and the Environment*, London
15. TEST (1991) *Trouble in Store: retail locational policies in Britain and West Germany*
16. Hurdle, D (1991) 'Towards a Policy for Regional Shopping Centres', *The Planner*, 1 Sep
17. de Loor, H (1990) *The Right Business in the Right Place*, paper presented at the TCPA Annual Dinner Conference, London
18. British Railways Board (1991) *Future Rail – the next decade*
19. Commission of the European Communities (1990) *Green Paper on the Urban Environment*, CEC, Luxembourg
20. Government of the Netherlands (1989) *National Environmental Policy Plan*; Gossop, C (1990) 'Close it or lose it – lessons from the Netherlands NEPP', *Town and Country Planning*, Jun
21. Potter, S (1991) 'The Changing Transport Agenda', *Town and Country Planning*, Oct
22. Open University Energy and Environmental Research Unit (1991) *Routes to Stable Prosperity*, Open University, Milton Keynes
23. de Loor, H (1990) *The Right Business in the Right Place*, paper presented at the TCPA Annual Conference
24. Potter, S (1990) *Vital Travel Statistics*, Open University, Milton Keynes
25. CEC (1990) *op cit*
26. Potter, S (1976) *Transport and the New Towns*, Open University, New Towns Study Unit, Milton Keynes
27. Barton, H (1991) *City Transport – Strategies for Sustainability*, paper to BSRSA conference

CHAPTER 8

1. Smith, S (1992) 'Strategic Management and the Business Environment', *Business Strategy and the Environment*, vol 1, part 1
2. Roberts, P (1992) 'Business and the Environment: an Initial Review of the Recent Literature', *Business Strategy and the Environment*, vol 1, part 2
3. Hemming, C, Moody, C and Attwood, D (1992) *Eco–labelling Criteria for Washing Machines and Dish Washers*, PA Consulting, Cambridge
4. Williams, J (1992) *Environmental Opportunities: Building Advantage Out of Uncertainty*, Centre for Exploitation of Science and Technology, London
5. Johnston, P (1992) 'Opportunities for Rural Areas', *XIII Magazine*, June, DG XIII, EC
6. Kitamura, R (1991) 'Home work clears air', *New Scientist*, 5 Oct

CHAPTER 9

1. Commission of the European Communities (1990) *Green Paper on the Urban Environment*, CEC
2. Breheny, M (1992) 'The Contradictions of the Compact City: A Review' in Breheny, M *Sustainable Development and Urban Form*, Pion, London; ECOTEC Research and Consulting Ltd (1992) *Reducing Transport Emissions Through Planning*, draft report to the DoE
3. Office of Population Censuses and Surveys (1992) 1991 Census – *Preliminary Report for England and Wales*, OPCS, London
4. Breheny, M, Gent, T, and Lock, D (1992) *Alternative Development Patterns: New Settlements*, draft report to the DoE
5. Elkin, T, McLaren, D and Hillman, M (1991) *Reviving the City: Towards Sustainable Urban Development*, Friends of the Earth, London
6. Sherlock, H (1990) *Cities are Good for Us*, Transport 2000, London

6. Sherlock, H (1990) *Cities are Good for Us*, Transport 2000, London
7. Green, R, & Holliday, J (1991) *Country Planning – A Time for Action*, TCPA, London
8. Robertson, J (1990) 'Alternative Futures for Cities' in Cadman, D, and Payne, G (eds) *The Living City: Towards a Sustainable Future*, Routledge, London
9. Owens, S (1991) *Energy Conscious Planning*, Campaign for the Protection of Rural England, London; Rickaby, P (1987) 'Six Settlement Patterns Compared' published in Environment and Planning Bulletin, Planning and Design, no 14
10. Rydin, Y (1992) 'Environmental Impacts and the Property Marker' in Breheny, M (ed) *Sustainable Development and Urban Form*, Pion. London
11. TCPA (1993) *Strategic Planning for Regional Development*, TCPA, London

CHAPTER 10

1. HMSO (1990) *This Common Inheritance* HMSO, London, p11
2. Timberlake et al (1991) *Defending the Future*, IIED/Earthscan, London
3. Pearce, D, Markandya, A and Barbier, E (1989) *Blueprint for a Green Economy*, Earthscan, London
4. Parry, M (1990) *Global Warming – What Threat?*, paper to the TCPA Annual Conference

Suggested Further Reading

This list indicates some of the sources which the authors have found stimulating or useful in preparing this report. It is intended to be an indication of the variety of mainly contemporary sources available, rather than an attempt to provide a select bibliography.

Among the books of **general interest** are: Breheny, M (ed) (1992) *Sustainable Development and Urban Form*, London, Pion; Dobson, A (1990) *Green Political Thought*, London, Unwin Hyman; Elkin, T and Mclaren, D (eds) (1991) *Reviving the City*, London, Friends of the Earth; Girardet, H (1992) *The Gaia Atlas of Cities*, London, Gaia Books Ltd.; Goldsmith, E, Hildyard, N, McCully, P and Bunyard, P (1990) *5000 Days to Save the World*, London, Paul Hamlyn Publishing; Hough, M (1984) *City Form and Natural Process*, London, Routledge; Houghton, J, Jenkins, G and Ephraims, J (eds) (1990) *Climate Change: The IPCC Scientific Assessment*, Cambridge, CUP; IUCN, UNEP and WWF (1991) *Caring for the Earth: A Strategy for Sustainable Living*, Switzerland, Gland; Jacobs, M (1991) *The Green Economy*, London, Pluto Press; Lovelock, J (1979) *Gaia: A New Look at Life on Earth*, Oxford, OUP; Lovelock, J (1988) *The Ages of Gaia: A Biography of our Living Earth*, Oxford, OUP; Meadows, D, Dennis, L and Randers, J (1992) *Beyond the Limits*, London, Earthscan; Pearce, D, Markandya, A and Barbier, E (1989) *Blueprint for a Green Economy*, London, Earthscan; Yearley, S (1991) *The Green Case*, London, Routledge; Redclift, M (1987) *Sustainable Development; Exploring the Contradictions*, London, Routledge.

A number of significant reports have been published including HMSO (1990) *This Common Inheritance*, Cm 1200, London; DoE (1991) *Land Use Policy and Climate Change*, HMSO; DoE (1992) *The UK Environment* HMSO; ACC, ADC, AMA, LGMB (1992) *Environmental Practice in Local Government*; CEC (1990) *Green Paper on the Urban Environment*, Brussels; CEC (1991) *Europe 2000: Outlook for the Develpoment of the Community's Territory*, Brussels; CEC (1992) *Towards Sustainability*, Fifth Environmental Action Plan, Brussels; World Commission on Environment and Development (1987) *Our Common Future*, Oxford, OUP; Netherlands Environmental Policy Plan (1989) *To Choose or to Lose*, The Hague; OECD (1991) *The State of the Environment*, Paris.

On the role of **town planning** there is the original work of Ebenezer Howard (1902) *Garden Cities of Tomorrow* (1941 edition, London, Faber); and a contemporary source is Sherlock, H (1991) *Cities are Good for Us*, London, Paladin. Policies for planning natural resources are covered in Green, R and Holliday, J (1991) *Country Planning: a Time for Action*, London, TCPA.

Of the many sources on **energy** the following relate to sustainability: Goldemberg, J, Johansson, T, Reddy, A and Williams, R (1987) *Energy for a Sustainable World*, World Resources Institute; Hawkes, D, Owers, J, Rickaby, P and Steadman, P (eds) (1987) *Energy Planning and Urban Form*, London, Butterworth; Owens, S (1986) *Energy Planning and Urban Form*, London, Pion; Patterson, W (1991) *The Energy Alternative* London, Boxtree Ltd.

The definitions, conflicts and policies covering **pollution** are discussed in Blowers, A (1984) *Something in the Air: Corporate Power and the Environment*, London, Harper and Row; Holgate, M (1979) *A Perspective of Environmental Pollution*, Cambridge, CUP;

Problems of **waste** management are discussed in Clark, M, Smith, D and Blowers, A (1992) *Waste Location: Spatial Aspects of Waste Management, Hazards and Disposal*, Routledge, London.

Further reading on sustainability in relation to **buildings and construction** is in Alexander, C (1979) *The Timeless Way of Building*, Oxford, OUP; DoE (1990) *The Potential of Town and Country Planning in Reducing Carbon Dioxide Emission*, London, HMSO; Fox, A and Murrell, R (1989) *Green Design*, London, Architecture Design and Technology Press; Olivier, D (1992) *Energy Efficiency and Renewables*, Hereford, Energy Advisory Associates; Vale, B and Vale, R (1991) *Green Architecture*, London, Thames and Hudson.

Transportation and sustainability is the subject of the following; CEC (1992) *Green Paper on the Impact of Transport on the Environment*; Transport and Environmental Studies (1991) *The Wrong Side of the Tracks: impact of road and rail transport on the environment*.

Sources covering the role of **business** and the development of sustainable livelihoods are British Standards Institute (1992) *BS7750, Specification for Environmental Management Systems*, London, BSI; Burall, P (1991) *Green Design*, London, Design Council; Camagni, R (ed) (1991) *Innovation Networks: Spatial Perspectives*, London, Bellhaven Press; Chambers, R (1987) *Sustainable Livelihoods, Environment and Development: putting poor rural people first*, Institute of Development Studies, Sussex University, Discussion Paper 240.

INDEX

Index compiled by Frank Pert